Marcus Braybrooke

1000 World Prayers

BOOKS

Copyright © 2003 O Books

Compiled by Marcus Braybrooke

Cover illustration: Andrew Milne Design

ISBN 1 903816 17 3

Typography: Nautilus Design

Write to:

John Hunt Publishing Ltd
46A West Street
Alresford
Hampshire SO24 9AU
UK

The rights of Marcus Braybrooke as compiler of this work have been asserted in accordance with the Copyright, Designs and Patents Act 1988.

A CIP catalogue record for this book is available from the British Library.

Printed and bound by CPI Group (UK) Ltd., Croydon, CR0 4YY

Visit us on the Web at: www.obooks.net

Contents

'I once asked Mother Teresa for advice. She replied "Oh, pray, pray, all the time, never cease to pray". In her wisdom, Mother Teresa knew that prayer is the path to the "deep inside where love and beauty reside." I believe this book of beautiful prayers will inspire its readers to ceaselessly travel the path of prayer to that place of peace inside and harvest all its treasures there'.

(Mairead Corrigan Maguire. Mairead is co-founder and President of the Peace People in Northern Ireland and winner, with Betty Williams, of the 1976 Nobel Peace prize)

'This anthology of prayers will help us appreciate other religious traditions, it will enrich our spiritual life and inspire us to work for a more peaceful world. It is a book to treasure and to read and re-read.'

Dr Daniel Gomez-Ibanez, Executive Director of the International Peace Council

'The Rev Marcus Braybrooke is a prolific writer, a pioneer researcher, and a leading light in the interfaith movement for the last thirty-five years.'

Dr K L Seshagiri Rao, Chief Editor of *Encyclopaedia of Hinduism*

'Marcus Braybrooke has been tireless in serving the cause of global inter-religious understanding, whilst being at the same time an active and faithful priest of the Church of England.'

Professor John Hick

Acknowledgements

We would like to thank all those who have given permission to include prayers in this book, as indicated in the list below, and if there are any omissions in the acknowledgements we apologize to those concerned. Every effort has been made to trace and contact authors and their agents and if they like to contact John Hunt Publishing we will include them in the Acknowledgements in the event of a reprint.

Anglican Church of Canada for excerpts from from *The Book of Alternative Services* of the Anglican Church of Canada, copyright © 1985 by the General Synod of the Anglican Church of Canada. Used with permission.

Angela Ashwin, for permission to reproduce 'This day, Lord, may I dream your dreams.'

Duncan Baird Publishers, © for permission to reproduce prayers from *The Bridge of Stars.* Edited by Marcus Braybrooke.

M. Lynn Baquie, for permission to reproduce her prayer 'One God'.

Mary Batchelor, for permission to reproduce her prayers from *The Lion Prayer Collection.*

John L. Bell and Graham Maule, for permission to reproduce 'We Cannot Measure How you Heal', copyright © 1989, WGRG, Iona Community, G2 3DH.

Rachel Bennett, for permission to reproduce prayers written by her father, George Appleton.

Ruth Burgess, for permission to reproduce prayers from *Bread of Tomorrow* and *The Book of a Thousand Prayers.*

John Carden, for permission to reproduce prayers.

Church of England. Extracts from *Common Worship: Pastoral Services and Prayers for the Church of England*, are copyright © The Archbishops' Council, 2000 and are reproduced by permission. Extracts from *The Alternative Service Book 1980* are copyright © The Central Board of Finance of the Church of England 1980; The Archbishops' Council, 1999 and are reproduced by permission.

Jason Clark for permission to reproduse 'Gaian Prayer' and 'Peace'.

Kenneth Cragg, for permission to reproduce prayers from *Alive to God.*

Darton, Longman and Todd Ltd, for permission to reproduce a prayer by Sheila Cassidy from *Good Friday People*, passages from *The Vedic Experience* by Raimundo Panikkar, and a prayer from *Becoming What I Am* by Harry Williams.

Esther De Waal, for permission to reproduce items from *The Celtic Vision.*

Rabbi Hadassah Davis, for permission to reproduce material from *Animal Kaddish.*

Families in Society, 11700 West Lake Park Drive, Milwaukee, WI, for permission to reproduce material from *Tales From My Teachers On The Alzheimer's Unit.*

Forest of Peace Publishing. Reprinted with permission from *Prayers for a Planetary Pilgrim* by Edward Hays, copyright © Forest of Peace Publishing Inc., 251 Muncie Road, Leavenworth, Kansas 66048 USA.

Brian Frost, for permission to reproduce prayers from *Prayers of Darkness and Light.*

Geoffrey Gardner, for permission to reproduce 'Spirit of peace, come to our waiting world'.

Gill & Macmillan Publishers, for permission to reproduce 'Lord, I have time' and 'The Telephone' from *Prayers of Life* by Michel Quoist.

Eric Gladwin, for permission to reproduce a number of his prayers.

Giles Harcourt, for permission to reproduce prayers from *Dawn Through Our Darkness*, and *Short Prayers for a Long Day*.

Fr. Edward Hays for prayers from his *Prayers for a Planetary Pilgrim*.

Idaratul Marif, Karachi, Pakistan, for permission to reproduce prayers from *Radiant Prayers*.

International Peace Council for prayer by Desmond Tutu.

Dadi Janki, for permission to reproduce extracts from *Wings of Soul*, Brahma Kumaris Information Services 1998.

John Johansen-Berg, for permission to reproduce a prayer from *Prayers of the Way* and from *Prayers for Pilgrims*.

Joan Johnson for permission to reproduce 'A Prayer for Each Day's Journey'.

Kathy Keay's literary executor for permission to reproduce her prayers from *Laughter, Shouting and Silence*.

Krishnamurti Foundation Trust. From J Krishnamurti's 'The Only Revolution', copyright © 1970 Krishnamurti Foundation Trust, Brockwood Park, Bramdean, Hampshire SO24 0LQ, in the *Second Penguin Krishnamurti Reader*.

Roger Lesser, for permission to reproduce extracts from his, *Breath of God*, and, *Saints and Sages of India*.

Ann Lewin, for permission to reproduce her work.

McCrimmons Publishing Company Ltd, for permission to reproduce from the work of Michael Hollings, copyright © McCrimmons Publishing.

Mercier Press, Cork, Eire, for permission to reproduce from *Prayer without Frills* by Juan Arias.

Lynne Milum, for permission to reproduce two prayers. Details on www.UniversalLight.org

Morehouse Publishing, for 'Difficult to Live With' from *A Barclay Prayer Book*, copyright © The Estate of William Barclay 1990. Reprinted by permission of Morehouse Publishing, Harrisburg, PA.

Janet Morley, for permission to reproduce her work.

Oxford University Press, for permission to reproduce prayers from *The Oxford Book of Prayer*, edited by George Appleton.

Quest Books, The Theosophical Publishing House, Wheaton, Illinois 60189-0270 for the prayer by Achaan Chah.

Palgrave Macmillan Ltd. John Hick, *God and the Universe of Faiths* 1988 © Palgrave Macmillan. Reproduced with permission of Palgrave Macmillan.

Parallax Press, for permission to reproduce material from *Being Peace* and *Present Moment, Wonderful Moment: Mindfulness Verses for Daily Living* by Thich Nhat Hanh.

Penguin for Quotations from *On Love and Barley: Haiku of Basho* by Basho, translated by Lucien Stryk (Penguin Classics, 1985) Copyright.

Reform Synagogues of Great Britain, for permission to reproduce material from

Reform Synagogues of Great Britain, for permission to reproduce material from *Forms of Prayer.*

SCM Press, for permission to reproduce 'Difficult to Live With' from *A Barclay Prayer Book* (1980).

Self-realization Fellowship, for permission to reproduce the prayers of Paramahansa Yogananda from *Whispers of Eternity* and *Metaphysical Meditations*

Shambhala Publications. For permission to reproduce 'My Heart was Free' *from Songs of the Sons & Daughter of Buddha,* translated by Andrew Schelling and Anne Waldman. © 1996 by Andrew Schelling & Anne Waldman. Reprinted by arrangement with Shambhala Publications Inc., Boston www.shambhala.com

Janet Shepperson, for permission to reproduce the prayer 'Help Us to Listen.'

SPCK, for permission to reproduce material from *Muslim Devotions* by Constance Padwick, *Beyond All Pain* by Dr Cecily Saunders, *Another Day* by John Carden, *The Edge of Glory* and *Tides and Seasons* by David Adam, *All Desires Known* by Janet Morley and *In the Silence of the Heart* by Kathryn Spink, for 'Harvest Prayer by Lilian Cox from *Little Prayers* (1988), for Prayers by Mechtild of Magdeburg from *Beguine Spirituality* (1989), for prayer by St Thérèse of Lisieux from SPCK Book of Christian Prayers (1995) and prayer by Amy Carmichael from *Prayers for the World Today*

David and Celia Storey, for permission to reproduce prayers from *Visions of an Interfaith Future.*

Sylvia Rothschild and Sybil Sheridan, for permission to reproduce material from *Taking up the Timbrel.*

Ta-Ha Publishers Ltd, for permission to reproduce prayers from *Selected Prayers* by Dr Jamal Badawi.

This England of Cheltenham, for permission to include 'High Flight' from *John Magee, The Pilot Poet.*

United Research for 'Seven Steps of Effective Prayer' by Jim Goure, copyright© April 1976, United Research, The Light Center, Black Mountain, North Carolina.

Urantia Foundation. Quotations from *The Urantia Book* used by permission. © 1955 Urantia Foundation. All rights reserved.

Greg Urick, for permission to reproduce 'Slow Dance.' (urickusn@yahoo.com)

Justice Muhammad Taqi Usmani, for permission to reproduce prayers from *Radiant Prayers.*

Ken Walsh, for permission to reproduce prayers from *Sometimes I Weep.*

Rabbi Lee Wax, for permission to reproduce prayers from *Taking up the Timbrel,* edited by Sylvia Rothschild and Sybil Sheridan.

John Wiley & Sons, Australia. 'Song' by Oodgeroo of the tribe Noonuccal, from *My People,* 3e, The Jacaranda Press, 1990, Reproduced by permission of John Wiley & Sons Australia.

Alexandra Wright, for permission to reproduce her prayer.

Extracts from the Authorized Version of the Bible (The King James Bible), the rights in which are vested in the Crown, are reproduced by permission of the Crown's Patentee, Cambridge University Press.

1000 World Prayers

An anthology of prayers from many countries, creeds
and centuries

Compiled and edited by

Marcus Braybrooke

For

Peter and Rachel,
Kathryn,
Helen,
Sarah,
and
Anna Hobin

Also for my friends in The World Congress of Faiths
And The International Interfaith Centre.

Royalties from the sale of this book will be given to
The World Congress of Faiths
And
The International Interfaith Centre
At Oxford.

Introduction

A rich inheritance of prayers from the religions of the world, thanks to the work of many scholars and translators, is now available in English and other modern languages. These prayers, of which this anthology is but a sample, provide us with a basis for the spiritual unity of a world that modern communications have made one.

This anthology, I hope will enrich the path of all who seek a deeper understanding of the Mystery of life. Those who are committed to one way may gain in appreciation of those who follow a different path, whilst spiritual seekers will become aware of the vast throng of fellow pilgrims.

It is significant how many people of prayer have also been active in the struggle for peace and justice and in service of those in need. Indeed, as the notes on contributors show, a large number have paid the price of imprisonment or even death for the causes to which they have dedicated their lives. This is not surprising. Prayer brings us into the presence of the Divine and as we begin to see the world as God sees it, we become more aware of the injustice and suffering which afflicts so many people. The pattern of the book reminds us that a turning to God should result in a renewed turning to the world in compassion and service. Only as people come together in the presence of the Divine and sense their spiritual oneness will we discover the resources to redeem globalisation from the strife and economic injustices which seem to be its entail.

I hope the book will enrich the lives of many individuals and also be useful to those who lead congregational prayer. The spiritual unity, of which I speak, is not some bland homogenised religiosity, but one in which the diversity of traditions enriches the whole. This is why there are a variety of styles and I have tried to honour the manner of writing of those whose prayers are included. My spell-check does not recognise 'Thee' or 'Thou', but to change all the prayers into modern English would lose the beauty of prayers which some people know by heart. In the same way, many prayers from the past are not gender inclusive, but I have hesitated to change what may have become sacred texts. Equally some of the prayers make reference to special names for God or holy persons. It seems right to preserve this particularity, although the sentiment expressed may have a more universal resonance.

I am very grateful to the many authors and publishers who have allowed me to use copyright material. I am also very grateful to John Hunt and his colleagues and once again to Mary for her support and patience.

The last year in which I have spent much time in choosing and typing prayers has been very enriching. It has helped me see how prayer should be part of every aspect of life. I now look forward to some leisure in which I can pray these prayers.

Marcus Braybrooke.   October 2002.

1 God

 ## 1.1 God: Prayer

1.1.1
Prayer is the Soul of Religion

I believe that prayer is the very soul and essence of religion, and, therefore,
prayer is the very core of the life of a person, for no one can live without prayer.

Mahatma Gandhi

1.1.2
More Things Are Wrought By Prayer

More things are wrought by prayer
Than this world dreams of. Wherefore, let thy voice
Rise like a fountain for me night and day.
For what are men better than sheep or goats
That nourish a blind life not within the brain,
If, knowing God, they lift not hands of prayer
Both for themselves and those who call them friend?
For, so the whole round earth is every way
Bound by gold chains about the feet of God.

Alfred Lord Tennyson

1.1.3
Disclosure

Prayer is like watching
For the kingfisher.
All you can do is
Be where he is likely to appear
And wait.
Often, nothing much happens:
There is space, silence
And expectancy.
No visible sign.
Only the Knowledge
That he's been there
And may come again.
Seeing or not seeing cease to matter,
You have been prepared.
But sometimes when you've almost
Stopped expecting it,
A flash of brightness
Gives encouragement.

Ann Lewin

1.1.4
Hoping to Meet Him

I have not seen his face, nor have I listened to his voice; only I have heard his gentle footsteps from the road before my house... I live in the hope of meeting with him; but this meeting is not yet.

Rabindranath Tagore

1.1.5
Face to Face

Day after day, O Lord of my life, shall I stand before thee face to face. With folded hands, O Lord of all worlds, shall I stand before thee face to face.
Under thy great sky in solitude and silence, with humble heart shall I stand before thee face to face.
In this laborious world of thine, tumultuous with toil and with struggle, among hurrying crowds shall I stand before thee face to face.
And when my work shall be done in this world, O King of kings, alone and speechless shall I stand before thee face to face.

Rabindranath Tagore

1.1.6
Prayer is...

White tapering fingers touching
 Cracked labouring fingers matching
 Seamless skin of youngness
 And branching paths of oldness...

   Purple robe; surplice and clean incense
   Oak pew, and voices seeking echo
   Deep man strength; and woman's
   Glorying, calling angels...

   A gentleness; and a refuge;
   Concentration, invocation
    of the Love that disarms hate.
    Invisible but ever waiting...

    Sometime a depth of gratitude
    For a peace which came unseen
    or for a quick-healed flesh
    (IN wrought coincidence of Time)...

Prayer...

Is murmuring voices
Stillness
And serenity of Blessing...
Limitless seeking... past countless human generations...

Long testimony to a birthright
Given outside Earth's existence...
A birthright born to the womb of Thought...
Of Love universal in creativity.

Prayer is power...

And is of all that has been or will be
Changing eternally
In created things of individual beauty
self maintained
Without desire... and alone can make us all one...

Eric Gladwin

1.1.7
May We Deserve to Be Heard

Grant us grace, Almighty Father,
so to pray as to deserve to be heard.

Jane Austen

1.1.8
Give Ear to My Prayer

Hear my cry, O God, and give ear unto my prayer.

Psalm 61:1

1.1.9
Love in My Heart

O God, some sought You for this world and You gave it to them. And others sought from You the next world and You did satisfy them. But I ask You neither for this world nor the next, but only for increase of love to You in my heart.

Muslim Devotions

1.1.10
Open the Door

Open to me the door of your generosity which you never close to your dear ones.

Muslim Devotions

1.1.11
Your Door is Open

Your door is open to the beggar...

Muslim Devotions

1.1.12
The Silent Cry of the Soul

We do not even know how we are supposed to pray. All we do is call for help because of the need of the moment. But what the soul intends is spiritual need, only we are not able to express what the soul means. That is why we do not merely ask God to hear our call for help, but also beg Him who knows what is hidden, to hear the silent cry of the soul.

A Hasidic Jewish prayer

1.1.13

True Prayer
Flowers, sesame-seed, bowls of fresh water, a tuft of kusha grass,
all this altar paraphernalia is not needed
by someone who takes the teacher's words in
and honestly lives them. Full of longing in meditation,
one sinks into a joy that is free of any impulse to act,
and will never enter a human birth again.

Lalla, a Kashmiri woman mystic

1.1.14
Help Me

O God, help me to pray better;
help me with words from the heart;
help me to know how to start
Please listen to the meaning not the letter.

Conrad Levasseur

1.1.15
Breathe Deeply

We breathe thy life, O God, as we breathe the air about us:
help us to breathe it more deeply.

A. Powell Davies

1.1.16
One Life in All

One life through all the immense creation runs,
One spirit is the moon's, the sea's, the sun's;
All forms in the air that fly, on earth that creep;
And the unknown, nameless creatures of the deep:
Each breathing thing obeys one Mind's control,
And in all substance is a single Soul.

Virgil

1.1.17
God Within Us

There is a God within us
And we glow when he stirs us.

Ovid

1. 1

1.1.18
Rhythms of Rest and Renewal

In order to grow towards wholeness,
accepting our brokenness
and gradually becoming more compassionate,
we need the power of the Spirit.
But we are humans
and must also know the ways of our own bodies and beings...
Each one of must find our own secret rhythm
of how to rest, relax and find re-creation
for each one of our bodies is different.
We need personal space and time.
God gave the Jewish people the Sabbath
as a day of rest.
Each of us must discover our own Sabbath,
our real nourishment...
We must learn
not just to free ourselves from tension and fatigue
on the Sabbath day, our day of rest.
We must also learn
as the mother must learn
in front of the never-ending needs of her children,
how to respect our energy
and relax in all the moments of our day
filled as they may be with arduous work
or often tiresome meetings,
and crises of all sorts,
and the hundred and one things that have to be done.
To do this we must discover how to harmonise
the active and the passive in us.
if we are just doers,
feeling terribly responsible and serious,
we will crack up one day.
We must nourish the passive part of us,
our hearts made for a personal love,
learning to listen to others,
to marvel at nature,
to rest a moment in the presence of Jesus,
to receive the love of those around us
and be nourished by their trust,
enjoying the little things of each day,
not taking ourselves too seriously,
accepting to become like little children.

Jean Vanier

1.1.19
The Light of Day

So long as we enjoy the light of day
may we greet one another with love.
So long as we enjoy the light of day
may we pray for one another.

A native North American payer: Zuni

1.1.20
Pray At All Times

The soul that is not nourished by prayer
Is like a tree without soil.
Pray in the woods,
Pray when you plough,
Pray in the fields,
Pray when you dig ditches,
Pray in silence
So that no one can see you. Amen.

Russian Orthodox prayer

1.1.21
A Prayer from Within

How sublime -   (Arigata ya)
a boat beneath the moon   (tsuk no funauta)
and from within a prayer.   (Namu Amida)

A Japanese haiku or verse

A haiku is a Japanese verse form consisting of three lines of five, seven and five syllables in length. Traditionally the poem contains a reference to one of the seasons of the year.

1.1.22
Our Father

Our Father, who art in heaven,
Hallowed be Thy name,
Thy kingdom come, Thy will be done
On earth as it is in heaven,
Give us this day our daily bread
And forgive us our trespasses,
As we forgive those who trespass against us;
For thine is the kingdom, the power and the glory
For ever and ever
Amen.

Jesus

1.1.23
A closer walk with God

O for a closer walk with God,
A calm and heavenly frame;
A light to shine upon the road
that leads me to the Lamb!

Return, O holy Dove, return,
Sweet messenger of rest;
I hate the sins that made thee mourn,
And drove thee from my breast.

The dearest idol I have known,
Whate'er that idol be,
Help me to tear it from thy throne,
And worship only thee.

So shall my walk be close with God,
Calm and serene my frame;
So purer light shall mark the road
That leads me to the Lamb.

William Cowper

1.1.24
Every Prayer Contains An Answer

He prayed, but to his prayer no answer came,
and choked within him sank his ardour's flame;
No more he prayed, no more the knee he bent,
While round him darkened doubt and discontent;
Till in his room, one eve, there shone a light,
And he beheld an angel-presence bright,
Who said, 'O faint heart, why hast thou resigned
Praying, and no more callest God to mind?'
'I prayed', he said, 'but no one heard my prayer,
Long disappointment has induced despair.'
'Fool', said the angel, 'every prayer of thine,
Of God's immense compassion was a sign;
Each cry of thine, 'O Lord', itself contains
The answer, 'Here am I'; the very pains,
Ardour, and love and longing, every tear,
Are His attraction, prove Him very near.
The cloud dispersed: once more the suppliant prayed
Nor ever failed to find the promised aid.

Jalal al-Din Rumi

1.1.25
Calm the Waves of this Heart

O Lord, calm the waves of this heart, calm its tempest!
Calm yourself, O my soul, so that the divine can act in you!
Calm yourself, O my soul, so that God is able to repose in you,
so that his peace may cover you!
Yes, Father in heaven, often have we found that the world cannot give us peace,
but make us feel that you are able to give us peace; let us know the truth of your
promise: that the whole world may not be able to take away your peace.

Sören Kierkegaard

1.1.26
A Short Prayer

A short prayer finds its way to heaven.

William Langland

1.1.27
Groans

The best prayers have more often groans than words.

John Bunyan

1.1.28
Offering the Soul to God

Prayer must mean putting our very soul upon our hands,
Offering it to God.

Babylonian Talmud

1.1.29
Asking for Compassion

Let not your prayer become a matter of routine,
But let it be a plea for mercy and compassion.

Babylonian Talmud

1.1.30
Centring in God

Fix the centre of my heart in yourself, O Lord,
for only thus will I resist temptation
and live according to your will.

After Meister Eckhart

1.1.31
Come, Holy One

When the heart is hard and parched up, come upon me with a shower of mercy.
When grace is lost from life, come with a burst of song.
When tumultuous work raises its din on all sides shutting me out from beyond,
come to me, my Lord of silence, with thy peace and rest.

When my beggarly heart sits crouched, shut up in a corner, break open the door, my king, and come with the ceremony of a king.
When desire blinds the mind with delusion and dust, O thou Holy One, thou wakeful, come with thy light and thy thunder.

Rabindranth Tagore

1.1.32
He Ever Comes

Have you not heard his silent steps?
he comes, comes, ever comes.
Every morning and every age, every day and every night he comes, comes, ever comes.
Many a song have I sung in many a mood of mind, but all their notes have always proclaimed, "He comes, comes, ever comes."
In the fragrant days of sunny April through the forest path he comes, comes, ever comes.
In the rainy gloom of July nights on the thundering chariot of clouds he comes, comes.
In sorrow after sorrow it is his steps that press upon my heart, and it is the golden touch of his feet that makes my joy to shine.

Rabindranath Tagore

1.1.33
I Will Hear You

When you call Me and come and pray to Me, I will hear you.
When you seek Me, you will find Me.
If you search for Me with all your heart.
I shall let you find Me, says the Lord.

Bible: Jeremiah 29:12-14

1.1.34
Ye Shall Find

I say unto you,
Ask and it shall be given unto you,
Seek and ye shall find
Knock and the door shall be opened unto you.

Jesus

1.1.35
Garment of Holiness

As the flame clothes the black, sooty clod in a garment of fire, and releases the heat imprisoned therein, even so does prayer clothe a man in a garment of holiness, evoke the light and fire implanted within him by his Maker, illumine his whole being, and unify the Lower and the Higher Worlds.

From the Zohar, a Jewish mystical writing

1.1.36
Too Full of Prayer

The Baal Shem Tov once refused to enter a certain synagogue because he said that it was too full of prayer. Noting his followers' astonishment at his attitude, he explained that so many routine insincere prayers were uttered there that they could not rise to the heavenly throne and stayed on earth, cramming the synagogue full.

Baal Shem Tov

1.1.37
Ten Minutes

O God, I am hellishly angry; I think so-and-so is a swine; I am tortured by worry about this or that; I am pretty certain that I have missed my chances in life; this or that has left me feeling terribly depressed. But nonetheless here I am like this, feeling both bloody and bloody-minded, and I am going to stay here for ten minutes. You are most unlikely to give me anything. I know that. But I am going to stay for ten minutes nonetheless.

Harry Williams

1.1.38
The Simplest Form of Speech

> Prayer is the soul's sincere desire,
> Uttered or unexpressed;
> The motion of a hidden fire
> That trembles in the breast.
>
> Prayer is the burden of a sigh,
> The falling of a tear,
> The upward glancing of an eye
> When none but God is near.
>
> Prayer is the simplest form of speech
> That infant lips can try;
> Prayer the sublimest strains that reach
> The Majesty on high.

John Montgomery

1.1.39
God's Answer

No prayer unanswered is,
If He say 'yes', 'tis well,
Or He answer 'wait'
Rest suppliant at his gate.
He never answers 'no',
But that in time,
Some richer fuller gift is thine.

R. E. Cleeve

1.1

1.1.40
In Prayer

Be like the hill – still –
in touch with eternity.
Let your spines
Be like the stalk of the sunflower – straight;
Like the flower itself search –
always search for the Sun.
Be like the depth of the sea – calm,
whatever may stir above.
Like ivy cling
with every fibre of your being
to the Lord you love so much.
Let your words
mingle
with the song of the birds,
forever praising.
Be like the river
always giving, helping, serving.
Be like the moon,
give your light to all.
Like that of the moon –
It is not yours.
Remember your breath.
It comes from God
to make you live.
It goes to God...
Let your prayer float on your breath
from God – to God
To make you live
like God.
Be like the thirsting earth –
Open, silent, still, receiving
Whatever comes to you.

Roger Lesser, inspired by Fr. Seraphion of Mt Athos

# 1.2 God: Silence

1.2.1
Be still

Be still and know that I am God.

Psalm 46:10

1.2.2
Stilling the Body

I weave a silence on my lips
I weave a silence into my mind
I weave a silence within my heart
I close my ears to distractions
I close my eyes to attractions
I close my heart to temptations
Calm me O Lord as you stilled the storm
Still me O Lord, keep me from harm
Let all tumult within me cease
Enfold me Lord in your peace.

David Adam

1.2.3
A Time for Silence

O Lord, the Scripture says,
'There is a time for silence and a time for speech'.
Saviour, teach me the silence of humility,
the silence of wisdom,
the silence of love,
the silence of perfection,
the silence that speaks without words,
the silence of faith.
Lord, teach me to silence my own heart
that I may listen to the gentle movement of the Holy Spirit within me and be
aware of your depths.

Anonymous

1.2.4
Liberated By Silence

When I am liberated by silence,
when I am no longer involved
in the measurement of life, but in the living of it,
I can discover a form of prayer in which
there is effectively no distraction.

My whole life becomes a prayer.
My whole silence is full of prayer.
The world of silence in which I am immersed
contributes to my prayer.

Anonymous

1.2.5
Still Your Mind

When you pray you are speaking to God,
meditate, still your mind,
and then you can hear God.
Only when your mind becomes still
can you get clarity.

Shri Shivabalayogi Maharaj

1.2.6
Read Your Own Heart Right

We would have inward peace,
Yet will not look within;
We would have misery cease,
Yet will not cease from sin;
Once, read your own heart right
And you will have done with fears;
Man gets no other light
Though he search a thousand years.

Matthew Arnold - 'Empedocles on Etna'

1.2.7
Unspoken Language

No loud or whispered words of prayer shall cloak my love for Thee.
In divine unspoken language will I express my heart's devotion.
Thy voice is silence; in my soul silence may I hear Thee speak.
Tell me, O Eternal Mother, that though I knew it not,
Thou hast loved me always.

Paramahansa Yogananda

1.2.8
Quiet With You

My God, in You depressed hearts find rest
And in knowledge of You divided hearts are made whole.
Nor are hearts stilled, save by calling on You,
Nor are souls quieted till they meet with you

Muslim Devotions

1.2.9
Recollection of God

They who believe and whose hearts are stayed in the recollection of God:
Is there not serenity of heart in the recollection of God?

Qur'an: 13:28

1.2.10
Still Hearts

Send down O God, O Gentle, O Compassionate,
into my heart faith and tranquillity and stillness,
that I may be of those whose 'hearts are stilled by the mention of God'.

Muslim Devotions

1.2.11
Thy Peace Abides

Calm Soul of all things! Make it mine
To feel, amid the city's jar,
That there abides a peace of thine,
Man did not make, and cannot mar!

Matthew Arnold

1.2.12
Voice in My Silence

I believe that God is in me
as the sun is in the colour and fragrance of a flower –
the Light in my darkness, the Voice in my silence.

Helen Keller
Helen Keller became blind and deaf in infancy and never experienced the reality
of human speech.

1.2.13
Calmness

Let nothing disturb you
nothing frighten you,
all things are passing;
patient endurance
attains all things.
One whom God possesses
lacks nothing,
for God alone suffices.

Teresa of Avila – Teresa's Bookmark

1.2.14
Meditate Alone

Solitariness of place is the most appropriate place for meditation.
Retire from other people, if you want to talk with profit with yourself.

So Jesus meditates alone on the mount;
Isaac, in the fields;
John the Baptist, in the desert;
David, on his bed;
Chrysostom, in the bath:
Each, in different places; but all solitary.

Joseph Hall

1.2.15
Retire Into Thyself

Men seek out retreats for themselves, cottages in the country, lonely sea shores
and mountains. Thou too art disposed to hanker greatly after such things: and
yet all this is the very commonest stupidity; for it is in thy power whenever thou
wilt, to retire into thyself: and nowhere is there any place whereto a man may
retire quieter and more free from politics than his own soul.

Marcus Aurelius

1.2.16
The Lord's my Shepherd.

The Lord's my Shepherd, I'll not want;
he makes me down to lie
In pastures green; he leadeth me
the quiet waters by.

My soul he doth restore again,
and me to walk doth make
Within the paths of righteousness,
e'en for his own name's sake.

Yea, though I walk through death's dark vale,
yet will I fear none ill;
For thou art with me, and thy rod
and staff me comfort still.

My table thou hast furnished
in presence of my foes;
My head thou dost with oil anoint,
and my cup overflows.

Goodness and mercy all my life
shall surely follow me;
And in God's house for evermore
my dwelling place shall be.

Psalm 23 in Scottish Psalter (1650)

1.2.17
Dive Deep

Pearls lie not on the seashore.
If thou desirest one thou must dive for it.

Oriental proverb

1.2.18
Alone

Grant me the ability
to be alone
There is no place
on this wide earth –
Be it the vast expanse of Ocean's waste,
or peak of wildest mountain, sky-caressed –
In which the ever-present power divine
In every force of nature's not a shrine.
Alone
Grant me the ability to be alone;
May it be my custom to go outdoors each day
Among the trees and grasses,
Among all growing things,
And there may I be alone,
And enter into prayer
To talk with the one
That I belong to.

Lao Tsu

1.2.19
For Quiet Hearts

O Spirit of God,
Set at rest the crowded, hurrying anxious thoughts
within our minds and our hearts.
Let the peace and quiet of your presence take possession of us.
Help us to rest, to relax, to become open and receptive to you.
You know our inmost spirits,
the hidden unconscious life within us,
the frustrated desires,
the unresolved tensions and dilemmas.
Cleanse and sweeten the springs of our being,
that freedom, life and love may flow into both our conscious
and hidden life.
Lord, we lie open before you,
waiting for your peace, your healing and your Word.

George Appleton

1.2.20
God in Yourself

Settle yourself in solitude and you will come
upon God in yourself.

Teresa of Avila

1.2.21
Perfect Peace

You will keep in perfect peace those whose minds are stayed on you.

Bible: Isaiah 26:3

1.2.22
Stillness

Real silence, real stillness, really holding one's
tongue comes only as the sober consequence of spiritual stillness.

Dietrich Bonhoeffer

1.2.23
Silence

I see no way of truthfully praising you
For except silence you do not put on any other ornament.
Your true praise consists in perfect silence
Your worship is no outer act,
And union with you is being nothing myself.
But, if, like one whose mind is crazed
And wildly babbles,
I sing your praise:
Bear with it,
O dear Mother.

Dnyanadev
A prayer from his commentary on the Bhagavad Gita.

1.2.24
A Still Small Voice

The Lord was not in the wind: and after the wind an earthquake; but the Lord
was not in the earthquake:
And after the earthquake a fire: but the Lord was not in the fire: and after the
fire a still small voice.
And it was so, when Elijah heard it, that he wrapped his face in his mantle, and
went out, and stood in the entering in of the cave. And behold there came a
voice unto him, and said, What doest thou here, Elijah?

Bible: 1 Kings 19:11-13

1.2.25
Adoring Jesus in the Silence

Let us adore Jesus in our hearts, who spent thirty years out of thirty-three in silence; who began his public life by spending forty days in silence; who often retired alone to spend the night on a mountain in silence. He who spoke with authority, now spends his earthly life in silence. Let us adore Jesus in the eucharistic silence.

Mother Teresa of Calcutta

1.2.26
The Real Word

The real word, the word of words,
can only be sensed in the heart of silence.

Julian Green

1.2.27
Breathing

As I breathe in, I am aware of joy.
As I breathe out, I am aware of joy.

As I breathe in, I am aware of my mind.
As I breathe out, I am aware of my mind.

As I breathe in, I calm the activities of my mind.
As I breathe out, I calm the activities of my mind.

As I breathe in, I compose my mind.
As I breathe out, I compose my mind.

As I breathe in, I concentrate my mind.
As I breathe out, I concentrate my mind.

As I breathe in, I free my mind.
As I breathe out, I free my mind.

Adapted from Buddhist teaching on breath control

1.2.28
Stillness

This, I say, is the stillness:
A retreat to one's roots;
Or better yet, return
To the will of God.

From the Taoist Tao te Ching

1.2.29
A Still Place

Make me
    a still place of light
    a still place of love
    of you
    your light radiating
    your love vibrating
    your touch and your healing
far flung and near
to the myriads caught
in darkness, in sickness
in lostness, in fear
make a heart-centre here
Light of the World.

From Malling Abbey

1.2.30
The Still Depth

Like weary waves
thought flows upon thought
but the still depth beneath
is all thine own.

George Macdonald

1.2.31
Silence is a Sign From God

The sign (from God) of the intellect is contemplation and the sign of
contemplation is silence, because it is impossible for a person to do two things at
one time – he cannot both speak and meditate...
Through the faculty of meditation a person attains to eternal life; through it he
receives the breath of the Holy Spirit – the bestowal of the Spirit is given in
reflection and meditation.

Adapted from a talk by Abdu'l-Baha

1.2.32
Silence

Dear Lord and Father of mankind
    Forgive our foolish ways!
Re-clothe us in our rightful mind,
In purer lives thy service find,
    In deeper reverence praise.

In simple trust like theirs who heard,
    Beside the Syrian sea,
The gracious calling of the Lord,

Let us, like them, without a word
       Rise up and follow thee.

O Sabbath rest by Galilee!
       O calm of hills above,
Where Jesus knelt to share with thee
The silence of eternity,
       Interpreted by love!

Drop thy still dews of quietness,
       Till all our strivings cease;
Take from our souls the strain and stress,
And let our ordered lives confess
       The beauty of thy peace.

Breathe through the heats of our desire
       Thy coolness and thy balm;
Let sense be dumb, let flesh retire;
Speak through the earthquake, wind, and fire,
       O still small voice of calm!

J. G. Whittier

1.2.33
Pray With All Our Strength

The prayer has great power
Which we pray with all our strength.
It makes an embittered heart mellow,
A sad heart joyful,
A foolish heart wise,
A timid heart bold,
A weak heart strong,
A blind heart clear-seeing,
A cold heart ardent.
It draws God who is great into a heart which is small.
It drives the hungry soul up to the fullness of God.
It unites the two lovers, God and soul, in a place of bliss
Where they converse long of love.

Mechtild of Magdeburg

1.2.34
Join Your Hands Gently

Join your hands gently;
Let the world be placed
Beyond their reach,
Beyond their itch
Always to be doing;

Exempt from speech
This little space thus formed
Between your folded fingers,
Between your going
And your slow return –
This still enclosure
With its own high walls:
Join your hands gently, so
No lovelier way than this of letting go.

Jean M. Watt

1.2.35
Silence Like a Mantle

Let silence be placed around us,
like a mantle,
Let us enter into it,
as through a small secret door;
stooping,
to emerge into
an acre of peace,
where stillness reigns,
and the voice of God
is ever present.

The voice of God,
is the startled cry
of a refugee child,
waking
in unfamiliar surroundings.
The voice of God,
in the mother,
fleeing with
her treasure
in her arms,
who says,
'I am here.'

The voice of God
in the father
who points to the stars
and says:
'there is our signpost
there is our lantern. Be of good courage.'

O Lord, may the mantle of silence
become a cloak of understanding

to warm our hearts in prayer.

Kate McIlhagga

1.2.36
Help Us to Listen

God of listening, God of peace,
In our hearts may you increase,
Till our flow of words shall cease,
and we hear you.

Listening is the hardest skill,
Silences we strain to fill,
Far too restless to be still
And just hear you.

If our well-planned words defeat
Words of others that we meet,
Hesitant and incomplete,
Father, hear them.

If the insights that we seek
Come from someone tired and weak,
Looking for a chance to speak,
Help us hear them.

Janet Shepperson

1.2.37
The Desert

The desert waits,
ready for those who come,
who come obedient to the Spirit's leading;
or who are driven,
because they will not come any other way.

The desert always waits,
ready to let us know who we are –
the place of self-discovery.
And whilst we fear, and rightly,
the loneliness and emptiness and harshness,
we forget the angels,
whom we cannot see for our blindness,
but who come when God decides
that we need their help;
when we are ready
for what they can give us.

Ruth Burgess

1.2

1.2.38
My Time of Prayer is Finished

My time of prayer is finished
    trailing its ashes like an incense stick
    burned to the end.

Quiet my mind
    before it passes judgement on this prayer,
    my gift of time to you.

How can I judge its worth
    this struggle to still my mind in you,
    my efforts to feel your presence in my prayers?

Only you can judge the simple song of love
    sung in the noisy chambers of my heart,
    often drowned by the wail of fear
    or the sweaty shouts of work that must be done.

You, my hidden Friend, waited in patience
    as memories called from the past
    and future prospects clamoured for attention
    filling my mind with yesterdays and tomorrows,
    stealing my sense of your presence.

As I prepare to go about my work today,
    may my intention to live in your present moment
    be the pattern for this day and my life.

With your help, may I forever do
    only one thing at a time –
    always in communion with you, my Beloved,
    with all my heart and mind and soul.

Edward Hays

 1.3 God's Glory

1.3.1
Now My Eyes See You

I have heard of you by the hearing of the ear:
but now my eyes have seen you.
Wherefore I abhor myself,
and repent in dust and ashes.

Bible: Job 42:4-5

1.3.2
God's Glory: Our Mercy

When the solitary reaches the divine cloud and enters the harbour of all service, and sees with his mind, face to face, the glory of the Lord, and is made radiating by it, and is transformed into His likeness – then his mercy is poured out over all, like that of God.

By an anonymous Syriac Christian mystic

1.3.3
Glory to Him

O You who art described though no description reaches your True Being nor does any deliminator draw limits for You. You who are absent in mystery yet not lost, You Seer who art not seen, You who are sought and found, for neither the heavens nor the earth nor the intervening space is void of You for the flicker of an eyelid... You are the Light of Light and Lord of Lords encompassing all things. Glory to Him whom nothing resembles, the all-Hearer, the all-Seer. Glory to Him who is thus and no other is thus.

Muslim Devotions

1.3.4
Most High Praise

Most high praise to Him who is robed in power and in power has spoken.
Most high praise to Him who clothes Himself with glory, and in glory is generous.
Most high praise to Him to whom praise is due as to no other.

Muslim Devotions

1.3.5
All Praise to the Lord

All praise to the Lord of greatness and magnitude, Lord of the great throne.
All praise to the Lord of power and abidingness, Lord of the noble throne.
All praise to Him whom all things praise, the Exalted, the August.
All praise to Him whose knowledge contains all things, the Everlasting, the Eternal.
All praise to Him to whose glorious Face such praise alone is due.

All praise to Him who alone knoweth the mode of his Being, the Powerful, the All-Wise.
All praise to Him the depth of whose eternal greatness is unthinkable by the minds of men.

Muslim Devotions

1.3.6
Praise be to God

Praise be to Him who when I call on Him answers me, slow though I am when He calls me.
Praise be to Him who gives to me when I ask, miserly though I am when He asks a loan of me.
Praise be to Him to whom I confide my needs whensoever I will and He satisfies them.
My Lord I praise, for He is of my praise most worthy.

Muslim Devotions

1.3.7
The Unnameable

The Tao that can be told
is not the eternal Tao.
The name that can be named
is not the eternal Name.
The unnameable is the eternally real.
Naming is the origin of all particular things.
Free from desire, you realize the mystery.
Caught in desire, you see only the manifestations.
Yet mystery and manifestations arise from the same source.
This source is called darkness. Darkness within darkness.
The gateway to all understanding.

Lao Tsu

1.3.8
My Timeless Love

The angels dance in your wake
The sun rises for your glory
Stars illume in your light
Magnificent and eternal
My Lord Jesus
My timeless love.

Justina M. Pernetter

1.3.9
God Hears and Knows All Things

God! There is no god but He –
The Living, The Self-subsisting. Eternal.
No slumber can seize him nor sleep.
His are all things in the heavens and on earth.
Who is there that can intercede in His presence except as He permitteth?
He knoweth what is before or after or behind them.
Nor shall they encompass aught of His knowledge except as He willeth.
His Throne doth extend over the heavens and the earth,
and He feeleth no fatigue in guarding and preserving them
For He is The Most High, The Supreme.
Let there be no compulsion in religion.
Truth stands out clear from error:
Whoever rejects Evil and believes in God
Hath grasped the most trustworthy handhold, that never breaks.
And God heareth and knoweth all things.
God is the Protector of those who have faith;
From the depth of darkness He will lead them forth into light.

Qur'an: 2:255-257

1.3.10
You Alone Are God

You alone are God,
You were from of old,
And You will be until eternity, always, first and last,
Now and always for ever and ever.
As for You, You are the same,
And Your epoch will not come to an end;
As for You, You are the same,
and Your kingdom will not be abolished,
And Your Power is invincible,
And Your strength is untiring,
And Your magnificence will not be humbled,
And the splendour of Your Name will not be dispelled,
And the praise of Your exalted fame will not be diminished,
And Your light will not be darkened,
And Your decree will not be abrogated,
The pillar of Your word will not be overthrown,
And Your wisdom will not fall into error,
And Your counsel will not be concealed.
You alone are God, God of all;
You alone are God, Lord of all;
You alone are God, King of all;
You alone are God, Creator of all;

You alone are God, Conqueror of all;
You alone are God, Omnipotent;
You alone are God, Slayer of all;
You alone are God, Destroyer of all;
You alone are God, Saviour of all;
You alone are God, Life of all;
You alone are God, Sustainer of all;
You alone are God, Protector of all;
You alone are God, Restorer of all;
You alone are God, Raiser of all;
You alone are God, Supporter of all;
You alone are God, Helper of all;
You alone are God, A righteous God over all creation.

Traditional Ethiopian Jewish prayer

1.3.11
The Kiss We Want

There is some kiss we want
with our whole lives,
the touch of Spirit on the body.
Sea water begs the pearl to break its shell.
And the lily, how passionately
it needs some wild Darling!
At night, I open the window
and ask the moon to come
and press its face into mine.
Breathe into me. Close the language-door,
and open the love-window.
The moon won't use the door,
only the window.

Jalal al-Din Rumi

1.3.12
God

Today is God.
In the beginning was God,
Today is God,
Tomorrow will be God.
Who can make an image of God?
He has no body...

From An African Pygmy Prayer

1.3.13
I Am It

I it am: the might and the goodness of the Fatherhood.
I it am: the wisdom and kindness of Motherhood.
I it am: the light and grace that is all blessed love.
I it am: the Trinity. I it am: the Unity.
I it am: the high Sovereign Goodness of all manner of things.
I it am: that maketh'thee to love.
I it am: that maketh thee to long.
I it am: the endless fulfilling of all true desires.

Julian of Norwich

1.3.14
Eternity

I saw Eternity the other night
Like a great Ring of pure and endless light,
    All calm, as it was bright,
And round beneath it, Time in hours, days, years
    driven by the spheres
Like a vast shadow moved, in which the world
    And all her train were hurled.

Henry Vaughan

1.3.15
Mother You Are Light

O Mother, you are light and your light is everywhere.
Streaming from your body are rays in thousands –
two thousand, a hundred thousand,
tens of millions, a hundred million –
there is no counting their numbers.
It is by you and through you that all things moving
and motionless shine. It is by your light,
O Mother, that all things come to be.

A Hindu Tantric prayer

Tantrism, which is an important current in Indian religious thought, emphasises the feminine aspect of the Deity.

1.3.16
God's Light

God is the Light of the heavens and the earth. His light is like a niche in which there is a lamp. The lamp is in a glass. The glass is, as it were, a shining star. This lamp is kindled from a blessed tree, an olive, neither of the East nor of the West, whose oil would almost glow forth of itself, though no fire touched it. Light upon light, God guides to His light whom God wills.

Qur'an: 24:35-38

1.3

1.3.17
God Fills Every Heart

Our Lord fills every heart
The Infinite is within as well as without.
Our Lord fills every heart.
He is the earth, the sky, and the underworld;
He fills the entire universe.

Guru Arjan

1.3.18
The Self

The Self is one. Unmoving, it moves faster than the mind. The senses lag, but Self runs ahead. Unmoving, it outruns pursuit. Out of Self comes the breath that is the life of all things.
Unmoving, it moves; it is far away, yet near; within all, outside all.
Of a certainty the man who can see all creatures in himself, himself in all creatures, knows no sorrow.
How can a wise man, knowing the unity of life, seeing all creatures in himself, be deluded or sorrowful?
The Self is everywhere, without a body, without a shape, whole, pure, wise, all knowing, far shining, self-depending, all transcending; in the eternal procession assigning to every period its proper duty.

Hindu Scriptures: Isha Upanishad

1.3.19
You and Only You

I will sing you a song
O, Lord of the Universe.
I will sing You a song.
Where can You be found,
And where can You not be found?
Where I pass – there You are.
Where I remain there, too, You are,
You, You and only You.

Jewish Hasidic song

1.3.20
Learn the Language of Adoration

Tell me, I beg, what I must do
To win Him for whom I yearn;
What virtue practise, what magic use,
What language must I learn.

Learn the language of adoration;
Let silence be your quest.

Practise submission to your Lord
and He will be your guest.

Baba Farid

1.3.21
By Love

By love may He be gotten and holden,
By thought never.

Attributed to Julian of Norwich

1.3.22
Waiting on God

In the centre of my heart I have a mystic throne for You. The candles of my joys are dimly lighted in the hope of Your coming. They will burn brighter when You appear.

Whether You come or not, I will wait for You until my tears melt away all material grossness. To please You my love-perfumed tears will wash Your feet of silence.

The altar of my soul will be kept empty until You come. I will talk not; I will ask nothing of You. I will realise that You know the pangs of my heart while I wait for You.

You know that I am praying; You know that I love no other. Yet whether You come to me or not, I will wait for You, though it be for eternity.

Paramahansa Yogananda

1.3.23
Life's Journey

O Father, give my spirit power to climb
To the fountain of all light, and be purified.
Break through the mists of earth, the weight of clay
Shine forth in splendour, you who are calm weather,
And quiet resting-place for faithful souls.
You carry us, and you go before;
You are the journey, and the journey's end.

Boethius

1.3.24
Clearness Beyond Measure

O clearness beyond measure
O burning mountain, O chosen sun,
O perfect moon, O fathomless well,
O unattainable height, O clearness beyond measure,

O wisdom without end, O mercy without limit,
O strength beyond resistance, O crown of all majesty,
The humblest you created sings your praise.

Mechtild of Magdeburg

1.3.25
Adoration

Where I wander – you
Where I ponder – you
Only you, you again, always you!
You! You! You!
When I am gladdened – you
When I am saddened – you!
You! You! You!
Sky is you, earth is you!
You above! You below!
In every trend, at every end,
Only you, you again, always you!
You! You! You!

Levi Yitzchak of Berditchev

1.3.26
Ask Not Who or Where

Who is like you, revealing the deeps,
Fearful in praises, doing wonders?

The creator who discovers all from nothing
Is revealed to the heart, but not to the eye;
Therefore ask not who nor where –
For God fills heaven and earth.

Judah Halevi

1.3.27
Where Shall I Find You

Creator, where shall I find you?
All hidden and exalted is your place.
And where shall I not find you?
Full of glory is the infinite space.

I have sought your nearness,
with all my heart I called you
and going out to meet you
I found you coming to meet me.

Judah Halevi

1.3.28
No God But Thee

O thou whose face is the object of my adoration
Whose beauty is my sanctuary,
Whose habitation is my goal,
Whose praise is my hope,
Whose providence is my companion,
Whose love is the cause of my being,
Whose mention is my solace,
Whose nearness is my desire,
Whose presence is my dearest wish and highest aspiration:
I entreat Thee not to withhold from me the things
Thou didst ordain for the chosen ones among Thy servants.
Supply me, then, with the good of this world and of the next.
Thou, truly, art the King of all men.
There is no God but Thee, the Ever-forgiving, the Most generous.

Baha'u'llah

1.3.29
One God

O God of many names –
Father, Mother, Spirit,
Compassionate One –
Look on us with mercy.

We close our eyes in prayer
And see your face
In our reflections,
Content with what we understand.

In our worship places
Of stone and wood, sunshine and air,
Surrounded by organ, pipes, incense,
Smoke and drums –

Teach us to see beyond
the clouds of eye and skin and hair.
To treasure rivers and children
And creatures running free.

And to refrain from using you
As an excuse to harm any part
Of your creation.

Lynn Baquie

1.3

1.3.30
Do Not Part Me From Thee

O God do not part me from thee,
Do not part me from thy sight.

To love you is my faith and belief,
Do not part my belief from my faith.

I've withered, become like the Autumn,
Do not part the leaf from the rose.

I, a nightingale in my love's garden,
Do not part his beak from his song.

All the fish breathe in the water they say,
Do not part the fish from the lake.

Esrefoglu

1.3.31
Eternal But Present

God is not external to any one, but is present in all things,
Though they are oblivious of His presence.

Plotinus

1.3.32
A Circle

God is a circle
Whose centre is everywhere,
Whose circumference is nowhere.

Anonymous

1.3.33
The Heart's Embrace

A heart can enclose God –
The Most High is without measure,
Unspeakably immense,
And yet a human heart can completely
Him embrace.

Angelus Silesius

1.3.34
True Light

Come, true light.
Come, life eternal.
Come, hidden mystery.

Come, treasure without name.
Come, reality beyond all words.
Come, person beyond all understanding.
Come, rejoicing without end.
Come, unfailing expectation of the saved.
Come, raising of the fallen.
Come, resurrection of the dead.
Come, Alone to the alone.
Come, for you are yourself the desire that is within me.
Come, the consolation of my humble soul.
Come, my joy, my endless delight.

Symeon the New Theologian

1.3.35
Circle Me

Circle me O God
Keep peace within
Keep turmoil out

Circle me O God
Keep calm within
Keep storms without

Circle me O God
Keep strength within
Keep weakness out.

David Adam

1.3.36
God the Unnameable

What can I say to you, my God? Shall I collect together all the words that praise your holy Name? Shall I give you all the names of this world, you, the Unnameable? Shall I call you 'God of my life, meaning of my existence, hallowing of my acts, my journey's end, bitterness of my bitter hours, home of my loneliness, you my most treasured happiness'? Shall I say: 'Creator, Sustainer, Pardoner, Near One, Distant One, Incomprehensible One, God both of flowers and stars, God of the gentle wind and of terrible battles, Wisdom, Power, Loyalty and Truthfulness, Eternity and Infinity, you the All-merciful, you the Just One, you Love itself'?

Karl Rahner

1.3.37
Cling to the Lord

Set your mind on your love
And still your wandering heart.

1.3

Like a patient tree clinging to earth
From your Love never part.

Baba Farid

1.3.38
Beauty so Ancient and So New

Late have I loved you,
O Beauty so ancient and so new.
You called, and broke through my defences,
and now I long for you.
You breathed your fragrance on me,
and I drew in my breath
and now I pant for you.
I tasted you, and now I hunger and thirst for you.
You touched me,
and I burn for your peace.

St Augustine of Hippo

1.3.39
Beyond Our Imagining

O God
whose beauty is beyond our imagining,
and whose poverty we cannot comprehend:
show us your glory
as far as we can grasp it,
and shield us
from knowing more than we can bear
until we may look upon you without fear
through Jesus Christ.

Janet Morley
In Exodus 33, Moses had to hide in a cleft of the rock when he saw the glory
of God, as no human could see the face of God.

1.3.40
Eternal Goodness

My God,
I pray that I may so know you and love you
that I may rejoice in you.
And if I may not do so fully in this life,
let me go steadily on
to the day when I come to fullness of life.
Meanwhile let my mind meditate on your eternal goodness,
let my tongue speak of it,
let my heart live it,
let my mouth speak it,

let my soul hunger for it,
and my whole being desire it,
until I enter into your joy.

St Anselm

1.3.41
The Sea of Love

O God, you are the unsearchable abyss of peace,
the ineffable sea of love,
and the fountain of blessings.
Water us with plenteous streams
from the riches of your grace;
and from the most sweet springs of your kindness,
make us children of quietness and heirs of peace.

From the Syrian Liturgy of St Clement of Alexandria

1.3.42
Eternity Within Me

The moon shines in my body, but my blind eyes cannot see it:
The moon is within me, and so is the sun.
The unstruck drum of Eternity is sounded within me;
but my deaf ears cannot hear it.

Kabir

1.3.43
God's Glory

All things are created by the Om;
The love-form is His body.
He is without form, without quality, without decay:
Seek thou union with Him!

But that formless God takes a thousand forms in the eyes of His creatures:
He is pure and indestructible,
His form is infinite and fathomless,
He dances in rapture, and waves of form arise from His dance.
The body and the mind cannot contain themselves, when they are touched by his great joy.
He is immersed in all consciousness, all joys, and all sorrows;
He has no beginning and no end;
He holds all within His bliss.

Kabir

Om is the most sacred syllable in Hinduism, the source of all origination and dissolution.

1.3.44
To Him One Must Pray

To Him of Whom one cannot speak
    To Him one must pray.
Ludwig Wittgensteing, adapted by Viktor E. Frankl

1.3.45
My Body is the Shrine

The rich
will make temples for Siva:
What shall I,
A poor man
Do? My legs are pillars,
The body is the shrine,
The head is the cupola
Of gold.
Listen, O Lord of the meeting rivers,
Things standing shall fall
But the moving ever shall stay.

Basavanna

1.3.46
Give My Heart

What can I give him
    Poor as I am?
If I were a shepherd
    I would bring a lamb;
If I were a wise man
    I would do my part;
Yet what I can I give him –
    Give my heart.

Christina Rossetti

The 'him' is the infant Jesus.

1.3.47
Worship for Your Sake Alone

O Lord, if I worship Thee from fear of Hell, burn me in Hell;
And if I worship thee from Hope of Paradise, exclude me thence;
But if I worship Thee for Thine own sake
Withhold not from me Thine eternal beauty.

Rabi'a of Basra

1.3.48
You Touch Me, Lord

Not because of your promised heaven
Do I wish to devote my love to you;
Nor from dread of a much-feared hell
Do I wish to cease from offending you.
You touch me, Lord, when I see you nailed –
Nailed on a cross – when I see you mocked;
I am stirred by the sight of your body bruised,
By your sufferings too and by your death.
I am stirred by your love in such a way
That even without hope of heaven I shall love you
And without any fear of hell I shall fear you.
Naught you need give me that I may love you,
For even without hoping for the hope that is mine
I shall love you as love you I do.

A Sonnet attributed to St Francis Xavier

1.3.49
Not Seeking A Reward

My God, I love thee, not because
    I hope for heaven thereby,
Nor yet because who love thee not
    Are lost eternally.

Thou, O my Jesus, thou didst me
    Upon the Cross embrace;
For me didst bear the nails and spear
    And manifold disgrace.

And griefs and torments numberless,
    And sweat of agony;
E'en death itself; and all for one
    Who was thine enemy.

Then why, O blessed Jesu Christ,
    Should I not love thee well,
Not for the sake of winning heaven,
    Or of escaping hell;

Not with the hope of gaining aught,
    Not seeking a reward;
But as thyself hast loved me,
    O ever loving Lord!

E'en so I love thee, and will love,
    And in thy praise will sing,
Solely because thou art my God,
    And my eternal King.

Translated from the Latin by E. Caswall

1.3.50
Pray With All Our Strength

The prayer has great power
Which we pray with all our strength.
It makes an embittered heart mellow,
A sad heart joyful,
A foolish heart wise,
A timid heart bold,
A weak heart strong,
A blind heart clear-seeing,
A cold heart ardent.
It draws God who is great into a heart which is small.
It drives the hungry soul up to the fullness of God.
It unites the two lovers, God and soul, in a place of bliss
Where they converse long of love.

Mechtild of Magdeburg

1.3.51
Longing for God

For thee, my God, the living God,
My thirsty soul doth pine;
O when shall I behold thy face,
Thou majesty divine?

N. Tate and N. Brady, based on Psalm 42

1.3.52
All Goodness

Most powerful, most high, most holy, most supreme Lord, you alone are good,
and all goodness comes from you. May we give you all praise, all glory, all
blessing and all honour. And may we offer back to you all the good things which
you have granted to us.

St Francis of Assisi

 1.4 God: Creator

1.4.1
Creation's Signs

Verily in the Creation of the heaven and the earth and the variations of night and day are signs to the possessors of intelligence.

Qur'an: 3:190

1.4.2
Lord of the Universe

Indeed, You alone know Yourself
By Your own potencies,
O Origin of all,
Lord of all beings,
God of gods,
O Supreme Person,
Lord of the Universe!

Hindu Scriptures - Spoken by Arjuna in the Bhagavad Gita

1.4.3
The World We Share

God, you have given life to all beings. Help me to appreciate that I live in a world shared by animals and birds, insects and fish and to show respect for all life. Help me to wonder at the beauty of sea and sky, mountain and valley and to reverence your creation.

Marcus Braybrooke

1.4.4
One God, Creator of All

There is but one God;
Eternal Truth is his name.
Creator of all things,
All-pervading spirit,
Fearless and without hatred,
Timeless and formless,
Beyond birth and death,
Self-existent,
Known through his grace.

Guru Nanak

1.4.5
Celebrate Often the Praises of God

O ye who believe!
Celebrate the praises of God,

And do this often;
And glorify Him
Morning and evening.
He it is who sends
Blessings on you, as do
His angels, that He may
Bring you out from the depths
Of darkness into Light:
And He is full of mercy
To the Believers.

Qur'an: 33: 41-43

1.4.6
Ever True

There is One god,
He is the Supreme Truth,
He, the Creator, is without fear
And without hate.
He, the Omnipresent, pervades the Universe,
He is not born, nor does He die to be born again.
True in the beginning, true throughout the ages,
True even now and forever shall be true.

Guru Nanak

1.4.7
Lord of All

(Praise be to You)
O Lord of the clear heavens and the light and the darkness in them;
O Lord of the outspread lands and the creatures and created things in them:
O Lord of the steadfast mountains:
O Lord of the sweeping winds:
O Lord of the airy clouds balanced between the heavens and the earth.
O Lord of the stars sent by You on their business and flashing in the air of heaven.

Muslim Devotions

1.4.8
The Delight of Being

What, you ask, is the beginning of it all?
And it is this...
Existence that multiplied itself for sheer delight of being
and plunged into numberless trillions of forms
so that it might find itself innumerably.

Sri Aurobindo

1.4

1.4.9
Worshipped by All

Tao gave them birth;
The power of Tao reared them,
Shaped them according to their kinds,
Perfected them, giving to each its strength.
Therefore of the ten thousand things there is not one that does not worship Tao,
and do homage to its power.
Yet no mandate ever went forth that accorded to Tao the right to be worshipped,
nor to its power the right to receive homage.
It was always and of itself so.

Taoist: Tao Te Ching 51

1.4.10
The Creative Principle

Vast indeed is the sublime Creative Principle, the Source of all,
co-extensive with the heavens.
It causes clouds to come forth, the rain to bestow its bounty
and all objects to flow into their respective forms.
It's dazzling brilliance permeates all things from first to last...
The Creative Principle functions through Change;
Accordingly, when we rectify our way of life by conjoining it
with the universal harmony,
Our Pure firm persistence is richly rewarded.
Confucian: I Ching 1

1.4.11
Grant Us Sight

May the God of Light
grant to us sight!
May the heavenly peaks
grant to us sight!
May God the creator
grant to us sight!

Give sight to our eyes
and sight to our bodies
that we may see.
May we see the world
at a single glance
and in all its details.

Thus, O Sun
may we gaze on you,
most fair to behold!

1.4

may we see clearly,
with the eyes of Men.

From the Hindu Scriptures: the Rig Veda

1.4.12
Prayers Filled With Beauty

O God help me to rejoice in your revelation in nature. May I recognise my interdependence with all life of our planet. May I discover an earth filled with song and landscapes of beauty. May the music of mountains and rivers and the artistry of skies, seas, and deserts enter into my prayer. Praise and Thanksgiving to you, Creator of all beauty.

Marcus Braybrooke

1.4.13
I Sparkle in the Waters

I, the fiery life of divine wisdom,
I ignite the beauty of the plains,
I sparkle in the waters,
I burn in the sun, and the moon, and the stars.
With wisdom I order all rightly.

I adorn all the earth.
I am the breeze that nurtures all things green.

I am the rain coming from the dew
That causes the grasses to laugh with the joy of life.
I call forth tears, the aroma of holy work.
I am the yearning for good.

Hildegard of Bingen

1.4.14
Love Encompasses the Whole Universe

To know that Love alone was the beginning of nature and creature,
that nothing but Love encompasses the whole universe of things,
that the governing hand that overrules all, the watchful Eye that sees
        through all, is nothing but omnipotent and omniscient Love,
using an infinity of wisdom, to save every misguided creature from the
            miserable works of his own hands,
and make happiness and glory the perpetual inheritance of all the creation,
is a reflection that must be quite ravishing to every intelligent creature that is
sensible of it.

William Law

1.4.15
Let Life be God

Let there be life said God.
Let there be God say I.
Let life be God.

Siegfried Sassoon

1.4.16
Inner Light

Help me to feel your presence
O You who has given me eyes
to see the light that fills my room,
give me the inward vision
to behold you in this place.
O you, who has made me to feel
the morning wind upon my limbs
help me to feel your Presence
as I bow in worship of You.

Chandran Devanesen

1.4.17
Thou Shalt Endure

Thou, Lord, in the beginning hast laid the foundation of the earth:
and the heavens are the work of thy hands.
They shall perish, but thou shalt endure:
they all shall wax old as doth a garment;
And as a vesture shalt thou change them and they shall be changed:
but thou art the same, and thy years shall not fail.

Bible: Psalm 102:25-27

1.4.18
The Lord of all Worlds

Say: Is it that ye
Deny Him Who created
The earth in two Days?
And do ye join equals
With Him? He is
The Lord of (all)
The Worlds.
He set on the (earth)
Mountains standing firm,
High above it,
And bestowed blessings on
The earth, and measured therein
Its sustenance

In four Days,
alike for
(All) who ask.

Then He turned to the sky
And it had been (as) smoke:
He said to it
And to the earth:
"Come ye together,
Willingly or unwillingly."
They said: "We do come
(Together), in willing obedience."

So He completed them
As seven firmaments
In two Days and He
Assigned to each heaven
its duty and command."

Qur'an: 41: 9-12

1.4.19
Whoso'er Thou Art

O thou that stayest the earth and hast thy firm
throne thereon: whoso'er thou art, unfathomable
to human knowledge
whether thou art Zeus
or the necessity of Nature
or the mind of man –
to thee I raise my voice.

Euripides

1.4.20
Who Knows?

At first was neither Being nor Nonbeing.
There was not air nor yet sky beyond.
What was its wrapping? Where? In whose protection?
Was Water there, unfathomable and deep?

There was no death then, nor yet deathlessness;
Of night or day there was not any sign.
The One breathed without breath, by its own impulse.
Other than that was nothing else at all.

Darkness was there, all wrapped around by darkness,

And all was Water indiscriminate. Then
That which was hidden by the Void, that One, emerging,
Stirring, through power of Ardour, came to be.

In the beginning love arose,
Which was the primal germ cell of the mind.
The Seers, searching in their hearts with wisdom,
Discovered the connection of Being in Non-being.

A crosswise line cut Being from Non-being.
What was described above it, what below?
Bearers of seed there were and mighty forces,
Thrust from below and forward move above.

Who really knows? Who can presume to tell it?
Whence was it born? Whence issued this creation?
Even the Gods came after its emergence.
Then who can tell from whence it came to be?

That out of which creation has arisen,
Whether it held firm or it did not,
He who surveys it in the highest heaven,
He surely knows – or maybe He does not!

Hindu Scriptures: Rig Veda X, 129

1.4.21
Fire

O Fire! Son of the most high!
Worthy of sacrifice, worthy of prayer!
In the dwellings of men,
Happiness may there be unto that one
Who shall sacrifice unto you
With fuel in his hand.

Zoroastrian litany

1.4.22
God who Gives Life

Cattle browse peacefully
Trees and plants are verdant,
Birds fly from their nests
And lift up their wings in your praise.
All animals frisk upon their feet,
All winged things fly and alight once more,
They come to life with your rising.

Boats sail upstream and boats sail downstream,
At your coming every highway is opened.
Before your face the fish leap up from the river
Your rays reach the green ocean.
You it is who place the male seed in woman,
Who create the semen in man;
You quicken the son (child) in the mother's belly
Soothing him so that he shall not cry.
Even in the womb you are his nurse.
You give breath to all your creation,
Opening the mouth of the new born
And giving him nourishment.

From Pharaoh Akhenaton's 'Hymn to the Sun'

1.4.23
Alone Existing

He was. Taaroa was his name.
He stood in the void: no earth, no sky, no people.
Taaroa calls the four corners of the universe;
Nothing replies.
Alone existing, he changes himself into the universe.
Taaroa is the light, he is the seed, he is the base, he is the incorruptible.
The universe is only the shell of Taaroa.
It is he who puts it in motion and brings forth its harmony.

Tahitian traditional hymn

1.4.24
Love is the Firstborn

Love is the firstborn, loftier than the Gods,
the Fathers and human beings.
You, O Love, are the eldest of all,
altogether mighty.
To you we pay homage!

Greater than the breadth of Earth and Heaven,
or of Waters and Fire,
You, O Love, are the eldest of all,
altogether mighty.
To you we pay homage! ...
In many a form of goodness, O Love,
you show your face.
Grant that these forms may penetrate
within our hearts.
Send elsewhere all malice.

Hindu Scriptures: Atharva Veda: 9.2.19-25

1.4.25
In Front of Our Eyes

What is wrong, O God, with this earth, that people want to rise up to the heavens?
Why can people not find you on earth, so they must seek you in the heavens?
Look at them staring upwards.
You are right before their eyes; yet their eyes cannot see.
You are in front of them; yet they are blind.

al-Hallaj: Diwan

1.4.26
My Spirit is God

My Form is the form of all women and men,
My Spirit is God.

Egyptian Book of the Dead, c 3500 BCE

1.4.27
Praise

The Creator, Lord of Light, we praise you
The Teacher, Lord of Purity, we praise you,
The day-times we praise.
The pure water we praise.
The stars, the moon, the sun, the trees we praise...
The well-created animals we praise.
We praise all good men; we praise all good women.
We praise you, our dwelling-place, O Earth.
We praise you, O God, Lord of the dwelling place.

Zoroastrian Zend-Avestas

1.4.28
Living in God

Watching a marvellous film
about the ocean depths
I felt a huge desire
to help the fish
understand how lucky they are
to live immersed
in so much splendour.
Imagine then my thirst
to cry to men, my brothers,
that we live immersed -
coming and going,
swimming to and fro -
not in the oceans
but in God himself.

Dom Helder Camara

1.4.29
Every Creature a Mirror

And if thy heart be straight with God, then every creature shall be to thee a mirror of life and a book of holy doctrine, for there is no creature so little or so vile, but that sheweth and representeth the goodness of God.

Thomas à Kempis

1.4.30
Walking the Sacred Path

Great Spirit, you are everything,
and yet above everything.
You are first and always have been.
Through you our children will have strong hearts
and they will walk the straight path in a sacred manner.
Help me to walk the sacred path of life without difficulty
with my mind and heart continually fixed on you.

Native American: Lakota prayer St Joseph's Indian School, Chamberlain, South Dakota

1.4.31
Open Our Hearts

Creator, open our hearts
to peace and healing between all people.
Creator, open our hearts
to provide for and protect all children of the earth.
Creator, open our hearts
to respect for the earth, and all the gifts of the earth.
Creator, open our hearts
to end exclusion, violence, and fear among all.
Thank-you for the gifts of this day and every day.

Native American

1.5 God's Love and Care

1.5.1
Thou Art There

O Lord, thou hast searched me out, and known me: thou knowest my down-sitting, and mine up-rising; thou understandest my thoughts long before.
Thou art about my path, and about my bed:
and spiest out all my ways.
For lo, there is not a word in my tongue: but thou, O Lord, knowest it altogether.
Thou hast fashioned me behind and before: and laid thine hand upon me.
Such knowledge is too wonderful and excellent for me: I cannot attain unto it.
Whither shall I go then from thy Spirit: or whither shall I go then from thy presence?
If I climb up into heaven, thou art there: if I go down to hell, thou art there also.
If I take the wings of the morning: and remain in the uttermost parts of the sea;
Even there also shall thy hand lead me: and thy right had shall hold me.
If I say, Peradventure the darkness shall cover me: then shall my night be turned to day.
Yea, the darkness is no darkness with thee but the night is as clear as the day: the darkness and light to thee are both alike.
For my reins are thine: thou hast covered me in my mother's womb.
I will give thanks unto thee, for I am fearfully and wonderfully made: marvellous are thy works, and that my soul knoweth right well.
My bones are not hid from thee: though I be secretly fashioned beneath in the earth.
Thine eyes did see my substance, yet being unperfect: and in thy book were all my members written;
Which day by day were fashioned: when as yet there was none of them.
How dear are thy counsels unto me, O God: O how great is the sum of them!
If I tell them, they are more in number than the sand: when I wake up I am present with thee.

Bible: Psalm 139: 1-18

1.5.2
God My Mother

O God my Mother,
You carried me
from conception.
You delivered me
from darkness.
You nourished me
and sustained me.
You let me crawl
and taught me to walk
You put the first word into my mouth.

You encouraged me.
You guided me.
You agonised
in my hurts
and my hurtfulness.
You let me go
but never stopped loving,
O God my Mother.

Anonymous; based on Hosea 11

1.5.3
Before Reading the Qur'an

Give me the joy of right listening to Thy Word and send down into my heart
those gifts of Thine which in that Word Thou hast granted to Thy purified ones.

Muslim Devotions

1.5.4
Longing for Your Word

Increase our longing for it; multiply our delight in it, to the number of the
raindrops and the leaves on the trees.

Muslim Devotions

1.5.5
Guide Us Lord

Thou art the giver of Life
the remover of pain and sorrow
the bestower of happiness.
O Creator of the Universe
May we receive thy supreme sin-destroying light.
May thou guide our intellect
in the right direction.

From the Hindu Scriptures: the Gayatri Mantra from the Rig Veda

1.5.6
Pure Love Be Here Now

O love, O pure deep love, be here, be now.
Be all; worlds dissolve into your stainless endless radiance,
Frail living leaves burn with you brighter than cold stars;
Make me your servant, your breath, your core.

Jalal al-Din Rumi

1.5.7
I Lift These Hands

I lift these hands, dear God, to You,
in praise and thanks for all you do.
You light the path through all my days

and bless me with your loving ways...
I lift these hands dear God, to You,
in troubled hours when joys are few.
You bear me up on eagles' wings and see
me through each test life brings.
I lift these hands, dear God, to You,
please grant me wisdom, patience, too.
Then fill my heart with love and caring,
precious gifts you've made for sharing.

Emily Matthews

1.5.8
Your Love, O God

O God,
I beg you to grant me your Love
And the Love of those who Love you
And the action that would lead me to win your Love
And make my love for you more dear to me
Than myself, my family, and cold refreshing water.

Attributed to the Prophet Muhammad

1.5.9
Shipwrecked

My comfortable boat of earthly happiness foundered, I was shipwrecked on the
ocean of life. I struggled amid the dreary waters of deceptive worldly dreams.

Sent by the winds of Thy mercy, a little raft of spiritual hope floated near me. I
grasped it – I held fast. Little by little I moved onward and reached a spacious
island of infinite charm.

Nymphs of Thy presence silently gathered to take me to thee. In Thy safe
presence all hurt from my hardships vanished.

Paramahansa Yogananda

1.5.10
Not An Umbrella

Lord, help us not to
Look on you as an umbrella,
But as someone who
Helps us to enjoy
The rain.

Ken Walsh

1.5.11
Easy to Believe

How easy it is for me to live with you, Lord.
How easy it is for me to believe in you.
When my mind is distraught and my reason fails,
When the cleverest people do not see further than this
 Evening and do not know what must be done tomorrow,
You grant me the clear confidence that you exist and
 That you will take care
 That all your ways of goodness are not stopped.
And you will enable me to go on doing
 As much as needs to be done.
And in so far as I do not manage it -
That means you have allotted the task to others.

Alexander Solzhenitsyn

1.5.12
No Other Helper

I have no other helper than you,
no other father,
no other redeemer,
no other support.
I pray to you
Only you can help me.
My present misery
is too great
despair grips me,
and I am at my wits' end.
I am sunk in the depths,
and I cannot pull myself up
or out.
If it is your will,
help me out of this misery.
Let me know
that you are stronger
than all misery and all enemies.
O Lord if I come through this,
please let the experience
contribute to my and my brother's blessing.
You will not forsake me;
this I know. Amen.

African Prayer From Ghana

1.5.13
God's Unfailing Help

Eternal God, the refuge of all your children,
in our weakness you are our strength, in our darkness our light,
in our sorrow our comfort and peace.
May we always live in your presence,
and serve you in our daily lives.

St Boniface

1.5.14
Jesus as a Mother

Jesus, as a mother you gather your people to you:
You are gentle with us as a mother with her children;
Often you weep over our sins and our pride:
tenderly you draw us from hatred and judgement.
You comfort us in sorrow and bind up our wounds:
in sickness you nurse us,
and with pure milk you feed us.
Jesus, by your dying we are born to new life:
By your anguish and labour we come forth in joy.
Despair turns to hope through your sweet goodness:
through your gentleness we find comfort in fear.
Your warmth gives life to the dead:
your touch makes sinners righteous.
Lord Jesus, in your mercy heal us:
in your love and tenderness remake us.
In your compassion bring grace and forgiveness:
for the beauty of heaven may your love prepare us.

St Anselm

1.5.15
Love That Will Not Let Us Go

O Love that wilt not let me go
I rest my weary soul in thee:
I give thee back the life I owe,
That in thine ocean depths its flow
May richer, fuller be.

O light that followest all my way,
I yield my flickering torch to thee:
My heart restores its borrowed ray,
that in thy sunshine's blaze its day
May brighter, fairer be.

O joy that seekest me through pain,
I cannot close my heart to thee:
I trace the rainbow through the rain,
And feel the promise is not vain,
That morn shall tearless be.

O cross that liftest up my head,
I dare not ask to fly from thee:
I lay in dust life's glory dead,
And from the ground there blossoms red
Life that shall endless be.

George Matheson

1.5.16
Brothers and Sisters

All ye under heaven! Regard heaven as your father, earth as your mother, and all things as your brothers and sisters.

Shinto; Oracle of Atsuta

1.5.17
Rescue me

O good Shepherd, seek me, and bring me home to your fold again. I am like the man on the road to Jericho who was attacked by robbers, wounded, and left half dead. You who are the good Samaritan, lift me up and deal favourably with me according to your good pleasure...

St Jerome

1.5.18
Divine Grace

In each of the three wondrous worlds of life –
The past, the present, and that yet to come –
The first before our birth, the second now,
The next to open when we breathe our last –
Through all we are maintained by grace Divine.

Tachibana-no-Sanki

1.5.19
Our Father and Mother

God is our Father and Mother
And has shown mercy to me.
In peace I will walk on the straight road.

Native American prayer of the Cheyenne people

1.5.20
I Believe

>   I believe in the sun even when it is not shining.
>   I believe in love even when feeling it not.
>   ` I believe in God even when He is silent.

Inscription on the wall of a cellar in Cologne, Germany, where Jews hid from the Nazis

1.5.21
You Open Wide Your Hand

You open wide your hand
The eyes of all look to you in hope
And you give them their food in due season.
You open wide your hand
And fill all things living with your bounteous gift.

Bible: Psalm 145:15-16

1.5.22
Trust Wholly Given

God are you there?
like an opening bud unaware
awareness awakes unafraid
in a trust wholly given
God's love flows out into his world
through the heart of a child.

Anonymous

1.5.23
Repentance

Great Spirit,
O our Father the Sky, hear us
    and make us bold.
O our Mother the Earth, hear us
     and give us support.
O Spirit of the East,
    send us your Wisdom.
O Spirit of the South,
    may we walk your path of life.
O Spirit of the West,
    may we always be ready for the long journey
O Spirit of the north, purify us
    with your cleansing winds.

Native American Sioux Prayer

1.5.24
God Will Help me

The Protector-of-the-Lowly will run to my help when in distress.
And through Him this body of mine will have peace.

What a Lord (Ram) I have, Giver of salvation!
Through Him all my concern has vanished.
What can I render to Him, Almighty One, in return?
I must at least praise Him with my lips for ever and ever.

Ramdas

1.5.25
God Hears

We can with certainty say these three things about God:
He knows;
He wills;
He speaks;
And He hears.

Ibn Sinai, also known as Avicenna

1.5.26
You Watch Over All

On you we call, Lord God,
All-wise, All-surveying, All-holy,
The only true Sovereign.
You created the universe:
You watch over all that exists.
Those who lie in darkness,
Overshadowed by death,
You guide into the right road, the safe road.
Your will is that all men should be saved
And come to the knowledge of the truth.

With one voice we offer you
Praise and thanksgiving.

Egyptian Christian papyrus

1.5.27
Love as a Guest

Love came a guest
Within my breast,
My soul was spread,
Love banqueted.

Ibn Hazm: The Ring of the Dove

1.5.28
Love Bade Me Welcome

Love bade me welcome; yet my soul drew back,
Guilty of dust and sin.
But quick-ey'd Love, observing me grow slack
From my first entrance in,
Drew nearer to me, sweetly questioning
If I lack'd anything.

'A Guest', I answer'd, 'worthy to be here.'
Love said, 'You shall be he.'
'I the unkind, ungrateful? Ah my dear,
I cannot look on thee.'
Love took my hand, and smiling did reply,
'who made the eyes but I?'

'Truth Lord, but I have marr'd them; let my shame
go where it doth deserve.'
'And know you not', says Love, 'who bore the blame?'
'My dear, then I will serve.'
'You must sit down', says Love, 'and taste my meat.'
so I did sit and eat.

George Herbert

1.5.29
I Found All Three

I sought my soul
And the soul I could not see
I sought my God
And God eluded me
I sought my brother
And found all three.

Anonymous

1.5.30
The Waters of Life

As the seashell contains the sand of the ocean
As the sun gives life to the universe
And the moon gives hope through another night,
Help me to contain the power of your love
Within my waiting, and to know
That such power is for me
A well very deep
Filled by the waters of real life,
Life with you, here.

Giles Harcourt

1.5

1.5.31
God Our Mother

God our Mother
Living Water,
River of Mercy,
Source of Life,
in whom we live
and move
and have our being,
who quenches our thirst,
refreshes our weariness,
bathes
and washes
and cleanses
our wounds,
be for us always
a fountain of life,
and for all the world
a river of hope
springing up in the midst
of the deserts of despair.

Miriam Therese Wint

1.5.32
Such Love

How can I tell of such love to me? You made me in your image
and hold me in the
palm of your hand, your cords of love, strong and fragile as silk
bind me and hold me.
Rich cords, to family and friends,
music and laughter echoing in memories,
light dancing on the water, hills rejoicing.
Cords that found me hiding behind carefully built walls and led me out,
love that heard my heartbreak and despair and rescued me,
love that overcame my fears and doubts and released me.
The questions and burdens I carry you take,
to leave my hands free – to hold yours and others,
free to follow your cords as they move and swirl in the breeze,
free to be caught up in the dance of your love,
finding myself in surrendering to you.
How can I tell of such love? How can I give to such love?
I am, here am I.

Catherine Hooper

1.5.33
We Must Come Back Together

Grandfather,
Look at our brokenness.
We know that in all creation
Only the human family
Has strayed from the Sacred Way.

We know that we are the ones
Who are divided
And we are the ones
Who must come back together
To walk in the Sacred Way.

Grandfather,
Sacred One,
Teach us love, compassion and honour
That we may heal the earth
And heal each other.

Native American: Art Solomon: Ojibway Canadian

1.5.34
Love That Cannot Be Broken

How could the love between Thee and me sever?
As the leaf of the lotus abides on the water:
So thou art my Lord and I am Thy servant.

Kabir

1.5.35
Silence

Hark to the unstruck bells and drums!
Take your delight in love!
Rains pour down without water, and the rivers are streams of light.
One Love it is that pervades the whole world, few there are who know it fully.

Kabir

1.5.36
The Blessing of Faithful Women

The blessing of the God of Sarah and Abraham,
The blessing of the Son, born of Mary,
The blessing of the Holy Spirit who broods over us
As a mother over her children
Be with you all. Amen.

Lois Wilson

1.5

1.5.37
Compassion for All

O perfect master, You shine on all things and all people, as gleaming moonlight plays upon a thousand waters at once!
Your great compassion does not pass by a single creature. Steadily and quietly the great ship of compassion sails over the sea of sorrow. You are the great physician of a sick and impure world.

From the Buddhist Amidista

1.5.38
Without You, I am Lost

Deep the river and dark the night,
I do not know the way.
Without you, Lover, I am lost,
So please, beside me stay.

I read the holy Scriptures
For many hours and long
But my poor mind could follow nothing –
Except to sing this song!

My Lover is my Saviour!
His name I sing once more
He will surely take me
To the further shore.

Meera Bai

1.5.39
I Have Saved You All

You are all my children,
And I am your Father.
For age upon age, you
Have been scorched by multitudinous woes
And I have saved you.

Buddhist: Lotus Sutra 3

1.5.40
Love Melts the Soul

Love penetrates the senses and storms the soul with all its power. When love grows in the soul, then it rises up with great longing to God and flowingly expands to receive the miracle that breaks in upon it. Love melts through the soul and into the senses. And so the body too gains its part and conforms in all ways to love.

Mechtild of Magdeburg

1.5.41
My Beloved Came

My beloved came,
I watched the road,
and I, the solitary, attained Him.
I decorated the plate
for *puja*,
I gave my jewels
to Him.

And finally,
he sent messages,
He came.

Bliss adorns me,
Hari is a sea
of love.

My eyes are linked
to his,
in Love,

Mira, a sea of bliss
admits
the Dark-one.
Meera Bai

Puja is an offering of worship. The 'Dark-one' is Krishna, often worshipped as Hari Krishna.

1.5.42
God's Desire

And God said to the soul:
I desired you before the world began.
I desire you now
As you desire me.
And where the desires of two come together
There love is perfected.

Mechtild of Magdeburg

1.5.43
God's Love Shall never Slacken

I learned that love was our Lord's meaning.
and I saw for certain, both here and elsewhere,
that before he ever made us, God loved us;
and that his love has never slackened,

nor ever shall.
In this love all his works have been done,
and in this love he has made everything serve us;
and in this love our life is everlasting.
Our beginning was when we were made,
but the love in which he made us
        never had any beginning.
In this we have our beginning.
All this we shall see in God for ever.
May Jesus grant this.

Mother Julian of Norwich

1.5.44
A Little Thing

And he showed me more, a little thing, the size of a hazel-nut, on the palm of my hand, round like a ball. I looked at it thoughtfully and wondered, 'What is this?' And the answer came, 'It is all that is made.' I marvelled that it continued to exist and did not suddenly disintegrate; it was so small. And again my mind supplied the answer, 'It exists, both now and for ever, because God loves it.' In short, everything owes its existence to the love of God.

Mother Julian of Norwich

1.5.45
Longing to Believe

While faith is with me, I am blest;
It turns my darkest night to day;
But, while I clasp it to my breast,
I often feel it slide away.

What shall I do if all my love,
My hopes, my toil, are cast away?
And if there be no God above
To hear and bless me when I pray?

Oh, help me, God! For thou alone
Canst my distracted soul relieve.
Forsake it not: it is thine own,
Though weak, yet longing to believe.

Anne Brontë

1.5.46
Thou Art Enough for Me

My Lord, whatever share of this world Thou dost bestow on me, bestow it on Thine enemies, and whatever share of the next world Thou dost give to me, give it to Thy friends – Thou art enough for me.

Rabi'a

1.5.47
Love God Now

My life is an instant,
An hour which passes by;
My life is a moment
Which I have no power to stay.
You know, O my God,
That to love you here on earth –
I have only today.

St Thérèse of Lisieux

1.5.48
He Will Meet Your Need

Of what avail this restless, hurrying activity?
This heavy weight of earthly duties?
God's purposes stand firm,
And thou, His little one,
Needest one thing alone,
Trust in His power and He will meet thy need,
Thy burden resteth safe of Him,
And thou, his little one,
Mayest play securely at His side,
This is the sum and substance of it all.
God is,
God loveth thee,
God beareth all thy care.

Tukaram

1.5.49
Footprints

One night a man had a dream. He dreamed he was walking along the beach with the Lord. Across the sky flashed scenes from his life. For each scene, he noticed two sets of footprints in the sand; one belonging to him, and the other to the Lord.

When the last scene of his life flashed before him, he looked back at the footprints in the sand. He noticed that many times along the path of life there was only one set of footprints. He also noticed that it happened at the very lowest and saddest times in his life.

This really bothered him and he questioned the Lord about it. "Lord, you said that once I decided to follow you, you'd walk with me all the way. But I have noticed that during the most troublesome times in my life, there is only one set of footprints. I don't understand why when I needed you most you would leave me."

1.5

The Lord replied, "My precious, precious child, I love you and I would never leave you. During your times of trial and suffering, when you see only one set of footprints, it was then that I carried you."

Anonymous

1.5.50
You Are There – You Are Here

You are there, O God, when a baby cries
You are there, O Lord, when someone dies.

You are there when they love and do your will –
You are there when they fight and hate and kill.

You are there and you love them, though they do not care
Though they laugh at and mock you, you are always there.

You are there with the youth as they feel their way
In a world that seems to have gone astray.

You are with the couples who try to obey
In a world that frustrates whatever you say.

With the sick and the wounded and the old you are there,
Though they may forget you, you always care.

You are here when in my distress I call –
You are here when in spite of your help I fall.

You are here in our minds, you read all our thoughts –
You are there with the criminal who sometimes gets caught.

You are here when we pray, when we sin you are here –
If only we remembered that you are so near.

You are here with me now in the dim candle light
You are here with the friend who reads what I write.

You are there in the darkness, in the light you are here,
Your presence brings hope – so why should we fear.

Roger Lesser

1.5.51
Thirsting for Love

Why am I thirsting for love
When love is the base of my being?
Why am I looking for shelter
When joy overwhelms my seeing?

Why am I hungry for friendship
When the best friend is always around?
Why do I seek words of comfort
When pierced by the sweetest sound?

Why am I blind and deaf?
Why am I dull like a stone?
Why am I stupid and stranded?
Why do I feel so alone?

Lord make me hear and accept;
Lord make me see and perceive;
Lord make me feel where you are –
Lord, help me to receive.

Lord you are wonderful to see;
You fill my every need –
Sound for the ears, joy for the heart,
The food on which I feed.

Roger Lesser

1.5.52
God's Donation

God fills our hearts with pure energy
of true love, true peace, and true happiness...
And the feeling on receiving it is, 'Yes, this is what I
Was missing, this is what I was looking for.'

And there is so much happiness –
Just as there always is on finding something
You had lost long ago.

Finding something that you had been looking for
over a long period of time always bringing a lot of happiness.

Dadi Janki

1.5.53
A Glorious Opportunity

Such a glorious opportunity stretches before each one of you. The trivialities of every day, the disappointments and the petty annoyances and the hurts which you allow yourselves to receive from daily life, are very small; but you yourselves allow them to seem very big. Let them recede, concentrate your whole being upon the love of God. Be His child! Surrender your self-will to the divine Will.

A Saying of White Eagle

1.5.54
My Loving Devotees

But those men of faith who make Me their Goal,
Adhering to the Truth,
Exceedingly dear are they to Me,
My loving devotees.

Hindu Scriptures: Bhagavad Gita, XII, 20

1.6 Gratitude and Thanksgiving

1.6.1
Be Thankful

O go your way into his gates with thanksgiving, and into his courts with praise: be thankful unto him and speak good of his name.
For the Lord is gracious, his mercy is everlasting: and his truth endures from generation to generation.

Bible: Psalm 100:3-4

1.6.2
Praise the Lord, O my Soul

Praise the Lord, O my soul: and all that is within me praise his holy name
Praise the Lord, O my soul: and forget not all his benefits;
Who forgiveth all thy sin: and healeth all thine infirmities:
Who saveth thy life from destruction: and crowneth thee with mercy and loving-kindness:
Who satisfieth thy mouth with good things; making thee young and lusty as an eagle.
The Lord executeth righteousness and judgement: for all them that are oppressed with wrong.
He shewed his ways unto Moses: his works unto the children of Israel.
The Lord is full of compassion and mercy: long-suffering and of great goodness.
He will not alway be chiding: neither keepeth he his anger for ever.
He hath not dealt with us after our sins: nor rewarded us according to our wickednesses.
For look how high the heaven is in comparison of the earth: so great is his mercy also toward them that fear him;
Look how wide also the east is from the west: so far hath he set our sins from us.
Yes, like as a father pitieth his own children: even so is the Lord merciful unto those that fear him.
For he knoweth whereof we are made: he remembereth that we are but dust.
For as soon as the wind goeth over it, it is gone: and the place thereof shall know it no more.
But the merciful goodness of the Lord endureth for ever and ever upon them that fear him: and his righteousness upon children's children.
Even unto such as keep his covenant: and think upon his commandments to do them.
The Lord hath prepared his seat in heaven: and his kingdom ruleth over all.
O praise the Lord, ye angels of his, ye that excel in strength: ye that fulfil his commandment, and hearken unto the voice of his words.
O praise the Lord, all ye his hosts: ye servants of his that do his pleasure.
O speak good of the Lord, all ye works of his, in all places of his dominion: praise thou the Lord, O my soul.

Bible: Psalm 103

1.6

1.6.3
All Wait On You, O Lord
The eyes of all wait upon you, O Lord: and you give them their food in due season.
You open your hand and fill all things living with abundance.

Bible: Psalm 145:15-16

1.6.4
Gratitude in all Seasons
When the summer of good fortune warms my tree of life, it easily burgeons with fragrant blossoms of thankfulness.
During winter months of misfortune, O Lord, may my denuded branches changelessly waft toward Thee a secret scent of gratitude.

Paramahansa Yogananda

1.6.5
Gladness in My Heart
You have put gladness in my heart, since the time that the corn and wine and oil increased.
I will lie down in peace and take my rest; for it is you, Lord, only, that makes me dwell in safety.

Bible: Psalm 4:8-9

1.6.6
Your Mercy reaches Unto the Heavens
My heart is fixed, O God. My heart is fixed: I will sing and give praise.
Awake up, my glory, awake, lute and harp; I myself will awake right early.
I will give thanks to you, O lord, among the people: and I will sing unto you among the nations.
For the greatness of your mercy reaches unto the heavens and your truth unto the clouds.

Bible: Psalm 57:7-10

1.6.7
Adoring Your Goodness
(To the deity Asclepios)
Adoring your goodness,
We make this our only prayer...
That you would be willing to keep us all our lives
In the love of your knowledge.

Apuleius

Asclepios was the Greek god of healing

1.6.8
No Words to Thank You

O my father, Great Elder,
I have no words to thank you,
But with your deep wisdom
I am sure that you can see
How I value your glorious gifts.
O my Father, when I look upon your greatness,
I am confounded with awe...

An African prayer of the Kikuyu people of Kenya

1.6.9
Thank You Lord

Thank you Lord for the sandy beach
Thank you Lord for human speech
Thank you Lord for the days that go by
Thank you Lord for the light blue sky
Thank you Lord for animals and plants
Thank you Lord for uncles and aunts
Thank you Lord for all we eat
Thank you Lord for our table and seat
Thank you Lord for everything
This is my prayer of Thanksgiving.

Helen Hobin

1.6.10
The Sustainer of the Universe

It is right to give you thanks and praise,
O Lord, our God, sustainer of the universe,
you are worthy of glory and praise.
 Glory to you for ever and ever.

At your command all things came to be:
the vast expanse of interstellar space,
galaxies, suns, the planets in their courses,
and this fragile earth, our island home;
by your will they were created and have their being.
 Glory to you for ever and ever.

From the primal elements
you brought forth the human race,
and blessed us with memory, reason, and skill;
you made us stewards of creation.
 Glory to you for ever and ever.

Canada: From the Book of Alternative Services of the Anglican Church of Canada

1.6

1.7 God's Forgiveness

1.7.1
There is Mercy With Thee

Out of the deep have I called unto thee, O Lord: Lord, hear my voice.

O let thine ears consider well: the voice of my complaint.

If thou, Lord, wilt be extreme to mark what is done amiss: O Lord, who may abide it?

For there is mercy with thee: therefore shalt thou be feared.

I look for the Lord, my soul doth wait for him: in his word is my trust.

My soul fleeth unto the Lord: before the morning watch, I say, before the morning watch.

O Israel, trust in the Lord, for with the Lord there is mercy: and with him is plenteous redemption.

And he shall redeem Israel: from all his sins.

Bible: Psalm 130

1.7.2
Grant Mercy

Say, "O my Lord!
Grant Thou forgiveness and mercy!
For Thou art the Best
Of those who show mercy."

Qur'an: 23:118

1.7.3
I Beg Forgiveness

I beg Forgiveness of Allah, my Lord
From all the sins which I have committed,
Consciously and unconsciously,
Hidden and evident. I repent and ask forgiveness for all my sins
Of which I am aware or not aware. O Allah!
You are the Knower of all things unknown
And the Veiler of disgrace,
The Forgiver of sins. There is no power or strength besides
Allah, the Exalted, The Supreme.

Muslim Devotions

1.7.4
Seven steps of effective prayer

1. I release all of my past, negatives,
     fears, human relationships, self-image, future,
     and human desires to the Light.
2. I am a Light Being.
3. I radiate the Light from my Light Centre

throughout my being.
4. I radiate the Light
   from my Light Centre to everyone.
5. I radiate the Light
   from my Light Centre to everything.
6. I am in a bubble of Light
   and only Light can come to me
   and only Light can be here.
7. Thank you God for everyone, for everything, and for me.

Jim Goure

Thanks to United Research, Black Mountain NC 28711 for permission to use.

1.7.5
My Only Refuge

From the blossoming lotus of devotion, at the centre of my heart,
Rise up, O compassionate master, my only refuge!
I am plagued by past actions and turbulent emotions:
To protect me in my misfortune
Remain as the jewel-ornament on the crown of my head, the mandala of great bliss,
Arousing all my mindfulness and awareness, I pray!

Tibetan Buddhist: Jikmé Lingpa

1.7.6
Hidden Memories

Penetrate these murky corners where we hide memories and tendencies on which we do not care to look, but which we will not disinter and yield freely up to you, that you may purify and transmute them. The persistent buried grudge, the half-acknowledged enmity which is still smouldering; the bitterness of that loss we have not turned into sacrifice, the private comfort we cling to, the secret fear of failure which saps our initiative and is really inverted pride; the pessimism which is an insult to your joy. Lord, we bring all these to you, and we review them with shame and penitence in your steadfast light.

Evelyn Underhill

1.7.7
Hidden springs

Help me, O Lord, to descend into the depths of my being, below my conscious and sub-conscious life until I discover my real self, that which is given me from thee, the divine likeness in which I am made and into which I am to grow, the place where your Spirit communes with mine, the spring from which all my life rises.

George Appleton

1.7.8
Blessed be God

Blessed be thou, O God, who alone can say 'I AM' in thine own right. Blessed be thou, O God, from whom I derive and in whom I too can say 'I am'.

George Appleton

1.7.9
Collect for purity

Almighty God, unto whom all hearts be open,
all desires known, and from whom no secrets are hid;
Cleanse the thoughts of our hearts by the inspiration of thy Holy Spirit, that we may perfectly love thee and worthily magnify thy holy Name...

Church of England: The Book of Common Prayer

1.7.10

Make me Better
I thank you, Lord, for knowing me better that I know myself and for letting me know myself better than others know me. Make me, I pray, better than they suppose and forgive me for what they do not know.

Abu Bakr, father-in-law of Muhammad

1.7.11
My Restless Soul

No deeds have I done, nor thoughts have I thought;
Save as your servant, Lord, I am naught.
Guard me, O God, O control
The tumult of my restless soul.

Ah do not, do not cast on me
The guilt of my iniquity.
My countless sins I, Tuka say
Upon your loving heart, I lay.

Tukaram

1.7.12
Repentance

May I,
who though experiencing impermanence
    still grasp at permanence,
And though having arrived at the gate of old age,
    am still proud of my youth
And all sentient beings with wrong notions as I
Receive the blessing of developing the feeling of impermanence.

May I,
who adhere to the three Refuges,
 but have little trust in my heart,
And know the three trainings,
 but have cast them aside by neglecting their application,
And all sentient beings as cowardly as I
Receive the blessings of stable, irreversible faith.

May I
who am proud of my development of Bodhicitta
 but have yet to give birth to it
And who have learned the path of the six perfections
but am still conceited
And all sentient beings with as narrow attitudes as I
Receive the blessings of practising
 the supreme Bodhicitta.

From the confession of a nineteenth-century Tibetan Buddhist lama

1.7.13

My Heart Cries to Come to You

As on the bank the poor fish lies
And gasps and writhes in pain,
Or as a man with anxious eyes
Seeks hidden gold in vain,
So is my heart distressed and cries
To come to you again.
You know, Lord, the agony
Of the lost infant's wail,
Yearning his mother's face to see.
(How oft I tell this tale)
O, at your feet the mystery
Of the dark world does unveil.
The fire of this tormenting thought
Upon my bosom preys.
Why is it I am thus forgot?
(O, who can know thy ways?)
Nay, Lord, thou seest my hapless lot;
Have mercy, Tuka says.

Tukaram

1.7.14

We Pray For Forgiveness

All that we ought to have thought
 and have not thought,
All that we ought to have said

and have not said,
All that we ought to have done
  and have not done;

All that we ought not to have thought
  and yet have thought,
All that we ought not to have spoken
  and yet have spoken,
All that we ought not to have done
  and yet have done:

For thoughts, words and works, we pray,
  O God
  for forgiveness.
And repent with penance.

Zoroastrian: from the Zend-avesta

1.7.15
May We Accept Our Limitations

Teach us, Lord, to accept our limitations.
it is of great advantage
that we shall know our place,
and not imagine that the whole universe
exists for us alone.

Maimonides

1.7.16
O Great Spirit

O Great Spirit,
whose voice I hear in the winds,
and whose breath puts life into all things,
hear my prayer!

I am small and weak,
I need your wisdom, and your strength.

Let me walk in beauty, and let me revere the red and purple sunset.
Make my hands respect all things you have made
and my ears sharp to hear your voice.
Make me wise so that I may understand
the things you have taught my people.
Let me find the lessons you have hidden in every leaf and rock.
I ask you for strength, not to be greater than another,
but to oppose my greatest enemy – myself.

Make me always ready to come to you
with clean hands and straight eyes.
So when life fades, like the dwindling daylight,
my spirit may come to you without shame.

Native American Prayer

1.7.17
Purify and Revive Me

God
Beloved Lord, Almighty God!
Through the rays of the Sun,
Through the waves of the air,
Through the all-pervading Life in space,
Purify and revive me, and, I pray,
Heal my body, heart and soul.

Hazrat Inayat Khan

1.7.18
Give Consolation

Have mercy on me, O Ishtar!
I have borne your yoke: give now consolation!
I have protected your splendour: let there be good fortune and prosperity!
I have sought your light: let my brightness shine!
I have turned toward your power: let there be life and peace!
Speak and let the word be heard!
Prolong my days, bestow life:
Let me live, let me be perfect, let me behold your divinity.

Ancient Babylonian Prayer

Ishtar was a Babylonian goddess of love and war

1.7.19
Failing to ask Forgiveness

I ask God's forgiveness for my lack of faithfulness in asking his forgiveness.

Jami

1.7.20
A Sin of Fear

Wilt thou forgive that sin, by man begun,
    Which was my sin though it were done before?
Wilt thou forgive that sin, through which I run,
    And do run still, though still I do deplore?
When thou hast done, thou hast not done,
                For I have more.

Wilt thou forgive that sin which I have won
    Others to sin, and made my sin their door?
Wilt thou forgive that sin which I did shun
    a year or two, but wallowed in a score?
When thou hast done, thou hast not done,
        For I have more.

I have a sin of fear, that when I've spun
    My last thread, I shall perish on the shore;
But swear by thyself, that at my death thy Son
    Shall shine, as he shines now and heretofore:
And, having done that, thou hast done:
        I fear no more.

John Donne

1.7.21
Forgive Me

Therefore I bow down prostrate and ask for pardon:
Now forgive me, God, as a friend forgives his comrade,
Father forgives son and man his dearest lover.

Hindu Scriptures: Bhagavad Gita

1.7.22
Accept Us in Thy Hevenly Kingdom

O GOD the Forgiver! O Heavenly Educator! This assembly is adorned with
the mention of thy holy Name. Thy children turn their face towards thy
Kingdom, hearts are made happy and souls are comforted.
Merciful God! Cause us to repent of our shortcomings! Accept us in thy
Heavenly Kingdom and give unto us an abode where there shall be no error.
Give us peace; give us knowledge, and open unto us the gates of thy heaven.
Thou art the Giver of all! Thou art the Forgiver! Thou art the Merciful!

'Abdu'l-Baha

1.7.23
No Admittance

With 'No Admittance' printed on my heart,
I go abroad and play my public part and
Win applause. I have no cause to be
Ashamed of that strange self that others see.

But how can I reveal, to you, and you,
My real self's hidden and unlovely hue?
How can I un-deceive, how end despair
Of this intolerable make-believe?

1.7

You must see with God's eyes, or I must wear
My furtive failures stark upon my sleeve.

Basil Dowling

1.7.24
My Nothingness

God in heaven
Let me really feel my nothingness,
Not in order to despair over it,
But in order to feel the more powerfully
The greatness of thy goodness

Sören Kierkegaard

1.7.25
Forgive Us and Direct Us

Forgive, O Lord, what we have been
Direct what we are,
And order what we shall be,
For thy mercy's sake. Amen.

Anonymous

1.7.26
Save Me

I am poor and wretched,
But I am Thine, O Lord:
Save me, O save me
Thou greatest of the great.
Thy Name, to thy slave Nanak
Is as his staff and his shield.
Only in the Name of the Lord
I have found comfort.

Guru Nanak

1.7.27
Fill Me Lord

As a kite needs the wind to fly,
as gloves need hands to be firm,
so I need to be filled, Lord,
with your guiding hand,
your strengthening Spirit
and your redeeming love.

Giles Harcourt

1.7.28
A Forgiving God

He is a forgiving God; kind to the distressed,
Responsive to love, and merciful always.
The Divine Herdsman places Himself at the head of His straying flock,
And feeds them, one and all.
He is the Primal Being, the Cause of all causes, the Creator,
The very breath of life to those who love him.
Whoever worships him is cleansed.
And is attached to love and devotion.
We are low, ignorant and devoid of virtue,
But we have come to your protection, O Lord of all resources.

Guru Arjan

1.7.29
The Vastness of Divine Favour

For arrogance in living unaware of the Divine Favour
We beg forgiveness
And pledge to amend our ways.
Let us live every day as an act of faith,
Rejoicing in the vastness of Divine Favour.
Let us care for those in pain
And invite them to the Way.
Let us guide those who are lost
And awaken them to a life of purpose.

A Shinto prayer

1.8 God's Care and Guidance

1.8.1
The Lord is My Shepherd

The Lord is my shepherd: therefore can I lack nothing.

He shall feed me in a green pasture: and lead me forth beside the water of comfort.

He shall convert my soul: and bring me forth in the paths of righteousness, for his name's sake.

Yea though I walk through the valley of the shadow of death, I will fear no evil: for thou art with me: thy rod and thy staff comfort me.

Thou shalt prepare a table before me against them that trouble me: thou hast anointed my head with oil, and my cup shall be full.

But thy loving kindness and mercy shall follow me all the days of my life: and I will dwell in the house of the Lord for ever.

Bible: Psalm 23

1.8.2
How Excellent is Your Mercy

Your mercy, O Lord, reaches unto the heavens and your faithfulness unto the clouds.

Your righteousness stands like the strong mountains: your judgements are like the great deep.

You, Lord, will save both man and beast. How excellent is your mercy, O God: and the children of men shall put their trust under the shadow of your wings.

They shall be satisfied with the plenteousness of your house and you will give them the drink of your pleasures, as out of a river.

For with you is the well of life and in your light shall we see light.

O continue forth your loving kindness unto those who know you: and your righteousness to those who are true of heart.

Bible: Psalm 36:5-10

1.8.3
In Your Keeping

Keep us O God and have the travellers in Your keeping and heal the sick and relieve the distressed and give security to those who are afraid.

Muslim: Radiant Prayers

1.8.4
Create Light

O God, create light in my heart and light in my eyes and light in my hearing and light on my right and light on my left and light above me, and light beneath me, and light in front of me, and light behind me, and appoint light for me, and magnify light for me, O God, bestow light upon me.

Muslim: Radiant Prayers

1.8

1.8.5
Right Guidance

Our Lord, bless us with mercy from Yourself and bless us with right guidance in all our matters.

Qur'an: 18:10

1.8.6
The Granter of Bounties

Our Lord,
Let not our hearts deviate
Now after you have guided us,
But grant us mercy
From Your own Presence;
For You are the granter
Of bounties without measure.

Qur'an: 3:8

1.8.7
God to Enfold Me

God to enfold me,
God to surround me,
God in my speaking,
God in my thinking.
God in my sleeping,
God in my waking,
God in my watching,
God in my hoping.
God in my life,
God in my lips,
God in my soul,
God in my heart.
God in my sufficing,
God in my slumber,
God in mine ever-living soul,
God in mine eternity.

Celtic oral tradition

1.8.8
Develop Heaven

Do not try to develop what is natural to man; develop what is natural to Heaven. He who develops Heaven benefits life; he who develops man injures life.

Chuang-Tsu 19 (Taoist Scripture)

1.8.9
God – the All Knowing

Oh God!
I consult You as You are all Knowing,
and I seek ability from Your power and I ask you for Your great favour,
for You have power,
but I do not,
and You have knowledge,
but I do not,
and You know all hidden matters.
Oh God!
If You know that this matter is good for me in my religion,
my livelihood and my life in the Hereafter,
then make it easy and bless it;
and if You know that this matter is evil for me in my religion,
my livelihood and my life in the Hereafter,
then keep it away from me and keep me away from it,
and choose what is good for me wherever it is,
and make me pleased with it.

Attributed to the Prophet Muhammad

1.8.10
Shelter Us

Shelter under Thy protection, O Thou Spirit of purity,
Thou Who art the All-Bountiful Provider,
this enthralled, enkindled servant of Thine.
Aid him in this world of being
to remain steadfast and firm in Thy love
and grant that this broken-winged bird
attain a refuge and shelter in Thy divine nest
that abideth upon the celestial tree.

Abdu'l-Bahá

1.8.11
God in all our activity

God be in my hands and in my making.
God be in my senses and in my creating.
God be in my heart and in my loving.
God be at my desk and in my trading.
God be in my pain and in my enduring.
God be in my plans and in my deciding.
God be in my mind and in my growing.
God be in my limbs and in my leisure.

Anonymous from the ruined walls of Coventry Cathedral

1.8.12
Lift Every Voice

Lift every voice and sing till earth and heaven ring,
ring with the harmonies of liberty,
Let our rejoicing rise high as the listening skies;
let it resound as the rolling sea.
Sing a song full of the faith that the dark past has taught us;
sing a song full of the hope that the present has brought us;
facing the rising sun of our new day begun,
let us march on, till victory is won.

Stony the road we trod, bitter the chastening rod,
felt in the days when hope unborn had died,
yet with a steady beat, have not our weary feet
come to the place for which our parents sighed?
We have come over a way that with tears has been watered;
we have come, treading our path through the blood of the slaughtered,
out from the gloomy past, till now we stand at last
where the white gleam of our bright star is cast.

God of our weary years, God of our silent tears,
you who have brought us thus far on the way;
you who have by might led us to the light;
keep us for ever in the path, we pray.
Lest our feet stray from the places, our God, where we met you;
lest our hearts drunk with the wine of the world we forget you
shadowed beneath your hand may we for ever stand,
true to our God, true to our native land.

African-American Anthem: Anonymous

1.8.13
Precious Lord

Take my hand, Precious Lord,
Lead me on, let me stand.
I am tired, I am weak, I am worn.
Through the storm, through the night, lead me on to the light.
Take my hand, Precious Lord, lead me home.

When my way grows drear, Precious Lord, linger near
When my life is almost gone.
Hear my cry, hear my call, hold my hand lest I fall.
Take my hand, Precious Lord, lead me home.

When the darkness appears and the night draws near
And the day is past and gone,

At the river I stand,
Guide my feet, hold my hand.
Take my hand, precious Lord, lead me home.

Thomas A Dorsey

'Precious Lord' was Martin Luther King Junior's favourite hymn.

1.8.14
Deliver Us from Fear

O Lord, we beseech you to deliver us from the fear of the unknown future, from fear of failure, from fear of poverty, from fear of bereavement, from fear of loneliness, from fear of sickness and pain, from fear of age, and from fear of death. Help us, O Father, by thy grace to love and fear you alone, fill our hearts with cheerful courage and loving trust in you, through our Lord and Master Jesus Christ.

Akanu Ibaim, Nigeria

1.8.15
Cast your Burden Upon the Lord

Holy God,
hear me when I call upon you.
There are times when I would like to hide away,
      to shelter like the dove from the raging storm.
Around me in the city I see violence and strife;
      by day and by night there is wrongdoing and trouble,
      there is fraud and oppression of the poor.
But I call upon you and you answer me;
      you give me wisdom and strength
      to proclaim to those in trouble and need.
'Cast your burden upon the Lord
      and he will sustain you.'

John Johansen-Berg

1.8.16
God will Give What is Needed

The devotee is always so close to God
The union is so very deep,
That God will give him whatever he needs –
His heart is never asleep.

Khwaja Moin-ud-din Chishti

1.8.17
I Trust in Thee

Unto thee, O Lord, will I lift up my soul; my God, I have put my trust in thee:
O let me not be confounded, neither let my enemies triumph over me.

1.8

For all they that hope in thee shall not be ashamed:
but such as transgress without a cause shall be put to confusion.
Shew me thy ways, O Lord: and teach me thy paths.
Lead me forth in thy truth, and teach me:
for thou art the God of my salvation; in thee hath been my hope all the day long.
Call to remembrance, O Lord, thy tender mercies:
and thy loving-kindnesses, which have been ever of old.

Bible: Psalm 25:1-6

1.8.18
My Master and I

I cannot do it myself
    the waves run fast and high
And the fogs close chill around
    And the light goes out in the sky
But I know that we two shall win in the end
    My Master and I

I cannot row it myself
    My boat on the raging sea
But beside me sits another
    who pulls or steers with me
But I know that we two shall come safe into port
    My Master and I

Coward and wayward and weak
    I change with the changing sky
Today so eager and brave
    tomorrow not caring to try
But he never gives in, so we two shall win,
    My Master and I.

Anonymous

This was my father's favourite prayer.

1.8.19
God's Answer

I asked for strength, that I might achieve,
I was made weak, that I might learn humbly to obey.
I asked for health, that I might do greater things,
I was given infirmity, that I might do better things.
I asked for riches, that I might be happy,
I was given poverty, that I might be wise.
I asked for power, that I might have the praise of men,
I was given weakness, that I might feel the need of God.

I asked for all things, that I might enjoy life,
I was given life, that I might enjoy all things.
I got nothing that I asked for - but everything I had hoped for.
Almost despite myself, my unspoken prayers were answered.
I am, among all men, most richly blessed.

American Confederate Soldier

1.8.20
Mother of Compassion

O Mother of the universe, there is nothing to be wondered at if You should be full of compassion for me, for a mother does not forsake her son, even if he has innumerable faults.

There is not such a sinner like me, neither such a destroyer of sins as You. O Mahadevi (or great God), having known all this, do as You think fit.

Sankara

1.8.21
Hear Me

Grandfather, Great Spirit, lean close to the earth that you may hear the voice I send. You towards where the sun goes down, behold me; Thunder Beings, behold me! ... You in the depths of the heavens, an eagle of power, behold! And you, Mother Earth, you who have shown mercy to your children!

Hear me, four quarters of the world – a relative I am! Give me the strength to walk the soft earth, a relative to all that is! Give me the eyes to see and the strength to understand, that I may be like you. With your power only can I face the winds.

Great Spirit, my Grandfather, all over the earth the faces of living things are all alike. With tenderness have these come up out of the ground. Look upon these faces of children without number and with children in their arms, that they may face the winds and walk the good road to the day of quiet.

This is my prayer; hear me! The voice I have sent is weak, yet with earnestness I have sent it. Hear me!

Black Elk

1.8.22
Remembrance of You Comforts Me

When the jewel of your love is buried in my mind
And the burden of your affliction weighs heavily on my soul -
Mere mention of your name refreshes me, heart and soul;
Remembrance of you is the comfort that supports me.
When my intellect has become a slave at your threshold,

Then the king of this world is my servant and doorkeeper.

Sharafuddin Maneri

1.8.23
Keep Me Straight

Lord,
Be the canoe that holds me in the sea of life,
Be the steer that keeps me straight,
Be the outrigger that supports me in times of great temptation.
Let your Spirit be my sail that carries me through each day.
Keep my body strong,
So that I can paddle steadfastly on,
In the long voyage of life.

A New Hebridean Prayer

1.8.24
Lead Me to Light

From the unreal lead me to the real
From darkness lead me to light
From death lead me to immortality.

Hindu Scriptures: Brihad-Aranyaka Upanishad

1.8.25
Dwell Within My Heart

O how you love the poor,
The humble and the true;
You make yourself their slave
Who give themselves to you...

Where can I find peace?
How to make a start?
Only if you come to me
And dwell within my heart.

Eknath

1.8.26
Don't Make It Impossible
Don't make it impossible!
O God,
you can make it tough,
but please
don't make it impossible!

Prayer of a Uruguayan survivor of a plane crash in the Andes

1.8.27
Help Me to be Righteous

Help me to be one of the righteous ones at all times. Strengthen me to work for the active propagation of righteousness... that I may prove a worthy worker in the inauguration of your kingdom of righteousness.

Based on a Zoroastrian Prayer

1.8.28
Guidance

O my God, my soul is a ship
adrift in the seas of her own will,
where there is no shelter from you except in you.

Appoint for her, O God, in the name of God,
her course and its harbour.

Muslim Prayer

1.8.29
My head on Your Lap

Lay me within Thy lap to rest;
Around my head Thine arms entwine;
Let me gaze into thy face,
O Father-Mother mine!

So let my spirit pass with joy,
Now at the last, O tenderest!
Saith Dasa, grant thy wayward child
This one, this last request!

Narayan Vaman Tilak

This was his last poem, written on his deathbed.

1.8.30
Light

O God, give me light in my heart
and light in my tongue
and light in my hearing
and light in my sight
and light in my feeling
and light in all my body
and light before me
and light behind me.

Give me, I pray Thee,
light on my right hand

and light on my left hand
and light above me
and light beneath me,
O Lord, increase light within me
and give me light
and illuminate me.

Attributed to Muhammad

1.8.31
God's Blessing

May God bless us with His grace and His qualities. May He bless us with His actions. May He bless us with His conduct and His unity, may He give us His compassion, and may He give us truth and that life which never leaves Him. May He gather us to His heart, accept us as babies, and protect us.

M. R. Bawa Muhaiyaddeen

1.8.32
An Understanding Heart

Grant us an understanding heart,
Equal vision, balanced mind,
Faith, devotion and wisdom.
Grant us inner spiritual strength.
     Free us from egoism, lust,
     Greed and hatred.
To resist temptations and to control the mind.
Fill our hearts with divine virtues.

Swami Sivananda

1.8.33
Show Me Your Ways

O Lord white as jasmine
show me
Your ways.
Call me: Child, come here,
Come this way.

Buddhist: Mahadeviyakka

1.8.34
Make Us Like You

Father, O mighty Force,
That Force which is in everything,
Come down between us, fill us,
Until we become like thee,
Until we become like thee.

African Susu prayer from Guinea

1.8.35
God Grant You Wisdom

And may God, who rules over all the world, give to you wisdom, intelligence, understanding, knowledge of his judgements, with patience. Farewell, children of love and peace. The Lord of glory and of all grace be with your spirit. Amen.

Letter of St Barnabas

1.8.36
Guidance

Steer the ship of my life, good Lord, to your quiet harbour, where I can be safe from the storms of sin and conflict. Show me the course I should take. Renew in me the gift of discernment, so that I can always see the right direction in which I should go. And give me the strength and the courage to choose the right course, even when the sea is rough and the waves are high, knowing that through enduring hardship and anger in your name we shall find comfort and peace.

St Basil the Great

1.8.37
You Are My Friend

Your name is deep within my heart
I worship you alone.
People may praise or blame me, yet
How can I change my tune!

Drunk as I am with lover's brew,
You are my friend at least.
If I love God – no fear of man
Can take me from this feast.

Meera Bai

1.8.38
Open Our Eyes

Open our eyes to your Presence
Open our minds to your grace
Open our lips to your praises
Open our hearts to your love
Open our lives to your healing
    And be found among us.

David Adam

1.8.39
Give Us Love

O God of love, we ask you to give us love;
Love in our thinking, love in our speaking,
Love in our doing,

And love in the hidden places of our souls;
Love of those with whom we find it hard to bear,
And love of those who find it hard to bear with us;
Love of those with whom we work,
And love of those with whom we take our ease;
That so at length we may be worthy to dwell with you
Who are eternal love.

William Temple

1.8.40
God is Not Forgetful

Let us not think in our heart that God is forgetful of us.
Let us give ourselves to Him for He is able to guide us...

Manichaean Psalm

1.8.41
Shield Us, O Lord

Lord God Almighty, shaper and ruler of all creatures, we pray for your great mercy to guide us to your will, to make our minds steadfast, to strengthen us against temptation, to put far from us all unrighteousness. Shield us against our foes, seen and unseen: teach us that we may inwardly love you before all things with a clean mind and a clean body. For You are our Maker and our redeemer, our help and our comfort, our trust and our hope, now and for ever.

King Alfred

1.8.42
The Wonders of Thy Mercy

Magnified be Thy name, O Lord my God! Behold Thou mine eye expectant to gaze on the wonders of Thy mercy, and mine ear longing to hearken unto Thy sweet melodies, and my heart yearning for the living waters of Thy knowledge... Cast not out, I entreat Thee, O my Lord, them that have sought Thee, and turn not away such as have directed their steps towards Thee, and deprive not of Thy grace all that love Thee.

Baha'u'llah

1.8.43
Prayer for a Stalled Heart

My heart is cold today, O God,
    I feel no burning desire
    no zeal to pray or be with you.
My heart is frozen by the chill of emptiness –
    sluggish and stalled.

Send forth your Spirit
    to revive my heart.

Spark it with a relish for service,
    with a longing to pray.

Take me beyond the need to feel
    the reassurance of a lover's heart.
May I seek to love and serve you,
    even when my wintry heart
    declines to dance
    with springtime grace.
Remind me of the ageless truth
    that we become what we pretend to be.
And as this long day passes,
    may I begin to glimpse a growing warmth
    beyond my words and deeds
    the marriage of what I would be
    and what I am.

And may my desire
    to be your flame of warmth and love
    spark other stalled souls
    to come alive, aflame in you.
May this be so, O God, may this be so.

Edward Hays

1.8.44
Safe with God

In heav'nly love abiding,
no change my heart shall fear;
and safe is such confiding,
for nothing changes here.
The storm may roar without me,
my heart may low be laid,
but God is round about me,
and can I be dismayed?

Anna Laetitia Waring

1.8.45
Seeking a Kind God

Under vaults of cathedrals eternal,
Barefoot where dusty roads wind,
With nakedly trembling candles
People seek a God who is kind.

That He'll understand and take pity
Through the murders, the raving and lies,

That He'll put his hands on temples
As on cruel injuries.

That He'll see the shouting faces
Dark of souls, eyes that light never knew,
That the fool and the whore He will pardon,
And the priest, and the poet, too.

That He'll save the fleer from pursuers,
That He'll give to the hungry bread...
Perhaps God is a cross in a hand's palm?
Perhaps God is a sky as dark as lead?

The road to Him, how discover?
With what measure the hope, pain and grief?
People seek God, a kind one.
God grant they may find and believe.

Irina Ratushinskaya, Odessa, 1970

1.8.46
For Protection

O God, who are the only hope of the world, the only refuge for unhappy men, abiding in the perfect harmony of heaven, give me courage and strength amidst the conflicts here on earth. Protect me from the utter ruin that would befall me if my weak faith gave way under the many blows which assail me. Remember that I am mere dust and wind and shadow, whose life is as fleeting as that of a wild flower in the grass. But may your eternal mercy, which has shone since time began, rescue me from the jaws of evil.

Venerable Bede

1.8.47
My Lord Will See Me Through

God restored me for a season
That I might know the more
Of His loving plan and purpose
Which, as yet, are in His store

I sense His hand will bring forth change
In attitude and state.
He'll teach me greater stillness;
My whole life recreate.

I cannot tell what lies ahead –
What's just beyond my view –
But this I know: what e'er may come

My Lord will see me through!

Thelma Bailey

Thelma suffered from a wasting muscular disease, but her faith enabled her to play an active part in her local community.

1.9 Surrender to God

1.9.1
Take All That I Am

Take, O Lord, and receive my entire liberty,
my memory, my understanding and my whole will.
All that I am and all that I possess You have given me.
I surrender it all to You to be disposed of according to Your will.
Give me only Your love and Your grace;
with these I will be rich enough,
and will desire nothing more.

St Ignatius Loyola

1.9.2
Dedication

O God!
Refresh and gladden my spirit.
Purify my heart.
Illumine my powers.
I lay all my affairs in Thy hands.
Thou art my Guide and my Refuge.
I will no longer be sorrowful and grieved;
I will be a happy and joyful being.
O God! I will no longer be full of anxiety,
nor will I let trouble harass me.
I will not dwell on the unpleasant things of life.
O God! Thou art more friend to me than I am to myself.
I dedicate myself to Thee, O Lord.

'Abdu'l-Bahá

1.9.3
To You I Submit

To You, my Lord,
I complain of my weakness,
lack of support and the humiliation I am made to receive.
Most Compassionate and Merciful!
You are the Lord of the weak,
and You are my Lord.
To whom do You leave me?
To a distant person who receives me with hostility?
Or to an enemy You have given power over me?
As long as You are not displeased with me,
I do not care what I face.
I would, however,

be much happier with Your mercy.

I seek refuge in the light of Your face by which all darkness is dispelled and both
this life and the life to come are put in their right course against incurring Your
wrath or being the subject of Your anger.

To You I submit,

until I earn Your pleasure.

Everything is powerless without Your support.

Attributed to the Prophet Muhammad

1.9.4
Integrity

Seek the truth,
Listen to the truth,
Teach the truth,
Love the truth,
Abide by the truth,
And defend the truth
Unto death.

John Hus

1.9.5
Think on These Things

Whatsoever things are true,
Whatsoever things are honest,
Whatsoever things are just,
Whatsoever things are pure,
Whatsoever things are lovely
Whatsoever things are of good report;
If there be any virtue,
And if there be any praise,
Think on these things.

Bible: Philippians 4:8

1.9.6
Not Bound to Win

I am not bound to win –
But I am bound to be true.
I am not bound to succeed –
But I am bound to live up to what light I have
I must stand with anybody that stands right – stand with him while he is right –
    And part with him when he goes wrong.

Ascribed to Abraham Lincoln

1.9.7
Do All the Good You Can

Do all the good you can
By all the means you can,
In all the ways you can,
In all the places you can,
At all the times you can
To all the people you can,
As long as ever you can.

John Wesley

1.9.8
Ever Devoted to Thee

In sickness or health, in sorrow or joy, in poverty or prosperity, in disaster or security, in death or life, I stand unalterably, immutably, unchangeably loyal, devoted, and loving to Thee, my Heavenly Father, forever, forever and forever.

Paramahansa Yogananda

1.9.9
I Abandon Myself to You

My father, I abandon myself to you. Do with me as you will.
Whatever you may do with me, I thank you.
I am prepared for anything, I accept everything.
Provided your will is fulfilled in men and in all
creatures I ask for nothing more, my God.
I place my soul in your hands.
I give it to you, my God,
with all the love of my heart
because I love you.
And for me it is a necessity of love,
this gift of myself,
this placing of myself in your hands
without reserve
in boundless confidence
because you are my Father.

Charles de Foucauld

1.9.10
You Alone

Now I love you alone
You alone do I follow.
You alone do I seek
You alone am I ready to serve.
For you alone have just dominion.
Under your sway I long to be.

St Augustine of Hippo

1.9

1.9.11
Daring to Dance

Lord God,
Dancer of the universe,
Take my hand
And dare me
To dance with you
Until I am
Out of breath
And rejoicing.

Kathy Keay

1.9.12
Mary's Lament

O God, when I am tempted to doubt
to rage
to despair
Tempted to think
there's no place
for me anywhere;
When I am tempted to rebel
and crave after a love
nearer, more tangible
and negotiable
than Yours
Woo me, rescue me
and establish me
Once more in the safety of
Your everlasting Love.

Kathy Keay

1.9.13
Where Are You Leading

Oh God, you put into my heart this great desire to devote myself to the sick and the sorrowful; I offer it to you. Do with it what is best for your service. You know that through all these years I have been supported by the belief that I was working with you who were bringing every one of us, even our poor nurses, to perfection. O Lord even now I am trying to snatch the management of your world from your hands. Too little have I looked for something higher and better than my own work – the work of Supreme Wisdom, which uses us, whether we know it or not.

Florence Nightingale

1.9.14
To see My Faults

Lord and Master of my life, do not give me a spirit of sloth, idle curiosity, love of power, and useless chatter.
Rather accord to me, your servant, a spirit of chastity, humility, patience, and love.
Yes, Lord and King, grant me to see my own faults and not to condemn my brother; for you are blessed to the ages of ages.
Amen.

The Prayer of St Ephrem the Syrian

1.9.15
Set Us On Fire

Come, Lord
work on us,
set us on fire
and clasp us close,
be fragrant to us,
draw us to your love,
let us run to you.

St Augustine of Hippo

1.9.16
Perseverance

O Lord God, when You give to your servants to endeavour any great matter, grant us also to know that it is not the beginning, but the continuing of the same to the end, until it be thoroughly finished which yieldeth the true glory.

Attributed to Sir Francis Drake

1.9.17
Grant us to love you

O Lord, grant us to love You; grant that we may
love those that love You; grant that we may do the deeds that win Your love.
Make the love of You to be dearer to us than ourselves, than our families, than wealth, and even than cool water.

Attributed to the Prophet Muhammad

1.9.18
Claim my Heart

Claim Thou my heart,
Fill Thou my mind,
Uplift my soul and
Reinforce my strength,
That when I fail Thou mayest succeed in me
And make me love Thee perfectly.

Anonymous

1.9

1.9.19
Come Down, O Love Divine

Come down, O Love divine,
Seek thou this soul of mine,
And visit it with thine own ardour glowing;
O Comforter, draw near,
With my heart appear,
And kindle it, thy holy flame bestowing.

O let it freely burn,
Till earthly passions turn
To dust and ashes in its heat consuming;
And let thy glorious light
Shine ever on my sight,
And clothe me round, the while my path illuming.

Let holy charity
Mine outward vesture be,
And lowliness become mine inner clothing:
True lowliness of heart,
Which takes the humbler part,
And o'er its own shortcomings weeps with loathing.

And so the yearning strong,
With which the soul will long,
Shall far outpass the power of human telling;
For none can guess its grace,
Till he becomes the place
Wherein the Holy Spirit makes his dwelling.

Bianco da Siena, translated by R. Littledale

1.9.20
Surrender

Lord and Master, teach me to surrender totally to thee
To let go and give myself completely,
To abandon all petty self-centred concerns
And dissolve my illusory sense of separateness
in the great sea of your omnipresence,
To ignite my life as a lamp
To illumine the world
With that ever shining light
And to serve you by serving one and all –
And by constantly remembering
And following thy example,
Let my life reflect thy wisdom all day long.

Lama Surya Das

1.9.21
A Heart of Flame

To my God a heart of flame,
To my fellow men a heart of love,
To myself a heart of steel.

St Augustine of Hippo

1.9.22
Whatever You Give

Give me death, give me life.
Give me sickness, give me health.
Give me honour, give me shame.
Give me weakness, give me strength.
I will have whatever you give.

St Teresa of Avila

1.9.23
Treasures

I have three treasures;
Guard them and keep them safe:
The first is love,
The second is, Never too much,
The third is, Never be the first in the world.

Through love, one has no fear;
Through not doing too much, one has aptitude
    (of reserve power);
Through not presuming to be the first in the world,
one can develop one's talent and let it mature.

For love is victorious in attack,
    and invulnerable in defence.
heaven arms with love
those it would not see destroyed.

Lao Tsu

1.9.24
The Light of the Minds that Know You

O God, you are the light of the minds that know you,
    the life of the souls that love you,
    and the strength of the wills that serve you:
Help us so to know you that we may truly love you,
and so to love you that we may fully serve you,
    whom to serve is perfect freedom
    through Jesus Christ our Lord.

St Augustine of Hippo

1.9.25
Whatever You Say

O Lord
whatever the world may say,
may we only pay attention
to what you are saying to us,
and seek only your approval,
which far outweighs any honour or praise
that the world might bestow or withhold.

After General Gordon

1.9.26
Loving Others

Eternal goodness,
you want me to gaze into you
and see that you love me.
You love me freely,
and you want me
to love and serve my neighbours
with the same love,
offering them my prayers and my possessions,
as far as in me lies.
O God, come to my assistance!

St Catherine of Sienna

1.9.27

Take My Life

Take my life, and let it be
Consecrated, Lord, to thee;
Take my moments and my days,
Let them flow in ceaseless praise.
Take my hands, and let them move
At the impulse of thy love.
Take my feet, and let them be
Swift and beautiful for thee.

Take my voice, and let me sing
Always, only, for my King;
Take my lips, and let them be
Filled with messages for thee.
Take my silver and my gold;
Not a mite would I withhold.
Take my intellect, and use
Every power as thou shalt choose.

Take my will, and make it thine:
It shall be no longer mine.
Take my heart; it is thine own:
It shall be thy royal throne.
Take my love; my Lord, I pour
At thy feet its treasure-store.
Take myself, and I will be
Ever, only, all for thee.

Frances R. Havergal

1.9.28

My Covenant

I am no longer my own, but thine.
Put me to what thou wilt, rank me with whom thou wilt;
Put me to doing, put me to suffering;
let me be employed for thee, exalted for thee or brought low for thee;
let me be full, let me be empty;
let me have all things, let me have nothing;
I freely and heartily yield all things to thy pleasure and disposal.

And now, O glorious and blessed God, Father, Son and Holy Spirit,
thou art mine, and I am thine.
So be it.
And the covenant which I have made on earth,
Let it be ratified in heaven. Amen.

John Wesley: Prayer from the Covenant Service

1.9.29
The Prayer of the Chalice

Father, to You I raise my whole being,
a vessel emptied of self. Accept, Lord,
this my emptiness, and so fill me with
Yourself – Your light, Your Love, Your
Life – that these Your precious Gifts
May radiate through me and over-
Flow the chalice of my heart into
The hearts of all with whom I
Come in contact this day,
Revealing unto them
The beauty of
Your Joy
And Wholeness
And
The
Serenity
Of Your Peace.

The International Order of St Luke the Physician

1.9.30
Wholly Thine

Breathe on me, Breath of God,
Fill me with life anew,
That I may love what thou dost love,
And do what thou wouldst do.

Breathe on me, Breath of God,
Until my heart is pure;
Until with thee I will one will,
To do and to endure.

Breathe on me, Breath of God,
Till I am wholly thine;
Until this earthly part of me
Glows with thy fire divine.

Breathe on me, Breath of God:
So shall I never die,
But live with thee the perfect life
Of thine eternity.

E. Hatch

1.9.31
Strength to Live our Lives Courageously

Father, hear the prayer we offer;
Not for ease that prayer shall be,
But for strength that we may ever
Live our lives courageously.

Not for ever in green pastures
Do we ask our way to be;
But the steep and rugged pathway
May we tread rejoicingly.

Not for ever by still waters
Would we idly rest and stay;
But would smite the living fountains
From the rocks along our way.

Be our Strength in hours of weakness,
In our wanderings be our Guide;
Through endeavour, failure, danger,
Father, be thou at our side.

L. M. Willis

2 Times and Seasons

2.1 Time

2.1.1
Slow Dance

Have you ever watched kids
On a merry-go-round?
Or listened to the rain
Slapping on the ground?
Ever followed a butterfly's erratic flight?
Or gazed at the sun into the fading night?
You better slow down.
Don't dance so fast.
Time is short.
The music won't last.

Do you run through each day
On the fly?
When you ask "How are you?"
Do you hear the reply?
When the day is done
Do you lie in your bed
With the next hundred chores
Running through your head?
You'd better slow down
Don't dance so fast.
Time is short.
The music won't last.

Ever told your child,
We'll do it tomorrow?
And in your haste,
Not seen his sorrow?
Ever lost touch,
Let a good friendship die
'Cause you never had time
To call and say "Hi"?
You'd better slow down.
Don't dance so fast.
Time is short.
The music won't last.

When you run so fast to get somewhere
You miss half the fun of getting there.
When you worry and hurry through your day,
It is like an unopened gift....
Thrown away.
Life is not a race.
Do take it slower
Hear the music
Before the song is over.

This poem was written by a terminally ill young girl in a New York Hospital

2.1.2
The Passing of Time

By the passing of time
Surely one is in a state of loss
Except those who have faith
And perform righteous deeds.
And those who enjoin upon one another
Abiding by the truth,
Enjoin upon one another steadfastness.

Muslim: Dr Lila Fahlman

2.1.3
The World is A Bridge

Jesus, on whom be peace, has said:
The world is a bridge.
Pass over it.
But build not your dwelling there.

Anonymous inscription on the Great Mosque at Fateh-pur-Sikri near Agra

2.1.4
Be With Us Now

God who is with us
at our beginning and ending,
be with us now,
help us to find you
in the chaos of our lives,
Let your light shine in our darkness
so that we may be guided
to walk in your ways,
all the days of our life.

Ulla Monberg

2.1.5
Slow Down

God help me to slow down;
To move calmly;
To look kindly:
To find space;
So that there is room for You and for others
In my life.

Marcus Braybrooke

2.1.6

An Idle Day
On many an idle day have I grieved over lost time.
But it is never lost, my Lord.
Thou hast taken every moment of my life in thine own hands.
Hidden in the heart of things Thou art nourishing seeds into sprouts,
Buds into blossoms and ripening flowers into fruitfulness.
I was tired and sleeping on my idle bed and imagined all work had ceased
In the morning I woke up and found my garden full with wonders of flowers.

Rabindranath Tagore

2.1.7
Time

Take time to think: it is the source of power.
Take time to play: it is the secret of perpetual youth.
Take time to read: it is the fountain of wisdom.
Take time to pray: it is the greatest power on earth.
Take time to love and to be loved: it is a God-given privilege.
Take time to be friendly: it is the road to happiness.
Take time to laugh: it is the music of the soul.
Take time to give: it is too short a day to be selfish.
Take time to work: it is the price of success.
Take time to do charity: it is the key to heaven.

Anonymous

2.1.8
Sabbath Rest

Lord of all creation, You have made us masters of Your world, to tend it, to serve it, and to enjoy it. For six days we measure and we build, we count and carry the real and imagined burdens of our task, the success we earn and the price we pay. On this Sabbath day, give us rest.
For six days, if we are weary or bruised by the world, if we think ourselves giants or cause others pain, there is never a moment to pause, and know what we should really be.
On this Sabbath day give us time.

2.1

For six days we are torn between our private greed and the urgent needs of others, between the foolish noises in our ears and the silent prayer of our soul. On this Sabbath day give us understanding and peace.

Help us, Lord, to carry these lessons, of rest and time, of understanding and peace, into the six days that lie ahead, to bless us in the working days of our lives. Amen.

Forms of Prayer for Jewish Worship

2.1.9
Lord, I have Time

Lord I have time,
I have plenty of time,
All the time that you give me,
The years of my life,
The days of my years,
The hours of my days,
They are all mine.
Mine to fill, quietly, calmly
But to fill up to the brim,
To offer them to you.

Michel Quoist

2.1.10
Time

The time I have is your gift, Lord –
In fact it is your loan.
How do I use the time you lend me –
The time I call my own?

I work, I write, I think, I talk –
I somehow fill my day;
I read, I laugh, I amuse myself –
I sometimes even pray.

Time is something like your water –
The water you make wine.
Whatever I may do with it –
Please make my time divine.

Whether I work or if I play –
Whatever else I do –
Please enrich my time, dear Lord,
Fill it up with you.

Each thought I think, each word I speak,
Each action big or small;
Fill it up with you so that
You are all in all...

Roger Lesser

 2.2 Morning

2.2.1
Awake in Heaven

Your enjoyment of the world is never right till every morning you awake in heaven, see yourself in [God's] palace, and look upon the skies and the earth and the air as celestial joys, having such a reverend esteem of all as if you were among angels.

Thomas Traherne

2.2.2
Lean on the Window-Sill of Heaven

Every morning lean your arms awhile upon the window-sill of heaven and gaze upon the Lord. Then with the vision in your heart, turn strong to meet your day.

Anonymous

2.2.3
The Best Day in the Year

Write it on your heart
that every day is the best day in the year.
He is rich who owns the day, and no one owns the day
who allows it to be invaded with fret and anxiety.
Finish every day and be done with it.
You have done what you could.
Some blunders and absurdities, no doubt crept in.
Forget them as soon as you can, tomorrow is a new day;
begin it well and serenely with too high a spirit
to be cumbered with your old nonsense.
This new day is too dear,
with its hopes and invitations,
to waste a moment on the yesterdays.

Ralph Waldo Emerson

2.2.4
Waking Up, I Smile

Waking up this morning, I smile.
Twenty-four brand new hours before me.
I vow to live fully in each moment
and to look at all beings with eyes of compassion.

Thich Nhat Hanh

Reprinted from *Present Moment, Wonderful Moment: Mindfulness Verses for Daily Living* (1990) by Thich Nhat Hanh with permission of Parallax Press, Berkeley, California.

2.2.5
Awake to Beauty

Today, like every other day,
we wake up empty and frightened.
Don't open the door to the study and begin reading.
Take down a musical instrument.
Let the beauty we love be what we do.
There are hundreds of ways to kneel and kiss the ground.

Jalal al-Din Rumi

2.2.6
You Are...

You are the peace of all things calm
You are the place to hide from harm
You are the light that shines in the dark
You are the heart's eternal spark
You are the door that's open wide
You are the guest who waits inside
You are the stranger at the door
You are the calling of the poor
You are my Lord and keep me from ill
You are the light, the truth, the way
You are my Saviour this very day.

Celtic oral tradition

2.2.7
With a Mighty Strength

I arise today
Through a mighty strength:
God's power to guide me,
God's might to uphold me,
God's eyes to watch over me;
God's ear to hear me,
God's word to give me speech,
God's hand to guard me,
God's way to lie before me,
God's shield to shelter me,
God's host to secure me.

St Bridget

2.2.8
Morning
There is joy
in all:
in the hair I brush each morning,

in the Cannon towel, newly washed,
that I rub my body with each morning,
in the chapel of eggs I cook
each morning,
in the outcry from the kettle
that heats my coffee
each morning,
in the spoon and the chair
that cry "hello there, Anne,"
each morning,
in the godhead of the table
that I set my silver, plate, cup upon
each morning. All this is God,
right here in my pea-green house
each morning
and I mean,
though often forget,
to give thanks,
to faint down by the kitchen table
in a prayer of rejoicing
as the holy birds at the kitchen window
peck into their marriage of seeds. So while I think of it,
let me paint a thank-you on my palm
for this God, this laughter of the morning,
lest it go unspoken. The joy that isn't shared, I've heard,
dies young.
Welcome morning.

Anne Sexton

2.2.9
Good Advice

Arise early, serve God devoutly, and the world busily.
Do thy work wisely, give thine alms secretely; go to thy ways gravely.
Answer the people demurely, go to thy meat appetitely,
Sit thereat discreetly, arise temperately.
Go to thy supper soberly, and to thy bed merrily.
Be in thine inn jocundly.
Please thy love duly, and sleep surely.

Sulpicius

2.2.10
Do Not Forget Me.

Lord thou knowest how busy I must be today.
If I forget thee, do not thou forget me. Amen.

Lord Astley A prayer said before the Battle of Edgehill, 1642

2.2.11
Walk Straight

O God, you have prepared in peace the path I must follow today. Help me to walk straight on that path. If I speak, remove lies from my lips. If I am hungry, take away from me all complaint. If I have plenty, destroy pride in me. May I go through the day calling on you, you, O Lord, who know no other Lord.

A Prayer From Ethiopia

2.2.12
Let Me Pass the Day in Peace

O God, you have let me pass the night in peace,
Let me pass the day in peace.
Wherever I may go upon my way
Which you made peaceable for me,
O God, lead my steps.
When I have spoken, keep lies away from me.
When I am hungry, keep me from murmuring.
When I am satisfied, keep me from pride.
Calling upon you, I pass the day, O God.

A Prayer from Kenya

2.2.13
A Prayer for Each Day's Journey

Touch me, Lord
With the promise of your dawning,
Prince of the Morning
Rising swift and sure.
Breaking through the shadows
Of my fitful sleeping
Bring me to awakening
Of your great love once more.

Touch me, Lord,
With the power of your rejoicing,
Day-star of the noon-time,
Rising on the wave
Of our Hope and Glory.
In your true light our story,
Unfolding realm of brightness
Your Spirit comes to save.

Be there, Lord,
When my day returns to evening,
Fragrant Rose of Sharon,
Fills this Day of grace

With perfumed oil of gladness
And joy from grief and sadness.
The skies reflect your presence
And the beauty of your face.

Be there, Lord,
When the nightfall veils my vision.
Light in darkness,
Guide me on the Way.
Bear me on the ocean
In the depths of your compassion.
Bring me safe to harbour
At the closing of my day.

Joan Johnson

2.2.14
Your Dreams

This day, Lord, may I dream your dreams;
this day, Lord, may I reflect your love;
this day, Lord, may I do your work;
this day, Lord, may I taste your peace.

Angela Ashwin

2.2.15
Come Into My Soul

Come into my soul, Lord,
as the dawn breaks into the sky;
let your Son rise in my heart
at the coming of the day.

Anonymous

2.2.16
We Praise You

Eternal God,
early in the morning, before we begin our work,
we praise your glory.
Renew our bodies as fresh as morning flowers.
Open our inner eyes, as the sun casts new light upon the darkness
which prevailed over the night.
Deliver us from captivity.
Give us wings of freedom like birds in the sky,
to begin a new journey.
Restore justice and freedom, as a mighty stream
running continuously as day follows day.
We thank you for the gift of this morning,

and a new day to work with you

Japanese: Masao Takenaka

2.2.17

Every Day is a Gift

Make me remember, O God, that every day is your gift
and ought to be used according to your command.

Samuel Johnson

2.2.18

Awake!

Awake my heart to be loved, awake, awake!
The darkness silvers away, the morn doth break
It leaps in the sky: unrisen lustres slake
the o'ertaken moon. Awake, O heart, awake...
Awake, the land is scattered with light, and see
Uncanopied sleep is flying from field and tree:
And blossoming boughs of April in laughter shake;
Awake, O heart, to be loved, awake, awake!

Robert Bridges

2.2.19

Daylight

I hold the splendid daylight in my hands...
Daylight like a fine fan spread from my hands,
Daylight like scarlet poinsettias,
Daylight like yellow cassia flowers,
Daylight like clean water,
Daylight like green cacti,
Daylight like sea sparkling with white horses,
Daylight like tropic hills,
Daylight like a sacrament in my hands.

George Campbell: Litany

2.2.20

Morning: After a Sleepless Night

Thank you, Father, that the longest night ends in dawn and a new day. Thank you
that your mercies are new every morning. Clear from my mind now all black
thoughts of the night and give me confidence in your loving care as I face today.
Give me your strength in my tiredness and the sure hope that your love will
guard and keep me.

Marcus Braybrooke

2.2.21
Children of Light

Rise up, O children of light, and let us give glory to the Lord who alone can save our souls. O Lord, as you withdraw sleep from the eyes of our body, grant us wakefulness of mind, so that we may stand before you in awe and sing your praises worthily.

Syrian Orthodox

2.2.22
Awakening

Great mystery of sleep,
Which has safely brought us to the beginning of this day
We thank you for the refreshment you daily provide,
And for the renewing cycle of your dreams
Which shelter our fantasies, nourish our vision,
And purge our angers and fears.
We bless you for providing a new beginning
Whose perennial grace is a tangible hope
For all the children of earth.
We praise the gift of another morning,
And pray that we may be worthy bearers of its trust
In the hours to come.
May life protect us and surprise us
And be no more harsh than our spirits may bear
Until we rest again in the vast emptiness
Of your everlasting arms.

Congregation of Abraxas

2.2.23
Morning

O our mother the earth, our father the sky,
Your children are we, and with tired backs
We bring you gifts that you love.
Then weave for us a garment of brightness;
May the warp be the white light of morning,
May the weft be the red light of evening,
May the fringes be the falling rain,
May the border be the standing rainbow.
Weave for us this garment of brightness
That we may walk fittingly where grass is green,
O our mother the earth, O our father the sky!

Native American: Tewa Pueblo prayer

2.2.24
With You There is Light

O God early in the morning I cry to you.
Help me to pray
And to concentrate my thoughts on you:
I cannot do this alone.
In me there is darkness,
But with you there is light;
I am lonely, but you do not leave me;
I am feeble in heart, but with you there is help;
I am restless, but with you there is peace.
In me there is bitterness, but with you there is patience;
I do not understand your ways,
But you know the way for me.

Dietrich Bonhoeffer awaiting execution by the Nazis

2.2.25
May We Arise to Glorify You

Strengthen, O Lord, our weakness in your compassion, and comfort and help the
wants of our soul in your loving-kindness.
Waken our thoughts from sleep, and lighten the weight of our limbs; wash us
and cleanse us from the filth of our sins. Enlighten the darkness of our minds,
stretch forth thy helping hand, confirm and give us strength; that we may arise
and confess you and glorify you without ceasing all the days of our life, O Lord of
all.

From the Liturgy of the Nestorian Church

2.2.26
Your Will Today

May my mouth praise the love of God this morning.
O God, may I do your will this day.
May my ears hear the words of God and obey them.
O God, may I do your will this day.
May my feet follow the footsteps of God this day.
O God, may I do your will this day.

Prayer from Japan

2.2.27
Prayer at Dressing

Bless to me, O God
My soul and my body;
Bless to me, O God
My belief and my condition;

Bless to me, O God,

My heart and my speech,
And bless to me, O God,
The handling of my hand;

Strength and busyness of morning,
Habit and temper of modesty,
Force and wisdom of thought,
And Thine own path, O God of virtues,
Till I go to sleep this night;

Thine own path, O God of virtues,
Till I go to sleep this night.

The Celtic Vision

2.2.28
Strength for the Coming Day

O Lord, grant me to greet the coming day in peace. Help me in all things to rely upon thy holy will. In every hour of the day reveal thy will to me. Bless my dealings with all who surround me. Teach me to treat all that comes to me throughout the day with peace of soul and with firm conviction that thy will governs all. In all my deed and words guide my thoughts and feelings. In unforeseen events let me not forget that all are sent by thee. Teach me to act firmly and wisely, without embittering and embarrassing others. Give me strength to bear the fatigue of the coming day with all that it shall bring. Direct my will, teach me to pray, pray thou thyself in me.

Metropolitan Philaret of Moscow

2.2.29
A Fresh Beginning

Every day is a fresh beginning,
Listen my soul to the glad refrain.
    And, spite of old sorrows
    And older sinning,
    Troubles forecasted
    And possible pain,
Take heart with day and begin again.

Susan Coolidge

2.2.30
Continue to Watch Over Me

Living Lord, you have watched over me, and put your hand on my head, during the long, dark hours of night. Your holy angels have protected me from all harm and pain. To you, Lord, I owe life itself. Continue to watch over me and bless me during the hours of day.

Jacob Boehme (1575-1624)

2.2.31
The Guiding Light of Eternity

O God, who broughtest me from the rest of last night
Upon the joyous light of this day,
Be Thou bringing me from the new light of this day
Unto the guiding light of eternity.
> Oh! From the new light of this day
> Unto the guiding light of eternity.

The Celtic Vision

2.2.32
I Saw

I slept and dreamt that life was joy
I woke and saw that life was service
I acted and behold! Service was joy.

Rabindranath Tagore

 # 2.3 Day

2.3.1
Blessed is...

Blessed is the spot
and the house,
and the place,
and the city,
and the heart,
and the mountain,
and the refuge,
and the cave,
and the valley,
and the land,
and the sea,
and the island,
and the meadows
where mention of God has been made
and His praise glorified.

Baha'u'llah

Travel

2.3.2
Travel

Be thou a bright flame before me,
Be thou a guiding star above me,
Be thou a smooth path below me,
Be thou a kindly shepherd behind me,
Today – tonight – and for ever.

St Columba

2.3.3
Deep Peace

Deep Peace of the Running Wave to you,
Deep Peace of the Flowing Air to you,
Deep peace of the Quiet Earth to you,
Deep peace of the Shining Stars to you,
Deep peace of the Son of Peace to you.

Celtic Blessing

2.3.4
May the Road Rise Up

> May the road rise up to meet you,
> may the wind be always at your back,
> may the sun shine upon your face,
> the rains fall soft upon your fields
> and, until we meet again,
> may God hold you in the palm of His hand.

Ancient Celtic Blessing

2.3.5
God Direct You

In thy journeys too and fro,
    God direct you;
In your happiness and pleasure
    God bless you;
In care, anxiety, or trouble
    God sustain you;
In peril and in danger
    God protect you.

Archbishop Timothy Olufosoye of Nigeria

2.3.6
Before Travel

He who wishes not to see anything objectionable on a journey should say what the Prophet of God used to say: O God I take refuge with Thee from the hardships of travel and from collision and overturning, and from the evil eye upon property or family or child.

Muslim Devotions

2.3.7
When Mounting a Means of Transport:

Glory to Him who has subjected these to our (use), for we could never have accomplished this (by ourselves). And to our Lord, surely must we turn back!

Muslim: Select Prayers

2.3.8
When the Conveyance is About to Stop and You are About to Get Out

O Lord, make my descent at a place full of blessings and you are the best of those who causes one to descend.

Qur'an: 23:29

It is said in the Qur'an that this prayer was made by Noah, when his ark was about to anchor on land

2.3.9
Exploring

Away O Soul, hoist instantly the anchor!
Cut the hawsers – haul out – shake out every sail!
Sail forth – steer for the deep waters only;
Reckless O Soul, exploring, I with thee and thou with me,
For we are bound where mariner has not yet dared to go,
And we will risk the ship, ourselves and all.
O my brave Soul.
O farther, farther sail!
O daring joy, but safe! Are they not all the seas of God?
O farther, farther, farther sail!

Walt Whitman

2.3.10
Journeys

I read in a book
that a man called
Christ
went about doing good.
It is very disconcerting
that I am so easily
satisfied with
just going about.

Toyohiko Kagawa

2.3.11
Journey Blessings

May God make safe to you each steep,
May God open to you each pass,
May God make clear to you each road,
      And may He take you in the clasp of His own two hands.

The Celtic Vision

2.3.12
New Homeland

I arrive where an unknown earth is under my feet.
I arrive where a new sky is above me,
I arrive at this land
A resting place for me
O spirit of the earth!
The stranger humbly offers his heart as food for you.

Maori chant upon arriving at their new homeland

2.3.13
Birthday

My Jesus, my King, my Life, my All: I again dedicate my whole self to Thee, Accept me, and grant, O gracious Father, that ere this year is gone I may finish my task. In Jesu's name, I ask it.

David Livingstone

A prayer written in his Last Journal, 19 March 1872 – his birthday.

Thank you for food and every blessing

2.3.14
Meals

This ritual is One.
The food is One.
We who offer the food are One.
The fire of hunger is also One.
All action is One.
We who understand this are One.

Traditional Hindu Blessing

2.3.15
A Mealtime Blessing

O Thou,
Sustainer of our body, heart, and soul.
Bless all we receive
In thankfulness.
Amen.

Hazrat Inayat Khan

2.3.16
For Food in a World of Hunger

For food in a world where many walk in hunger;
For faith in a world where many walk in fear;
For friends in a world where many walk alone,
We give you humble thanks, O Lord.

A Girl Guide world hunger grace

2.3.17
No Ordinary Meal

No ordinary meal – a sacrament awaits us
On our table spread.
For men are risking lives on sea and land
That we may dwell in safety and be fed.

Anonymous: A Scottish Grace

2.3.18
Bless my Kitchen

Bless my kitchen, Lord,
I love its every nook
And bless me as I do my work
Wash pots and pans and cook.

May the meals that I prepare
Be seasoned from above
With thy blessing and thy grace
But most of all thy love.

As we partake of earthly food,
The table thou hast spread,
We'll not forget to thank, thee, Lord
For all our daily bread.

So bless my kitchen, Lord,
And those who enter in.
May they find naught but joy and peace
And happiness therein.

Anonymous

2.3.19
Blessing on a Meal

Bless, O Lord, before we dine,
Each dish of food, each glass of wine
And Bless our Hearts that we may be
Aware of what we owe to Thee.

Anonymous: Nineteenth-century Leathersellers' Company anthology

2.3.20
A Grace for Airmen and Women

For the spirit of adventure which takes us into the air,
For God's grace which brings us safely back to earth,
For the comradeship which draws us together,
For the blessing of food,
For these and all his mercies God's holy name be praised.

A grace by R. Widdup, commended for use by chaplains of the Royal Air Force

2.3.21
A Grace for Sportsmen and Women

For the challenge and excitement of sport,
For the test of skill,
The sense of partnership in playing with a team,
For the friendships made
And for the food and fellowship we enjoy,
Thanks be to God.

Marcus Braybrooke

2.3.22
A Soldier's Grace

You have walked with us in the valley
You have stood with us on the hill.
We ask only your Pity on the living
And your Mercy on the dead.

J. Stanleigh Turner

2.3.23
A Humorous Grace

Lord, make us not like porridge,
Slow and difficult to stir
But make us like cornflakes
Quick and ready to serve.

Anonymous

2.3.24
For Healthy Appetites

Give me a good digestion, Lord
And also something to digest.
Give me a healthy body, Lord,
With a sense to keep it at its best.
Give me a healthy mind, good Lord,
To keep the pure and good in sight,
Which, seeing sin, is not appalled,
But finds a way to set it right.
Give me a mind that is not bored,
That does not whimper, whine or sigh.
Don't let me worry overmuch
About the fussy thing called 'I'.
Give me a sense of humour, Lord,
Give me the grace to see a joke,
To get some happiness in life,
And pass it on to other folk.

Sir Thomas More (1478-1535)

2.3

2.3.25
Bless My Wife and My Children

Bless to me, O God, the moon that is above me,
Bless to me, O God, the earth that is beneath me,
Bless to me, O God, my wife and my children,
And bless, O God, myself who have care of them;
   Bless to me my wife and my children,
And bless, O God, myself who have care of them...

The Celtic Vision

2.3.26
Blessing of the House

God bless the house,
From site to stay,
From beam to wall,
From end to end,
From ridge to basement,
From balk to roof-tree,
From found to summit,
    Found and summit.

The Celtic Vision

2.3.27
A Grateful Heart

Thou hast given so much to me,
Give one thing more – a grateful heart;
Not thankful when it pleases me,
As if thy blessings had spare days;
But such a heart whose very pulse may be
Thy praise.

George Herbert

2.3.28
Thanksgiving for a Sense of Humour

Lord, thank you for the gift of humour,
which adds enjoyment to life,
enables us to cope with difficulties,
and helps us to relax and to ease tensions.
Give us a sense of fun and
the ability to laugh at ourselves,
confident that you love us as we are.

Marcus Braybrooke

2.3.29
Thanks

The eyes of all wait upon Thee O Lord,
and Thou givest them their food in due season.
Thou openest Thy hand and fillest all things
living with plenteousness.

Ancient Armenian Liturgy

2.3.30
You Give Food to All

Blessed are You, O Lord our God,
King of the Universe
who feeds the whole world with
Your goodness, grace, kindness and mercy.
You give food to all flesh,
for Your mercy endures for ever.
Through Your great goodness,
we have never lacked food:
may it never fail us,
for the sake of Your great Name,
for You nourish and sustain all beings,
and do good to all,
and provide food for all Your creatures
whom you have created.
Blessed are You, O Lord,
who gives food to all.

A Jewish grace

2.3.31
Thank You God for Being There

When I wake up in the morning,
Thank you God, for being there.
When I come to school each day,
Thank you, God, for being there.
When I am playing with my friends,
Thank you, God, for being there.
And when I go to bed at night,
Thank you, God, for being there.

Anonymous: From Infant Prayer

2.3.32
The Great Spirit Takes Care of Me

I'm an Indian
I think about the common things like this pot.
The bubbling water comes from the rain cloud.

It represents the sky
The fire comes from the sun
which warms us all, men, animals, trees.
The meat stands for the four legged creatures,
our animal brothers,
who gave themselves so that we should live.
The steam is living breath.
It was water, now it goes up to the sky,
becomes a cloud again.
These things are sacred.
Looking at that pot full of good soup,
I am thinking how, in this simple manner,
The Great Spirit takes care of me.

Native American: John Lame Deer, Sioux Indian

2.3.33
For Rain

You, O Tsui-Goab!
Father of our fathers,
You, our father!
Let the thundercloud stream!
Let our flocks live!
Let us also live please.
I am so very weak indeed
from thirst
From hunger!
let me eat field fruits!
The father of the fathers
You, Tsui-Goab.
That we may praise you!
That we may bless you!
You father of the fathers!
You, our Lord!
You, O Tsui-Goab.

Hottentot prayer against drought

2.3.34
Bread for the Hungry

O God,
to those who have hunger
give bread:
And to those who have bread
give the hunger for justice.

Latin American prayer

2.3.35
Christ in the Stranger's Guise

I saw a stranger today
I put food for him in the eating-place
And drink in the drinking-place
And music in the listening-place.
In the Holy Name of the Trinity
Be blessed myself and my house
My goods and my family.
And the lark said in her warble
Often, often, often
Goes Christ in the stranger's guise
O, oft and oft and oft,
Goes Christ in the Stranger's guise.

Celtic: A Rune of Hospitality

2.3.36
When Enjoying Some Blessing

O my Lord, give me the ability to thank You for the blessing You have bestowed upon me and my parents, and to do good which pleases You and admit me, with Your mercy, among Your righteous servants.

Muslim: Al Ahqaf

2.3.37
After a Meal

Praise be to God who gave us food and drink and took care of our needs and housed us and blessed us amply.

Muslim prayer from Radiant Prayers

2.3.38
Meal

We give you thanks
For this food which is our life,
For the fruits of the earth,
Conceived in darkness
Rooted in the secret soil.
We offer you our part in the mess of creativity.
We wash, prepare, cook, present;
We eat and taste and enjoy with our bodies;
We clear away the mess.
We embrace with you the chaos that fulfils,
The secret labour that maintains life.

Janet Morley

2.3.39
The Lord be Thankit

Some hae meat and canna eat,
And some wad eat that want it;
But we hae meat, and we can eat,
And sae the Lord be thankit.

Robert Burns

2.3.40
Worthy of Prayer

O Fire! Son of the most high!
Worthy of sacrifice, worthy of prayer!
In the dwellings of men,
Happiness may there be unto that one
Who shall sacrifice unto you
with fuel in his hand.

Zoroastrian litany

2.3.41
You Open Wide Your Hand

The eyes of all look to you in hope
and you give them their food in due season.
You open wide your hand
and fill all things living with your bounteous gift.

Bible: Psalm 145:15-16

2.3.42
Bless Our Food and Drink

God bless the poor
God bless the sick
And bless the human race.
God bless our food.
God bless our drink.
All homes, O God, embrace.

St Bridget of Kildare

2.3.43
Chez Nous

When people turn
from the table
where bread is broken
and candles glow,
be sure you have invited them
not to your house
but to their own,

and offered not your wisdom
but your love.

Anonymous

2.3.44
Friends

Lord God
Friend of the Friendless,
Thank you
For our friends.
Help us to be faithful
In loving those
You have brought into our lives.
Keep us free from
Needless distractions
And excessive business
So that we can give
Our best energies
In making friendship
With them
And with You.

Kathy Keay

The day in your hands

2.3.45
Disturb Us

Disturb us, Lord, when
We are too well pleased with ourselves,
When our dreams have come true
Because we have dreamed too little,
When we arrived safely
Because we sailed too close to the shore.
Disturb us, Lord, when
With the abundance of things we possess
We have lost our thirst
For the waters of life;
Having fallen in love with life,
We have ceased to dream of eternity
And in our efforts to build a new earth,
We have allowed our vision
Of the new Heaven to dim.
Disturb us, Lord, to dare more boldly,
To venture on wider seas
Where storms will show Your mastery;

Where losing sight of land,
We shall find the stars.
We ask You to push back
The horizons of our hopes;
And to push us into the future
In strength, courage, hope, and love.

Attributed to Sir Francis Drake

2.3.46
Fulfilment

We thank you, God, for the moments of fulfilment:
    the end of a day's work
    the harvest of sugar cane,
    the birth of a child,
for in these pauses, we feel the rhythm of the eternal.

Prayer from Hawaii

2.3.47
The Servant's Prayer

May no one who encounters me
ever have an insignificant contact.
May the mere fact of our meeting
contribute to the fulfilment of their wishes.

May I be a protector of the helpless,
a guide to those travelling the path,
a boat to those wishing to cross over,
or a bridge or a raft.

May I be a lamp for those in darkness,
a home for the homeless,
and a servant to the world.

Buddhist: From the Bodhicaryavatara of Shantideva

2.3.48
Christ's Hands

Christ has no body now on earth but yours,
no hands but yours,
no feet but yours.
Yours are the eyes through which is to look out
Christ's compassion to the world;
Yours are the feet with which he is to go about doing good;
Yours are the hands with which he is to bless people now.

St Teresa of Avila

2.3.49
Daily Tasks

Let me use suspense as material for perseverance:
Let me use danger as material for courage
Let me use reproach as material for longsuffering:
Let me use praise as material for temperance:
Let me use pain as material for endurance.

John Baillie

2.3.50
Dance

Dance as though no one is watching you,
Love as though you have never been hurt before,
Sing as though no one can hear you,
Live as though heaven is on earth.

Anonymous

2.3.51
Perseverance

O Lord God, when You give to your servants to endeavour any great matter, grant us also to know that it is not the beginning, but the continuing of the same to the end, until it be thoroughly finished which yieldeth the true glory.

Attributed to Sir Francis Drake

2.4 Evening and Night

Evening

2.4.1
Signs for Humankind

The night and the day, the sun and the moon, are some of God' signs.
Do not prostrate yourself in worship to sun and moon.
Worship God, He who made them – if it be He whose servants you are.

Qur'an, sura 41:37

2.4.2
When Evening Comes

When evening comes
I will leave the door open beforehand and then wait
For him who said he would come
To meet me in my dreams.

Yakamochi

2.4.3

O Strength and Stay.
O Strength and Stay upholding all creation,
      Who ever dost thyself unmoved abide,
Yet day by day the light in due gradation
      From hour to hour through all its changes guide;

Grant to life's day a calm unclouded ending,
      An eve untouched by shadows of decay,
The brightness of a holy death-bed blending
      With dawning glories of the eternal day...

Ascribed to St Ambrose

2.4.4
Evening

It is a beauteous evening, calm and free;
The holy time is quiet as a nun
Breathless with adoration; the broad sun
Is sinking down in its tranquillity;

The gentleness of heaven is on the Sea:
Listen! The mighty Being is awake,
And doth with his eternal motion make
A sound like thunder everlastingly.

William Wordsworth

2.4.5
The Day is No More

The day is no more, the shadow is upon the earth. It is time that I go to the stream to fill my pitcher. The evening air is eager with the sad music of the water. Ah, it calls me out into the dusk. In the lonely lane there is no passer-by, the wind is up, the ripples are rampant in the river. I know not if I shall come back home. I know not whom I shall chance to meet. There at the fording in the little boat the unknown man plays upon his lute.

Rabindranath Tagore

2.4.6
Lighten Our Darkness

Lighten our darkness, we beseech Thee, O Lord, and by thy great mercy defend us from all the perils and dangers of this night, through Jesus Christ our Lord.

Church of England: Book of Common Prayer (1662)

2.4.7
Evening

Support us, O Lord, all the day long of this troublesome life, till the shadows lengthen, and the evening comes, the busy world is hushed, and the fever of life is over and our work is done. Then in Thy mercy grant us a safe lodging, a holy rest and peace at the last. Amen.

Church of England: Book of Common Prayer (1928)

2.4.8
Twilight

Blessed are You, Lord our God, king of the universe. By His word He brings on the evening twilight; in His wisdom He opens the gates of dawn, and with foresight makes times pass and seasons change. He sets the stars in their courses in the sky according to His plan. He creates day and night, turning light into darkness and darkness into light. He makes the day fade away and brings on the night, and separates day and night, for He is the Lord of the hosts of heaven. Blessed are You Lord, who brings on the evening twilight.

Forms of prayer for Jewish Worship

Sleep

2.4.9
Bed-time

Cause us, our Father, to lie down in peace, and rise again to enjoy life. Spread over us the covering of your peace, guide us with your good counsel and save us for the sake of your name. Be a shield about us, turning away every enemy, disease, violence, hunger and sorrow.

Shelter us in the shadow of your wings, for you are a God who guards and protects us, a ruler of mercy and compassion. Guard us when we go out and when we come in, to enjoy life and peace now and forever, and spread over us the shelter of your peace.

From the Jewish Daily Service

2.4.10
Sleep

Sweet Spirit of Sleep, who brings peace and rest to weary bodies,
Empty us of aches and pains,
for we struggle as seed through unyielding earth.
Bring us to the timeless nature of your presence –
the endless void of our slumber.
Make us aware of the work we can do while in your time.
Make us to know our dreaming,
where past and future are reconciled.
Come let us honour sleep, that knits up
the ravelled sleeve of care, the death of each day's life,
sore labour's bath, balm of hurt minds,
great nature's second course
chief nourisher in life's feast.

Congregation of Abraxas

2.4.11
Sleep in Your Arms

Now that the sun has set,
I sit and rest, and think of you.
Give my weary body peace.
Let my legs and arms stop aching,
Let my nose stop sneezing,
Let my head stop thinking.
Let me sleep in your arms.

African Dinka prayer

2.4.12
Strong to Endure

Go with each of us to rest; if any awake, temper to them the dark hours of watching; and when the day returns, return to us, our sun and comforter, and call us up with morning faces and with morning hearts, eager to labour, eager to be happy, if happiness should be our portion, and if the day be marked for sorrow, strong to endure it.

Robert Louis Stevenson

Written the night before he died.

2.4

2.4.13
Going to Bed

As my head rests on my pillow
Let my soul rest in your mercy.

As my limbs relax on my mattress,
Let my soul relax in your peace.

As my body finds warmth beneath the blankets,
Let my soul find warmth in your love.

As my mind is filled with dreams,
Let my soul be filled with visions of heaven.

Johann Freylinghausen

2.4.14
Thy Door is Open

My God and my Lord, eyes are at rest, stars are setting, hushed are the movements of birds in their nests, of monsters in the deep. And Thou art the Just who knowest no change, the Equity that swerveth not, the Everlasting that passeth not away. The doors of kings are locked, watched by their bodyguards; but Thy door is open to him who calls on Thee. My Lord, each lover is now alone with his beloved, and Thou art for me the Beloved.

Muslim Devotions

2.4.15
After a Good Dream

Grace be to God through Whose blessings good things are accomplished.

Muslim: Hasan Al Bânna's Al-Mathoorat

2.4.16
After a Bad Dream

Grace be to God under all circumstances.

Muslim: Hasan Al Bânna's Al-Mathoorat

2.4.17
You Are My Mother and My Father

O God, you have let me pass this day in peace,
let me pass the night in peace.
O Lord who has no Lord
there is no strength but in you.
You alone have no obligation.
Under your hand I pass the night.
You are my mother and my father.

A prayer from Kenya

2.4.18
Shelter Me in the Shadow of Your Wings

Lord Jesus Christ, who received the children who came to you,
receive this evening prayer from the lips of me, your child.
Shelter me in the shadow of your wings
that I may lie down and sleep in peace;
and wake me at the proper time to give you glory,
for you alone are good and love humankind.

From the Orthodox Church

2.4.19
Afraid

As I looked
a mist blurred
my mirror vision
my face dissolved
into a cloud of confusion
worries seized my brain
my head seemed to contain
an excessive burden
then your words encouraged me
'Let tomorrow's troubles come tomorrow'
the mist cleared
and I trusted in You.

Ellen Wilkie

2.4.20
I Am Not Afraid

The sun has disappeared
I have switched off the light
And my wife and children are asleep.
The animals in the forest are full of fear,
And so are the people on their mats.
They prefer the day with your sun
To the night.
But still I know that your moon is there,
And your eyes and also your hands.
Thus I am not afraid.
This day again
You led us wonderfully.
Everybody went to his mat
Satisfied and full.
Renew us during our sleep,
That in the morning we may come afresh to our daily jobs.

Be with our brothers far away in Asia
Who may be getting up now.

Prayer of a young Ghanaian Christian

2.4.21
The Day is Ended

The day thou gavest, Lord, is ended,
    The darkness falls at thy behest;
To thee our morning hymns ascended,
    Thy praise shall sanctify our rest...

The sun that bids us rest is waking
    Our brethren 'neath the western sky,
And hour by hour fresh lips are making
    Thy wondrous doings heard on high.

J. Ellerton

2.4.22
Too Tired to Pray

In the night of my weariness let me give myself up to sleep without struggle,
resting my trust upon thee.
Let me not force my flagging spirit into a poor preparation for thy worship.
It is thou who drawest the veil of night upon the tired eyes of the day to renew
its sight in a fresher gladness of awakening.

Rabindranath Tagore

2.4.23
I Don't Like the Man Who Does Not Sleep

I don't like the man who doesn't sleep, says God.
Sleep is a friend of man.
Sleep is the friend of God.
Sleep is perhaps the most beautiful thing I have created.
And I myself rested on the seventh day.
He whose heart is pure, sleeps.
And he who sleeps has a pure heart.

Charles Péguy, from God Speaks

Night

2.4.24
Hymn to Night

Night shield us from the wolf and the thief.
Throughout your hours let there be calm.
Pitch dark has brought a shroud for me.
Dawn, drive it, like my debts, away.

Child of Day, to you, as to a calf,
My hymn is offered.

Hindu Scriptures: Rig Veda

2.4.25
May Angels Attend Us

Watch, dear Lord, with those who wake, or watch, or weep tonight,
and give your angels charge over those who sleep;
Tend your sick ones, O Lord Christ, rest your weary ones,
bless your dying ones, O Lord Christ, soothe your suffering ones,
pity your afflicted ones, shield your joyous ones,
and all for your love's sake. Amen.

St Augustine of Hippo

2.4.26
Sleepless Nights

As I toss restless in my bed, help me O Lord to turn to you and not to worry that I
will be too tired tomorrow. You will give me the strength and the rest you know
that I need. In my sleeplessness deepen my sympathy for those who work at
night, for all in pain, for those giving birth and those who are dying and for all
victims of torture who are frightened and alone. Free or imprisoned, awake or
asleep, alive or dead, we are all in your care now and at all times.

Marcus Braybrooke

2.4.27
All Our Problems to the Setting Sun

All our problems
    We send to the setting sun
All our difficulties
    We send to the setting sun
All the devil's works
    We send to the setting sun
All our hopes
    We set on the Risen Son.

Kenyan Revised Liturgy for Holy Communion

2.4.28
Too Tired for Words

O Lord my heart is all a prayer,
But it is silent unto thee;
I am too tired to look for words,
I rest upon thy sympathy
To understand when I am dumb;
All well I know thou hearest me.

I know thou hearest me because
A quiet peace comes down to me,
And fills the places where before,
Weak thoughts were wandering wearily;
And deep within me it is calm,
Though waves are tossing outwardly.

Amy Carmichael

2.4.29
A Peaceful Night

Lord, let Your light be only for the day,
And the darkness for the night.
And let my dress, my poor humble dress
Lie quietly over my chair at night.

Let the church-bells be silent,
My neighbour Ivan not ring them at night.
Let the wind not awaken the children
Out of their sleep at night.

Let the hen sleep on its roost, the horse in the stable
All through the night.
Remove the stone from the middle of the road
That the thief may not stumble at night.

Let heaven be quiet during the night.
Restrain the lightning, silence the thunder,
They should not frighten mothers giving birth
To their babies at night.

And me too protect against fire and water,
Protect my poor roof at night.
Let my dress, my poor humble dress
Lie quietly over my chair at night.

Nachum Bomze

2.5 Seasons of the Year

2.5.1
New Year

I said to the man who stood at the gate of the year 'Give me a light that I may tread safely into the unknown'. And he replied: 'Go out into the darkness and put your hand into the hand of God. That shall be better than light and safer than a known way.'

Minnie Loise Haskins (1875-1957) quoted by King George VI in his Christmas broadcast 1939

2.5.2
Ring Out, Wild Bells

Ring out, wild bells, to the wild sky,
The flying cloud, the frosty light:
The year is dying in the night;
Ring out, wild bells, and let him die.

Ring out the grief that saps the mind,
For those that here we see no more;
Ring out the feud of rich and poor,
Ring in redress to all mankind.

Ring out a slowly dying cause,
And ancient forms of party strife;
Ring in the nobler modes of life,
With sweeter manners, purer laws.

Ring out false pride in place and blood,
The civic slander and the spite;
Ring in the love of truth and right,
Ring in the common love of good.

Ring out old shapes of foul disease,
Ring out the narrowing lust of gold;
Ring out the thousand wars of old,
Ring in the thousand years of peace.

Ring in the valiant man and free,
The larger heart, the kindlier hand;
Ring out the darkness of the land,
Ring in the Christ that is to be.

Alfred Lord Tennyson

2.5.3
The Bells on Christmas Day

I heard the bells on Christmas Day
Their old familiar carols play,
And wild and sweet
The words repeat,
Of 'Peace on earth, goodwill to all!'

I thought how, as the day had come,
The belfries of all Christendom
Had rolled along
The unbroken song,
Of 'Peace on earth, goodwill to all!'

Till ringing, singing on its way,
The world revolved from night to day,
A voice, a chime,
A chant sublime,
Of 'Peace on earth, goodwill to all!'

And in despair I bowed my head;
'There is no peace on earth,' I said.
'For hate is strong
And mocks the song
Of Peace on earth, goodwill to all!'

Then pealed the bells more loud and deep:
'God is not dead; nor doth God sleep
The wrong shall fail,
The right prevail,
'With Peace on earth, goodwill to all!'

H. W. Longfellow

2.5.4
Winter

Winter is so beautiful
and the wintry portions of my life
are those which often give birth
to a deeper understanding of who you
created me to be, O God.

Winter for me is an eye-opener.
I learn to appreciate
instead of bemoaning
to delight at the sight

of freshly fallen snow
looking in awe
at the frost-frozen tree limbs
openly rejoicing and celebrating.

Winter gives me more time to explore,
to reach out,
a time to make new plans
with a ripple of hope
within my soul.

Penny Tressler

Spring

2.5.5
Kiss of Spring

Who but You O God can rescue the earth
from the grip of winter?
You take the bare fields, bleak and desolate
and dress them in green,
splashing us with colours,
reminding us that Life comes
through You.
All about me buds are bursting,
I am dwarfed by Your great universe
when spring arrives.

Tammy Felton

2.5.6
Spring

Nothing is so beautiful as spring –
When weeds, in wheels, shoot long and lovely and lush;
Thrush's eggs look little low heavens, and thrush
Through the echoing timber does so rinse and wring
The ear, it strikes like lightnings to hear him sing;
The glassy pear tree leaves and blooms, they brush
The descending blue; that blue is all in a rush
With richness; the racing lambs too have their fling.
What is all this juice and all this joy?
A strain of the earth's sweet being in the beginning
In Eden garden...

Gerard Manley Hopkins

2.5.7
Winter is Past

For, lo, the winter is past, the rain is over and gone;
The flowers appear on the earth; the time of the singing of birds is come, and the voice of the turtle is heard in our land;
The fig tree putteth forth her green figs, and the vines with the tender grape give a good smell.

Bible: Song of Solomon 2:11-13

2.5.8
Spring

Spring - through
Morning mist,
What mountain's there?

Japanese Haiku

2.5.9
New Beings

Under the influence of the Vernal yang, the vegetation was reborn
The time of fertilising rains, the time of love
the thunder resounds and awakes the hibernating creatures.
That which seemed dead revives and pursues its destiny.
May the immeasurable new beings live their life to its end.
May the crowd of the living fully enjoy the happiness of the vernal spring.

Emperor Ou of China

2.5.10
Spring Rain

Spring rain -
Under trees
A crystal stream.

Japanese Haiku

2.5.11

Seed silence
I did not hear you fall
from pod to mother earth.

I did not hear you call
or cry your humble birth.

I did not hear you sigh
as silently you grew.

I did not hear a Why

2.5

because God made you you.
And yet your silence spoke
of confidence and might
and purpose as you broke
through earth into the light.

Harry Alfred Wiggett

Summer

2.5.12
Summer Moon

Summer moon –
Clapping hands,
I herald dawn.

Japanese Haiku

2.5.13
A Psalm of Summer's Siren

I salute you, God of rest and vacations,
>who laid down the law
>that every seventh day must be free.
No work for beast, man or woman
>was your legal word.
On this summer day, when my heart longs for leisure,
>my head tells me, 'It's time to go to work'.
I wish I had an extra sabbath
to enjoy your gift of liberty and peace.

Part of me is so grown-up,
and knows how to be productive,
to be responsible and to achieve.
>I have learned to listen to that inner adult
>and how to successfully silence
>the echoes of childhood's play.
I may know and possess more, but I've lost something
>in being a repeat offender, O God,
and in breaking your law of Seventh Day Vacations.
I have forgotten how to vacate my work,
to come out of my head and go out-of-doors,
to play with you in the summer sun.

Edward Hays

Autumn – Harvest

2.5.14
Stir the Soil

God stir the soil
Run the ploughshare deep,
Cut the furrows round and round,
Overturn the hard, dry ground,
Spare no strength nor toil
Even though I weep.
In the loose, fresh-mangled earth
Sow new seed.
Free of withered vine and weed
Bring fair flowers to birth.

Anonymous: A Prayer from Singapore

2.5.15
Harvest

We dare not ask you bless our harvest feast
Till it is spread for poorest and for least.
We dare not bring our harvest gifts to you
Unless our hungry brothers share them too.

Not only at this time, Lord, every day
Those whom you love are dying while we pray.
Teach us to do with less, and so to share
From our abundance more than we can spare.

Now with this harvest plenty round us piled,
Show us the Christ in every starving child;
Speak, as you spoke of old in Galilee,
'You feed, or you refuse, not them but me!'

Lilian Cox

2.5.16
The Everlasting Mercy

O Christ who holds the open gate,
O Christ who drives the furrow straight,
O Christ, the plough, O Christ, the laughter
Of holy white birds flying after,

Lo, all my heart's field red and torn,
And thou wilt bring the young green corn,
The young green corn divinely springing,
The young green corn for ever singing;

And when the field is fresh and fair
The blessèd feet shall glitter there,
And we will walk the weeded field,
And tell the golden harvest's yield,

The corn that makes the holy bread
By which the soul of man is fed,
The holy bread, the food unpriced,
Thy everlasting mercy, Christ.

John Masefield

2.5.17
Early Autumn

Early autumn –
rice field, ocean,
Once green.

Japanese Haiku

Winter

2.5.18
End of the Year

Year's end, all
Corners of this
Floating world, swept.

Basho, Japanese Haiku

2.5.19
Christmas

Beneath the Christmas tree of civilization, with its many branches of races, may
we lay imperishable presents of goodwill, spiritual service, and unconditional love
for all. These are the gifts that Christ wants to receive.

Paramahansa Yogananda

3 Through All the Changing Scenes of Life

3.1 Birth

3.1.1
Womb of God

Transforming womb of God
Conceive in us;
Create in us;
Create a new Life;
Faith, the confidence to bear
Hope, continuously expectant
Love, the true beginning.

Sally Dyck

3.1.2
Our Desire For a Child

Our loving Father in heaven, we bring to you our deep desire to have a child. You created the family and we believe that our desire comes from you. You are the giver of life. Hear our prayer and grant us our request.
Take the stress and anxiety from our lives that we may not become so obsessive that we forfeit your peace or miss the opportunities of life that the present offers.

Marcus Braybrooke

3.1.3

For the Gift of Children
Lord, if it is not your plan to give us children, begin to give us the grace to accept your will. Help us never to feel belittled or lessened by what seems like failure but to know our worth as your children.
Above all we pray for those qualities of a father and a mother that will make us more like you and enable us to love and care for all those you bring our way.

Marcus Braybrooke

3.1.4
Unexpected Child

Father, we commit to you the child that I am carrying. You know that we had not planned or wanted a baby and we bring to you all our feelings of shock, resentment, worry and inability to cope.
Help us to be accepting, that, even now, this child may never experience rejection or disfavour. Help us to welcome the one that you are sending as a gift from you. Provide where we have no resources and give us the joy of seeing, in the fullness of time, your perfect will fulfilled in the gift of a son or a daughter.

Marcus Braybrooke

3.1.5
Before Birth: A Waiting Prayer

Here, Lord
We await your gift of life,
Grown in secret
Now in ripeness
Full fruited
Ready to be received.

Lord, we long for our child,
Born out of covenant love
Nurtured in love, hope, forgiveness,
Received as a gift, blessing, joy.

Release in her abundant grace,
Enjoyment of all that earth affords,
Gentleness to those whose way has been hard,
Patience, kindliness and faith.

We receive, nurture and set free your gift,
Not only our child, but yours,
Yours to enjoy and delight in,
Ours to marvel at your generosity.

Lord of all the living
God of the uncreated and yet to be
Create in us community
As we await your gift.

Barrowby

3.1.6
Beating With Joy

My heart, beating with joy
My heart, beating with joy
Fills the tall air beneath the forest trees with song
Fills the forest, my home, my mother, with singing.
I have captured a tiny songbird in my net
A tiny bird,
And my own singing heart
Is caught with that bird in my net.

African: Adapted from a pregnancy song of the Efé peoples

3.1.7
Psalm During Pregnancy

I knew at once that something new had happened,
    a feeble, fleeting flutter of awareness.
I am now not I, but we: someone's deep within me,
    part of me but not me.
O Sacred Source of all, I am in awe at this new life within me,
    and I pray for the grace to carry it well,
to honour the rhythms and seasons of the birthing cycle.

May I respect the morning sickness
    that comes to me even at sunset
    and the inner dance that keeps me awake
    through half-sleepless nights.
As I am sensitive to the changing contours of my body
    which are now beyond my ability to control –
    I wonder if my husband will still find me lovely –
    may I celebrate this season of change
    and the energy to provide for the needs
    of this growing life within me
    that these changes make possible.

Teach me the art of patient waiting,
    especially at those times when I wish
    that I could just take a peek inside
    to find out who this little person is
    who's tap dancing on my ribs while I try to sleep.
I want so much to be a good mother,
    to care for and nourish this new life.
Help me to gift this child with all the love I can,
    now during this time of pregnancy
    and also at each stage of life when I am called
    to set my baby free into fuller life.

O Holy Womb of Life, help me, for I am frightened;
    I do not feel ready for this awesome task.
free me from my fear of a painful delivery;
    may it be a holy, harmonious experience for us both.
Free me from my fear of inadequacy
    about raising this child into maturity and holiness.
Please help me, Holy Parent,
    to protect my child who's yours as well;
    bring this baby safely through this birthing
    and the many other birthings in life.

Edward Hays

3.1.8
Birth

Our Birth is but a sleep and a forgetting; The soul that rises with us, our life's star, hath had elsewhere its setting and cometh from afar: Not in entire forgetfulness and not in utter nakedness but trailing clouds of glory do we come from God who is our home.

William Wordsworth

3.1.9
At the Moment of Birth

(Barukh/a habah/haba'ah b'sheim Adonai)
Blessed be s/he who comes in the name of the Eternal.

My child, I have known you for many months.
I have felt the first stirrings of your limbs firm and harden against my belly.
I have seen your faint form on the hospital scanner.
But only now do I see you in your wondrous wholeness, your wondrous smallness, your wondrous perfection.
I hear your cry, I feel your smoothness, I smell your newness and I give thanks.

Eternal, our God, how magnificent is your name throughout the earth.
Your splendour is recounted over the heavens.
From the mouths of babies and sucklings you have founded strength...
When I see your heavens and the work of your fingers,
the moon and stars that you have established,
what is humanity that you remember it?
and the children of human beings that you take notice?
and that you have made them little less than angels?
and have crowned them with glory and honour?

And God created humanity in the divine image. In the image of God was humanity created. Male and female God created them. Thus says the Eternal, your redeemer, who formed you from the womb, I the Eternal make all things.

There are three partners in the making of a person: the blessed Holy One, the father and the mother. The father and the mother create the bodily form... the blessed Holy One gives the child spirit and soul, beauty of appearance, the powers of speech, sight and hearing, the ability to walk, understanding and intelligence.

The pain of labour is over, the apprehension and fear is past. I have experienced a miracle in the creating of you.

We praise you, Eternal, our God ruler of the universe, who shows goodness to the undeserving, that you have shown every goodness to me.

(Those attending the birth respond:)
May God who has shown goodness to you, continue to favour you with all that is good.

Sybil Sheridan

3.1.10
Birth

That she was taken out of her mother,
thanks be for that!
That she, the little one, was taken out of her, we say,
thanks be for that.

Eskimo Prayer from West Greenland

3.1.11
Baby

I lift up this newborn child to you.
You brought it to birth, you gave it life.
This child is a fresh bud on an ancient tree,
A new member of an old family.
May this fresh bud blossom.
May this child grow up strong and righteous.

African Kalahari Bushman Prayer

3.1.12
Our Share in Creation

God our Father and Mother, the source of all life
we praise you for our share in the wonder and joy of creation.
We thank you from our hearts for the gift of this child, for a safe delivery and for
the privilege of parenthood. Renew our gratitude during sleepless nights and
make us worthy of our new responsibilities.

Marcus Braybrooke

3.1.13
New Born Child

O You who have created
All human beings,
You have conferred
A great benefit on us
By bringing us this child.

African Kamba Prayer from Kenya

3.1.14
My Baby

O Lord my God, shed the light of your love on my child. Keep him safe from all illness and all injury. Enter his tiny soul, and comfort him with your peace and joy. He is too young to speak to me, and to my ears his cries and gurgles are meaningless nonsense. But to your ears they are prayers. His cries are cries for your blessing. His gurgles are gurgles of delight at your grace. Let him as a child learn the way of your commandments. As an adult let   him live the full span of his life, serving your kingdom on earth. And finally in his old age, let him die in the sure and certain knowledge of your salvation. I do not ask that he be wealthy, powerful or famous. Rather I ask that he be poor in spirit, humble in action, and devout in worship. Dear Lord, smile upon him.

Johann Starck

3.1.15
Grant You Intelligence.

May God grant you intelligence.
May his Power grant you intelligence,
May his two divine Messengers, lotus-wreathed
Grant to you intelligence.

Buddhist Scriptures: Asvalayana Grhya Sutra I, 15, 2

3.1.16
Birth and Death

I was not aware of the moment when I first crossed the threshold of this life. What was the power that made me open out into this vast mystery like a bud in the forest at midnight! When in the morning I looked upon the light I felt in a moment that I was no stranger in this world, that the inscrutable without name and form had taken me in its arms in the form of my own mother. Even so, in death the same unknown will appear as ever known to me.

Rabindranath Tagore: Gitanjali 95

3.1.17
After an adoption

We receive this child into our family with thanksgiving and joy.
Through the love of God we receive her (him);
With the love of God we will care for her (him);
By the love of God we will guide her (him);
And in the love of God may we all abide for ever.

From the Alternative Service Book of the Church of England

3.1.18
One Parent

Lord, give me your help to be a good parent to my child.
Give me energy when I am tired,
Companionship when I am lonely,
Your guidance when I am anxious
And your forgiveness when I am angry or impatient.

Marcus Braybrooke

3.1.19
Fontal Being

Give me a candle of the Spirit, O God, as I go down into the deep of my own being. Show me the hidden things. Take me down to the spring of my life, and tell me my nature and name. Give me freedom to grow so that I may become the self, the seed of which you planted in me at my making. Out of the deep I cry unto you, O Lord.

George Appleton

 3.2 Children

3.2.1
For Our Family

Our Lord, bless us with the delight of our eyes through our spouses and children and make us leaders for the God-fearing.

Muslim: Radiant Prayers

3.2.2
For Parents

O my Lord, have mercy on both of them
as they nurtured me when small.

Muslim: Radiant Prayers

3.2.3
Grateful For Your Favour

Oh my Lord!
Grant me that I may be
Grateful for Your Favour
Which You have bestowed
Upon me, and upon both my parents, and that I
May work righteousness
Such as you may approve;
And be gracious to me
In my issue.
Truly I turn to You
And truly do I bow to you.

Qur'an: 46:15

3.2.4
For My Children

On this doorstep I stand
year after year
and watch you leaving

and think: may you not
skin your knees. May you
not catch your fingers
in car doors. May
your hearts not break.

May tide and weather
wait for your coming
and may you grow strong

to break
all webs of my weaving.

Evangeline Paterson

3.2.5
Hope Reborn to My Daughter

Sleep gently, baby, dream your little dreams,
While I watch your face with love, and wonder
What the future holds in store for you.
Let life be kind to you I pray
All your days.

Let love be your guide in your lifetime,
Love of God, Love of Life and Humanity.
Learn compassion, gentleness and truthfulness,
And have the courage to be just yourself,
All your lifetime.

K. McLaughlan

3.2.6
A Mother's Blessing

The joy of God be in thy face
Joy to all who see thee,
The circle of God around thy neck
    Angels of God shielding thee,
    Angles of God shielding thee.

Joy of night and day be thine,
Joy of sun and moon be thine,
Joy of men and women be thine,
    Each land and sea thou goest,
    Each land and sea thou goest.

Be every season happy for thee,
Be every season bright for thee,
Be every season glad for thee,
    And the Son of Mary Virgin at peace with thee,
The Son of Mary Virgin at peace with thee.

Be thine the compassing of the God of life,
Be thine the compassing of the Christ of love,
Be thine the compassing of the Spirit of Grace,
    To befriend thee and to aid thee,
    Thou beloved one of my breast.
(Oh! To befriend thee and to aid thee,

Thou beloved one of my heart.)

The Celtic Vision

3.2.7
Illness of a Child

Some pray 'Let me not lose my little child'
Do thou pray 'Let me not fear to lose him!'
In short, pray in this spirit, and await the outcome.

Marcus Aurelius: Meditations

3.2.8
For a Child Who is Ill

Most powerful Lord, beneath whose wings we find protection and shelter, you are invisible and untouchable, like the night and like the air. I appear before you, stammering with nervous uncertainty, as one who has stumbled and lost his way. I am afraid that my wrong-doing has provoked your wrath and aroused your indignation against me. For this is the only explanation I can find for the terrible sickness that has fallen upon my family. The misery of my children is surely the consequence of my wickedness.

Lord, do with my body whatever pleases. Heap upon me whatever diseases I deserve. Do not spare me any suffering or any indignity. Let me bear the punishment for my own actions. And so let my children be restored to health and happiness, that they may stand upright and follow your path of righteousness. Let me die, that they may live.

An Aztec payer

3.2.9
For a Daughter

May she be granted beauty and yet not
Beauty to make a stranger's eye distraught,
Or hers before a looking glass, for such, being made beautiful overmuch
Consider beauty a sufficient end,
Lose natural kindness and maybe
The heart-revealing intimacy
That chooses right and never finds a friend.

W. B. Yeats

3.2.10
Tell the Truth

Give us grace, Lord, to tell our children
the truth and nothing but the truth.
To issue no idle threats or promises.
To keep our word.
To apologise when we have been wrong.
To be disciplined over time.

To be courteous in all our dealings.
To answer children's questions as honestly and simply as we can.
To let them help in all the ways we can devise.
To expect from them no higher standard of honesty, unselfishness, politeness
than we are prepared to live up to ourselves.

Adapted from a prayer by Joan Kendall

3.2.11
God's Gifts

Grant to your Sikhs the gift of true discipleship,
The gift of discipline, the gift of discrimination,
The gift of trusting each other,
The gift of faith,
Above all the greatest gift of all,
The gift of thy Name.
May the Khalsa in all its actions remember God,
And in remembering God bring peace and comfort to the whole world.

From a Sikh baptism (amrit) prayer

The Khalsa is the fellowship of those who have received amrit.

3.2.12
Speak to Us of Children

And a woman who held a babe against her bosom said,
Speak to us of Children.
And he said:
Your children are not your children.
They are sons and daughters of Life's longing for itself.
They come through you but not from you,
And though they are with you yet they belong not to you.

You may give them your love but not your thoughts,
For they have their own thoughts.
You may house their bodies but not their souls,
For their souls dwell in the house of tomorrow,
which you cannot visit, not even in your dreams.
You may strive to be like them, but seek not to make them like you.
For life goes not backward nor tarries with yesterday.
You are the bows from which your children as living arrows
are sent forth.

The archer sees the mark upon the path of the infinite,
and He bends you with His might that His arrows may go
swift and far.
Let your bending in the Archer's hand be for gladness;

For even as He loves the arrow that flies,
so He loves also the bow that is stable.

Kahlil Gibran

3.2.13
Grandparents

Lord, teach me to love my grandchildren as a grandparent should:
not interfering, only understanding;
not pushing myself, just being there when wanted.
Teach me to be the sort of grandmother
my children and children's children
would want me to be.

Rosa George

3.2.14
Unhappy Children

Father, we pray for all children whose lives have been damaged by the death of a
parent or by their parents splitting up or by cruelty and abuse. We pray you that
time and loving care may heal the deep wounds that have been made. May these
children have such a sense of your parental love and care that they may develop
a healthy emotional life, able to form good and loving relationships with others.

Marcus Braybrooke

3.2.15
Help

I am so weak that I can hardly write,
I cannot read my Bible,
I cannot even pray,
I can only lie still in God's arms like a little child, and trust.

Hudson Taylor

3.2.16
Calmness

O Lord, calm the waves of this heart, calm its tempest!
calm yourself, O my soul, so that the divine can act in you...

Anonymous

3.2.17
Still Birth

Heavenly Father, by your mighty power you gave us the promise of life. Be with
us in our disappointment and desolation. Help us to believe that you make
nothing in vain and that the child we do not know is alive with you.

Marcus Braybrooke

3.2.18
The Vision

(from a conversation)
"When I was small I saw an Angel.
But only once"... she said.
"For years and years the Presence stayed.
His tender beauty brimmed my memory.
Until I grew, and lost my childhood
To fleeting years that dimmed the vision...
Till now, today, new childish voices
Innocent in loud child-laughter
Recall that lovely angel Being
And give me knowing of heaven's perfection..."

Eric Gladwin

3.2.19
Menarche Ritual: A Mother's Prayer

(Eloheinu velohei avoteinu v'immotenu,) Our God and God of our ancestors, I ask your blessing on my daughter... as she enters this new phase in her life. I have been blessed with watching her grow from a child into a woman, and I have grown with her. I have been privileged to care for her in her dependence, and nurtured her towards independence. May you grant me wisdom in supporting her through her teenage and adult years. The wine I hold in my hand is a symbol of God's fruitfulness and God's provision - reflected in our ability to bear children and care for them. It also celebrates the sweetness of this moment. May my daughter's life contain sweetness and fruitfulness.

Lee Wax

3.2.20
Menarche Ritual: A Young Woman's Prayer

(Eloheinu velohei avoteinu v'immotenu,) God and God of our ancestors, I give thanks for reaching this time. I am grateful for the love and support of the women here today, and pray that I will continue to feel supported and guided by them in the months and years ahead. As I become a Jewish woman, may I learn from the strength and wisdom of other Jewish women, past and present. At this very important stage in my life, I invoke the strength and teachings of the four matriarchs to help me on my way.
(Elohei Sarah,) God of Sarah, give me strength and courage as I leave the familiarity of childhood and go forward on my journey into an unknown stage in my life.
(Elohei Rivkah,) God of Rebecca, may I learn to bear the physical discomfort of menstruation, and know that as a blessing, as a sign of the miraculous, God-given potential to create life within me.
(Elohei Rachel,) God of Rachel, may I always treat my body with pride and with respect.

(*Elohei* Leah,) and God of Leah, with your blessing may I one day come to know the joy of motherhood.

Lee Wax

3.2.21
The Real Gurus

God knows that there is nothing as important as a mother.

The mother is the one who sustains the family.
God knows that the mothers are the real teachers,
the real gurus of the world.

After all, is it not the mother who educates her children
through her own example?

Dadi Janki

3.2.22

Orphans
Did he not find thee an orphan and sheltered thee?
Find thee wandering and led thee?
Find thee needy and suffice thee?

Then do not oppress the orphan,
Nor repel the suppliant.
The grace of your Lord – let that be your theme.

Qur'an: 5:6-11

3.2.23
Prayer for an Adopted Child

Not flesh of my flesh
nor bone of my bone
but still, miraculous, my own.
Never forget
for a single minute,
that you didn't grow under my heart
but in it.

Anonymous

3.2.24
Death of a Child

In his love he clothes us, enfolds us and embraces us, that tender love completely surrounds us, never to leave us.

O God, you have dealt very mysteriously with us. We have been passing through deep waters; our feet were well-nigh gone. But though you slay us, yet we will trust in you... You have reclaimed your lent jewels. Yet, O Lord, shall I not thank you now? I will thank you not only for the children you have left to us, but for those you have reclaimed. I thank you for the blessing of the last ten years, and for all the sweet memories of these lives... I thank you for the full assurance that each has gone to the arms of the Good Shepherd, whom each loved according to the capacity of her years. I thank you for the bright hopes of a happy reunion, when we shall meet to part no more.

Campbell Tait

Five of his six children died of scarlet fever in one month in 1856.

3.2.25
Your Friendly Voice

O Christ, the little girl on her deathbed, the young man on the way to his grave and Lazarus three days in the tomb, could all hear your voice. May each soul as it passes through death, hear your friendly voice, see the look of love in your eyes and the smile of welcome in your face and be led by you to the Father of all souls.

George Appleton

3.2.26
Prayer for a Very New Angel

God, God, be lenient for her first night there,
The crib she slept in was so near my bed;
Her blue and white wool blanket was so soft;
Her pillow hollowed so to fit her head.

Teach me that she'll not want small rooms or me
When she has you and Heaven's immensity!
I always left a light out in the hall;
I hoped to make her fearless in the dark.
And yet – she was so small – one little light,
Not in the room, it scarcely mattered. Hark!

No, no! She seldom cried! God, not too far
For her to see, this first night, light a star!

And, in the morning, when she first woke up,
I always kissed her on the left cheek where
The dimple was. And, oh, I wet the brush!
It made it easier to curl her hair.

Just – just tomorrow morning, God, I pray,
When she wakes up, do things for her my way.

Violet Alleyn Storey

3.3 Education and Growing Up

3.3.1
Excel When You Must

Do not seek too much fame,
but do not seek obscurity.
Be proud.
But do not remind the world of your deeds.
Excel when you must,
but do not excel the world.
Many heroes are not yet born,
many have already died.
To be alive to hear this song is a victory.

A West African song

3.3.2
Strong Friendships

Let our friendships be strong, O Lord,
that they become a blessing to others...
Let our friendships be open, O Lord,
that they may be a haven for others...
Let our friendships be gentle, O Lord,
that they may bring peace to others...
(for Jesus' sake. Amen.)

C. Herbert

3.3.3
Truth

From the cowardice that dare not face new truth
From the laziness that is contented with half truth
From the arrogance that thinks it knows all truth,
Good Lord, deliver me.

Prayer from Kenya

3.3.4
A Hint of Your Will

Grant, O Lord, that we may wait anxiously, as servants standing in the presence of
their lord, for the least hint of your will; that we may welcome all truth, under
whatever outward forms it be uttered; that we may have grace to receive new
thoughts with grace, recognising that your ways are not as our ways nor your
thoughts our thoughts; that we may bless every good deed, by whomsoever it
may be done; that we may rise above all party strife and cries to the
contemplation of the eternal Truth and Goodness, O God Almighty who never
changes.

Charles Kingsley

3.3.5
Education

O Father give me a passport
O Mother give me a passport
Elder brother give me a passport
To job and life
Give me education.

African: Prayer of a Ugandan Christian

3.3.6
Think Ahead

If you give a man a fish, he will eat once.
If you teach a man to fish, he will eat for the rest of his life.
If you are thinking a year ahead, sow seed.
If you are thinking ten years ahead, plant a tree.
If you are thinking one hundred years ahead, educate the people.
By sowing seed you will harvest once.
By planting a tree, you will harvest tenfold.
By educating the people you will harvest one hundredfold.

Chuang-tsu

3.3.7
For a School

O God, our heavenly Father, by whose Spirit we are taught knowledge, you give wisdom to all that ask you. Grant your blessing, we beseech you, upon this school, and help us in the work you have given us to do. Enable us all to labour diligently, not with eye-service, but in singleness of heart, remembering that without you we can do nothing, and that in your fear is the beginning of wisdom.

Based on a prayer by F. D. Maurice

3.3.8
For a School

Almighty God, in whom we live and move and have our being: Make this school as a field which the Lord has blessed; that whatsoever things are true and pure, lovely and of good report, may here abound and flourish.

Marcus Braybrooke

3.3.9
For Teachers

Let your Spirit, O God, rest upon all who teach. Enable them both by word and by example to lead their pupils to reverence truth, to desire goodness, and to delight in beauty; that, following after these things, both those who learn and those who teach may come to know and worship you, the giver of all that is good.

Marcus Braybrooke

3.3

3.3.10
For Students

Grant, O Lord, to all students to love that which is worth loving, to know that which is worth knowing, to praise that which pleaseth thee most, to esteem that which is most precious unto you, and to dislike whatsoever is evil in thine eyes. Grant that with true judgment they may distinguish things that differ, and, above all, may search out and do what is well-pleasing unto thee.

Thomas à Kempis

3.3.11
For Those Preparing for or Sitting Examinations

O God, you know the secrets of the heart: be with those now preparing for [sitting] examinations. Help them to face their task with calmness, confidence, and courage; with wisdom, faithfulness, and honesty; that they may do justice both to themselves and to their teachers, and acknowledge you, who are the source of all wisdom and truth.

Marcus Braybrooke

3.3.12
Examination Results

I believe you have a purpose for my life, O Lord.
Help me to hold onto this belief even if my results are disappointing
 And I cannot get the college place that I hope for.
If I am successful, make me grateful rather than bigheaded.
Help me to see my course as an opportunity to learn how to be of more use
In your service and in helping others.

Marcus Braybrooke

3.3.13
For a College

Almighty God, you are the source of truth
and your Spirit leads us into the truth:
may all who teach and all who learn
in our schools, colleges and universities
be set free from everything that might hinder
their search for the truth;
and finding truth, may they learn to use it
for the good of all people.

James M. Todd

3.3.14
For the New Generation

Lord of all Life, we pray that as young people in each new generation discover your world in their own way, they may catch a glimpse of your glory and use their energies creatively in your service and for the benefit of others.

Marcus Braybrooke

3.3.15
Sport and Recreation

God our creator, we thank you for opportunities for recreation and sport. Give us a sense of enjoyment and fair play so that while we strive to do our best we never take unfair advantage of others.

Marcus Braybrooke

3.4 Marriage and Friendship

3.4.1
Smiling

(What to say if you see a Muslim brother smiling:)
May God bring smiles to you.

Muslim: Hasan Al Bânna's Al-Mathoorat

3.4.2
A Prayer to Recite on One's Engagement

I rejoice in my happiness, O God,
My soul exults with joy.
You have blessed me with love and companionship,
With the affection and friendship of one whom my soul loves.
Guide me, O God, as I enter this new part of my life.
Help me to acknowledge the loss of being single and free,
And to understand that in this new relationship, my freedom acquires a different
aspect.
I am enriched, and my consciousness is deepened by this love.
Help me as I bring him into the house of my mother and father.
May they see my happiness and the qualities I see in him.
May I be gentle and giving in the months that lie ahead,
Tender and kind as we shape the beginning of our marriage.
Loving God, may Your steadfast love and faithfulness always be with us,
May we be guided by Your righteousness and peace.
Trusting in you, Eternal God,
May we learn to trust each other and be strengthened by this happiness
And the blessing of love and companionship. Amen.

Alexandra Wright

3.4.3
I Love You

(When one is told "I love you")
May he, for Whose sake you love me, love you also.

Muslim: Hasan Al Bânna's Al-Mathoorat

3.4.4
Born Together

You were born together, and together you shall be for evermore.
You shall be together when white wings of death scatter your days.
Aye, you shall be together even in the silent memory of God.
But let there be spaces in your togetherness,
And let the winds of the heavens dance between you.
Love one another but make not a bond of love:

Let it rather be a moving sea between the shores of your souls.
Fill each other's cup but drink not from one cup.
Give one another of your bread but eat not from the same loaf.
Sing and dance together and be joyous, but let each one of you be alone,
Even as the strings of a lute are alone though they quiver with the same music.
Give your hearts, but not into each other's keeping.
For only the hand of Life can contain your hearts.
And stand together, yet not too near together:
For the pillars of the temple stand apart,
And the oak tree and the cypress grow not in each other's shadow.

Kahlil Gibran

3.4.5
The Bonds of Our Love

The winter will lose its cold,
as the snow will be without whiteness,
The night without darkness,
the heavens without stars,
the day without light.
The flower will lose its beauty,
all fountains their water,
the sea its fish,
the tree its birds,
the forest its beasts,
the earth its harvest –
All these things will pass before
anyone breaks the bonds of our love,
And before I cease caring for you in my heart.
May your days be happy in number as flakes of snow,
May your nights be peaceful, and may you be without troubles.

Matthew of Rievaulx

3.4.6
Home

Home is where the heart is.

Ovid

3.4.7
Love Expands

The love that is kindled in the home
Expands itself over the whole human race.

Asoka

3.4.8
How a Home is Built

A house is built of logs and stone,
Of tiles and posts and piers;
A home is built of loving deeds
That stand a thousand years.

Victor Hugo

3.4.9

This House
O God make the door of this house wide enough to receive all who need human love and fellowship; narrow enough to shut out all envy, pride and strife.

Make its threshold smooth enough to be no stumbling block to children, nor to straying feet, but rugged and strong enough to turn back the tempter's power.

God, make the door of this house the gateway to your eternal kingdom.

Anonymous: From the ruins of St Stephen's Walbrook, London

3.4.10
No Strangers

There are no strangers here
Only friends we have not met.

Anonymous

3.4.11
He Who Would Marry a Childless Woman

O God –
This man's love is awesome!
Who can deny the inbuilt urge
Of seed to multiply
And trust that You have something else
That needs his fathering, conceive
And bring to birth a shadow-child
With the woman that he loves
More than the treasured dreams
Of eager children in his arms
To show the sunflower
And the wild birds to,
To teach the names of stars.

O God –
How can I say I'll make it up to him?
Because I can't.
But I will take his precious gift

3.4

Because I never knew a love
So costly and so fine.
It can't be treated lightly

Rowena Eldin White

3.4.12
For Childless Women: A Meditation on Psalm 139

'You knit me together in my mother's womb.'
I may as well add 'spun me, wove me' too,
Or better still, 'embroidered me'.
With care you picked the colour for my eyes,
Decided how much curl to give my hair
And whether it would match well with my skin.
If you knew my mother's womb so intimately
It stands to reason You know mine.
The dusty work-box, unfathomed, wasted,
Now rebellious. What can you see there
From which to fashion anything worthwhile,
Some rusty pins, a few old buttons,
Some faded silk wound round half a letter,
All neglected, left unused too long?
Oh God of miracles, what will You do with these?

Rowena Eldin White

3.4.13
Everything Good and Right

Almighty God, Giver of Life and Love, guide and guard N and N in their married life together. Grant them understanding and devotion, laughter and peace, that their home may be a place from which everything that is good and right may shine out to your glory, and in the service of others, to their own great happiness. May each be to the other a strength in need, a comfort in sorrow and a companion in joy. Unite their wills in your will and their spirits in your spirit, through Jesus Christ our Lord.

Church of England: From a Form of Blessing on a Second Marriage, produced by the Diocese of Bath and Wells

3.4.14
Marriage

May these vows and this marriage be blessed.
May it be sweet milk,
this marriage, like wine and halvah.
May this marriage offer fruit and shade
like the date palm.
May this marriage be full of laughter,
our every day a day in paradise.

May this marriage be a sign of compassion,
a seal of happiness here and hereafter.
may this marriage have a fair face and a good name,
an omen as welcome
as the moon in a clear blue sky.
I am out of words to describe
how spirit mingles in this marriage

Jalal al-Din Rumi

Halvah is a sweet confection.

3.4.15
A True Home

May obedience conquer disobedience within this house,
and may peace triumph over discord here,
and generous giving over avarice,
reverence over contempt,
speech with truthful words over lying utterance;
may the righteous order gain the victory
over the demon of the lie.

Zoroastrian prayer

3.4.16
Prayer for Entering a New House

My father built,
And his father built,
And I have built.
Ancestors: leave me to live here in success,
Let me sleep in comfort,
And have children.
There is food for you.

African: prayer of the Nyoro people of Uganda

3.4.17
A Wedding Blessing

May the God who is Love
– Eternally Loving –
Bless you both
And keep you sweethearts
As you inter-penetrate
Each Other's Being
And go through life together
In ever-growing tenderness,
Until you come hand in hand
To the joyful mystery of Love

– of Love eternal and divine –
May the God of Love
Bless you both
With Love Unending.

George Appleton

3.4.18
Marriage Anniversary

Through all the years of marriage
We've happily shared with others...
But God, you've given us one priceless gift
That belongs exclusively to us
Not to be shared with another –
The beautiful gift of physical intimacy.
Thank you for its mystery
Its wonder, its delight.
May we never mishandle it.
May we respect and cherish it always.
May our self-giving continue to be
An expression of oneness
A celebration of wholeness.
Keep it alive, fulfilling
And always full of surprises.
O God, what a marvellous expression
Of your own fathomless love!

Ruth Harms Calkin

3.4.19
A House Wide Enough for All

Father of all humankind, make the roof of our house wide enough for all
opinions,
Oil the door of our house so it opens easily to friend and stranger
And set such a table in our house that our whole family may speak kindly and
freely around it.

A Prayer from Hawaii

3.4.20
Blessing of a New House

May the inhabitants of this dwelling place be blessed with many children,
May they enjoy wealth, may they be generous to the poor;
May they escape disease and trouble, may they be safe these many Years.

Adapted from a prayer of the Nyola People of Kenya

3.4

3.4.21
Psalm During a Menstrual Cycle

O Divine One,
    Loving Source of sacred cycles,
    Life-force of the rising and setting sun,
    of the waxing and waning moon,
    help me to celebrate the cycles
    that are present within my own body.
May I listen to my bodily rhythms
    and embrace my menstrual cycle
    which I am experiencing today.

These are sacred days of the month:
    as I welcome and accept life-blood
    which is flowing from within me,
    may I also respect the full range of my feelings
    and honour the difficulty of these days,
    the low physical energy and deep sensitivity
    during this time of my menstrual cycle.

Help me to create space during these days
    for reflection, for quiet and dreaming,
    realising how thin at this sacred time
    is the veil between you and me.

O Endless Fountain of all life,
    may I embrace this time of my monthly cycle
    with awareness and sensitivity,
    reverence the life-force
    that is flowing through me.

Edward Hays

3.4.22
Psalm for a Woman who No Longer Bleeds

O Divine One
    Source of the feminine life-force,
    I thank you this day
    for your life-energy within my body,
    for the order of its rhythm and cycles.

Even though I no longer have
    my blood time to mark my cycles,
    teach me to listen with my inner ear
    to the other cycles and patterns
    of my body.

As I listen with attentiveness and respect,
    may I daily grow in understanding
    of how to care for my body
    with gentleness and love.

May I always remember
    that my femininity
    is an integral part of me,
    regardless of whether I am fertile or not.

And as I listen with greater reverence
    to that rhythm of your life within me,
    may I allow the special gifts
    of this stage of my life to emerge,
    creating space for the wise woman within me
    to find fuller expression in my life.

Edward Hays

3.4.23
Difficult to Live With

O God, forgive us for the faults which make us difficult to live with.
    If we behave as if we were the only people for whom life is difficult;
    If we behave as if we were far harder worked than anyone else;
If we behave as if we were the only people who were ever disappointed,
    or the only people who ever got a raw deal;
If we are far too self-centred and far too full of self-pity:
        Forgive us, O God.

If we are too impatient to finish work we have begun;
If we are too impatient to listen to someone who wants to talk to us
    Or to give someone a helping hand;
If we think that other people are fools, and make no attempt to conceal
    Our contempt for them:
        Forgive us, O God.

If we too often rub people the wrong way;
If we spoil a good case by trying to ram it down someone's throat;
If we do things that get on people's nerves, and go on doing them,
even when we are asked not to:
        Forgive us, O God.

William Barclay

3.4.24
A Baha'i Marriage Prayer

Glory be unto Thee, O my God! Verily, this Thy servant and this thy maid-servant have gathered under the shadow of Thy mercy and they are united through Thy favour and generosity. O Lord! Assist them in this world and Thy Kingdom and destine them for every good through Thy bounty and grace, O Lord! Confirm them in Thy servitude and assist them in Thy service. Suffer them to become the signs of Thy Name in Thy world and protect them through Thy bestowals which are inexhaustible in this world and the world to come. O Lord! They are supplicating the Kingdom of Thy mercifulness and invoking the realm of Thy singleness. Verily they are married in obedience to Thy command. Cause them to become the signs of harmony and unity until the end of time. Verily Thou art the Omnipotent and the Almighty.

'Abdu'l-Baha

3.4.25
A Home of Peace

... My home is the home of peace. My home is the home of joy and delight. My home is the home of laughter and exultation. Whoever enters through the portals of this home, must go out with gladsome heart. This is the home of knowledge; the one who enters it must receive knowledge. This is the home of love; those who come in must learn the lesson of love; thus may they know how to love each other...

'Abdu'l-Baha

3.4.26
Blessing of the Cup from an Orthodox Christian Marriage Service

O God, who hast created all things by thy might, and hast made fast the round worlds, and adornest the crown of all things which thou hast made: Bless now, with thy spiritual blessing, this common cup, which thou dost give to those who are now united for a community of marriage.

From an Orthodox Christian Marriage Service

The common cup is presented by the priest three times to the groom and then to the bride.

3.4.27
Blessing of the Bride and Groom

Blessed are you, O Lord our God,
For you have created joy and gladness,
Pleasure and delight, love, peace and fellowship.
Pour out the abundance of your blessing
Upon N and N in their new life together.
Let their love for each other be a seal upon their hearts
And a crown upon their heads.

Bless them in their work and in their companionship;
Awake and asleep,

In joy and in sorrow,
In life and in death.
Finally, in your mercy, bring them to that banquet
Where your saints feast for ever in your heavenly home.
We ask this through Jesus Christ, your Son, our Lord, who lives and reigns with
you and the Holy Spirit, one God, now and for ever.

From the wedding service in the Church of England's Common Worship.

Common Worship: Services and Prayers for the Church of England is copyright ©
The Archbishop's Council, 2000. Extracts are reproduced by permission.

3.4.28
Prayer for the newly weds

Faithful God
Holy and eternal,
Source of life and spring of love,
We thank and praise you for bring N and N to this day,
And we pray for them,
Lord of life and love:

All   hear our prayer.

May their marriage be life giving and life-long,
Enriched by your presence and strengthened by your grace;
May they bring comfort and confidence to each other
In faithfulness and trust.
Lord of life and love:

All   hear our prayer.

May the hospitality of their home
Bring refreshment and joy to all around them;
May their love overflow to neighbours in need
And embrace those in distress.
Lord of life and love:

All   hear our prayer.

May they discern in your word
Order and purpose for their lives;
And may the power of your Holy Spirit
Lead them in truth and defend them in adversity.
Lord of life and love:

All   hear our prayer.

May they nurture their family with devotion,
See their children grow in body, mind and spirit
And come at last to the end of their lives
With hearts content and in joyful anticipation of heaven.
Lord of life and love:

All   *hear our prayer.*
From the wedding service in the Church of England's Common Worship.
Common Worship: Services and Prayers for the Church of England is copyright ©
The Archbishop's Council, 2000. Extracts are reproduced by permission

3.4.29
A Witness to God's Love

Eternal God, true and loving Father, in holy marriage you make your servants one.
May their life together witness to your love in this troubled world;
May unity overcome division,
Forgiveness heal injury,
And joy triumph over sorrow; through Jesus Christ our Lord.

Alternative Service Book of the Church of England.

The *Alternative Service Book 1980* is copyright © The Central board of Finance of
the Church of England 1980; The Archbishops' Council, 1999. Extracts are
reproduced by permission.

3.4.30
True Union

To be humble and true and to do God's bidding:
Only thus is true union attained.
They are not man and wife who only have physical contact;
Only they are truly wedded who have one spirit in two bodies.

Guru Amar Das

3.4.31
The Seven Benedictions

Praised be Thou, O Lord our God, King of the Universe,
     who hast created the fruit of the vine
Praised be Thou, O Lord our God, King of the Universe,
     who hast created all things to Thy glory.
Praised be Thou, O Lord our God, King of the Universe,
     who hast created man.
Praised be Thou, O Lord our God, King of the Universe,
     who hast made man in Thine image, after Thy likeness, and out of his very
     self, Thou hast prepared unto him a perpetual fabric.
     Praised be Thou, O Lord our God, King of the Universe,
     Praised be Thou, O Lord who hast created man.
May she who is childless be exceedingly glad and rejoice when her children shall

be reunited in her midst in joy ...

Praised be Thou, O Lord our God, King of the Universe, who hast created joy and gladness, bridegroom and bride, rejoicing, song, pleasure and delight, love and brotherhood, peace and fellowship. Soon may there be heard in the cities of Judah, and in the streets of Jerusalem, the voice of joy and gladness, the voice of the bridegroom and the voice of the bride, the jubilant voice of bridegrooms from their nuptial canopies and of youths from their feasts of song. Praised be Thou, O Lord, who gladdenest the bridegroom and the bride.

From Forms of Prayer for Jewish Worship

3.4.32
Perfect Love

O Perfect Love, all human thought transcending,
Lowly we kneel in prayer before thy throne,
That theirs may be the love which knows no ending
Whom thou for evermore dost join in one.

O perfect Life, be thou their full assurance
O tender charity and steadfast faith,
Of patient hope, and quite brave endurance,
With childlike trust that fears nor pain nor death.

Grant them the joy which brightens earthly sorrow,
Grant them the peace which calms all earthly strife;
And to life's day the glorious unknown morrow
That dawns upon eternal love and life.

Dorothy Frances Gurney

3.4.33
Truly Wedded

With woman is man's companionship,
Form woman originate new generationship,

Sikh scriptures: Adi Granth

3.4.34
We Two Shall Dwell Together

I am He, you are She;
I am Song, you are Verse,
I am heaven, you are Earth.
We two shall here together dwell,
Becoming parents of children.

Hindu scriptures: Atharva Veda 14:2.71

3.4.35
Enshrine Me in Your Heart

Sweet be the glances we exchange,
Our faces showing true concord.
Enshrine me in your heart and let
One spirit dwell within us.
I wrap around you this my robe
Which came to me from Manu,
So that you may be wholly mine
And never seek another.

Hindu scriptures: Atharva Veda 7:36-7

3.4.36
Carol of Beauty

Praise we the Lord, who made all beauty
For all our senses to enjoy;
Owe we our humble thanks and duty
That simple pleasures never cloy;
Praise we the Lord who made all beauty
For all our senses to enjoy.

Praise him who makes our life a pleasure,
Sending us things which glad our eyes;
Thank him who gives us welcome leisure,
That in our hearts sweet thoughts may rise;
Praise him who makes our life a pleasure
Sending us things which glad our eyes.

Praise him who by a simple flower
Lifts up our hearts to things above;
Thank him who gives to each one power
To find a friend to know and love;
Praise him who by a simple flower
Lifts up our hearts to things above.

Praise we the Lord who made all beauty
For all our senses to enjoy;
Give we our humble thanks and duty
That simple pleasures never cloy;
Praise we the Lord who made all beauty
For all our senses to enjoy.

Steuart Wilson

3.4.37
A Sign from God

And among his Signs is this, that he created for you mates from among yourselves, that ye may dwell in tranquillity with them and He has put love and mercy between your (hearts). Verily, in that are signs for those who reflect.

The Qur'an: 30:21

3.5 Abuse and Divorce

3.5.1
After A Divorce

Heavenly Father we thank you for our friends, for all who have stood by us in time of trouble, who give wise advice when we need it, who are there when we want them, who teach us so much by their quality of life. We thank you for those who have meant much to us and have now been called to their rest. Above all we thank you that again and again in our earthly lives you speak to us through your word, through people we know or meet, through nature, through art and literature, of the lasting things which really matter...

Church of England: From a Form of Blessing on a Second Marriage, produced by the Diocese of Bath and Wells

3.5.2
By His Wounds You have Been Healed

O God
through the image of a woman
crucified on the cross
I understand at last.

For over half my life
I have been ashamed of the scars I bear.
These scars tell an ugly story,
A common story,
about a girl who is the victim
of sexual abuse.

In the warmth, peace
and sunlight of your presence
I was able to uncurl
the tightly clenched fists.
For the first time
I felt your suffering presence with me
in that event.

I have known you as a vulnerable baby,
as a brother, and as a father.
Now I know you as a woman.
You were there with me
as the violated girl
caught in helpless suffering.

The chains of fear

no longer bind my heart and body.
a slow fire of compassion and forgiveness
is kindled.
My tears fall now
for man as well as woman.

You were not ashamed of your wounds.
You showed them to Thomas
as marks of your ordeal and death,
I will no longer bear them gracefully.
They will tell a resurrection story

Anonymous – based on 1 Peter 2:24

Inspired by the figure of a woman, arms outstretched as if crucified, hung below the cross in a chapel in Toronto.

3.5.3
Rape

O God, I feel terrible... I feel sick... I want to die... I've been raped! Raped! Do you hear?... It's horrible... horrible...! O God, I feel terrible... violated, used, discarded, utterly rejected, alone and scared stiff... I don't know if I am pregnant or diseased or needing an abortion or irreparably harmed... I feel sick... I want to die... How can I face my family, my friends, myself... O God help me to forget the feeling of utter filth I feel, forget his body on me and in me. Clean me, O God, in the way only you can. For if you don't I'll never be clean, never forget, never forgive. Never!

Giles Harcourt

3.5.4
Wash Me

Wash me, O Lord and I shall be clean.

Bible: Psalm 51:2

3.5.5
A Male Confession

We seek forgiveness for the injustice of assuming that females are mere offspring for males; for the imprisonment of women in kitchens, offices and bedrooms. We seek forgiveness for the crimes of racism and prejudice; for our inability to create a world of understanding and compassion, O Lord. We ask for righteousness, for a deeper understanding of who the other really is, for an authentic and comprehensive justice which overcomes all forms of discrimination, be it of race, caste, religion or gender.

A Unitarian Universalist prayer

3.5.6
The Multifaith Power of Womanhood

O God
Who has been from the dawn of Time
With compassionate understanding see this form of mine.
Give me pride in womanhood
The feminine and all it brings:
Of joy in creation of beautiful things.

Give us all awareness of the power of the mind.
The will we use in prayer and gentle Thought...
The power of Love
That lies within all nations, skin, tints, creeds,
Yet moves the violets, tall trees and the stars,
We sense unending in the great streams of Light
Enwrapping our fair mother-earth
With ties of sisterhood
In your great Name.

Eric Gladwin

3.6 Work and Unemployment

3.6.1
Prayer When in Debt

O God, I seek refuge with You from anxiety and grief and I seek refuge with You from weakness and lethargy, and I seek refuge with You from cowardice and miserliness, and I seek refuge with You from being defeated by debt and subdued by people.

Muslim: Radiant Prayers

3.6.2
Failure

What is wrong with failure?
A glorious failure -
I mean, to fail well
Means you've got to put in a tremendous effort in the first place,
And having gone to all this effort and trouble
Look at what you have learned,
What experience you have gained,
What knowledge from trial and error you have,
How very much farther on you are,
Than if you had never ventured -
And risked failure.
And now that calamity and collapse have blessed your venture,
You're still in one piece,
Been through the storm,
More knowledgeable, more calm, more humble,
More mature and likely to succeed the next time -
And maybe you will have learned something about faith.

Ken Walsh

3.6.3
Something Real

No matter what field your work lies in
If you do something real
Something genuine in that field,
It will live on after you -
And that part of you will be eternal.

Ken Walsh

3.6.4
Risk

If man is centred upon himself the smallest risk is too great for him, because both success and failure can destroy him. If he is centred upon God, then no risk is too great, because success is already guaranteed - the successful union of Creator and creature, beside which everything else is meaningless.

Morris West – The Shoes of the Fisherman

3.6.5
Give Me Work

God give me work
Till my life shall end
And life
Till my work is done.

Written on the grave of the novelist Winifred Holtby at Rudstone, Yorkshire

3.6.6
To be a Woman is to Work

They say to me,
as we stop and talk in the street,
'Are you working?'
Well, my Lord,
I'd like to know when
you ever met a woman who
wasn't working?
who wasn't washing and feeding,
fetching and carrying
cooking and cleaning.
We listen to them politicians
on the radio
women as well as men,
but it's us who runs
both home and country
Don't you think, my Lord,
really?

Sometimes I get discouraged.
Help me and all women workers
the world over
to remember that you're our God
and after all is said and done,
Help us to find our rest in You.

Anonymous

3.6.7
Be a Gardener

Be a gardener, dig a ditch,
toil and sweat,
And turn your earth upside down

And seek the deepness
and water the plants in time.
Continue this labour
and make sweet floods to run
and noble and abundant fruits
to spring.
Take this food and drink
and carry it to God as your true worship.

Mother Julian of Norwich

3.6.8
Plants of the Garden

The garden is rich with diversity
With plants of a hundred families
In the space between the trees
With all the colours and fragrances.
Basil, mint and lavender,
God keep my remembrance pure,
Raspberry, Apple, Rose,
God fill my heart with love,
Dill, anise, tansy, (any of several plants of the genus Tanacetum)
Holy winds blow in me.
Rhododendron, zinnia,
May my prayer be beautiful
May my remembrance O God be as incense to thee
In the sacred grove of eternity
As I smell and remember
The ancient forests of earth.

Native American: Chinook Psalter

3.6.9
Music

As a conductor and musicians are part of one orchestra,
as limbs and muscles, sinews and blood part of one body,
help us to see that each of us is important to creation as a whole;
that your rhythms and your tempos are music to our lives as long as we keep in harmony with you,
now and through all eternity.

Giles Harcourt

3.6.10
Music

Countless are your names, countless your dwelling places;
The breadth of your kingdom is beyond our imagination.
Even to try and imagine your kingdom is foolish.

Yet through words and through music
We speak your name and sing your praise.
Words are the only tools we have to proclaim your greatness,
And music our only means of echoing your virtue.

You put words in our hearts and minds.
With words we can describe the glory of your creation,
And so our words can reflect your glory.
You put music in our hearts and minds.
With music we can echo the beauty of heaven,
And so our music can express our deepest wish.

How can someone as insignificant as me
Express the vastness and wonder of your creation?
How can someone as sinful as me
Dare to hope for a place in heaven?

My only answer lies in the words and the music
Which you yourself have given me.

Guru Nanak

3.6.11
Praise God

O praise God in his holiness: praise him in the firmament of his power.
Praise him in his noble acts: praise him according to his excellent greatness.
Praise him in the sound of the trumpet: praise him upon the lute and harp.
Praise him in the cymbals and dances: praise him upon the strings and pipe.
Praise him upon the well-tuned cymbals: praise him upon the loud cymbals.
Let every thing that hath breath: praise the Lord.

Bible: Psalm 150

3.6.12
Artists

O God, whose Spirit in our hearts teaches us to desire your perfection, to seek for
truth and to rejoice in beauty; enlighten and inspire all musicians, artists,
architects and crafts men and women in whatever is true, pure and lovely, that
all may be done to your glory and for the benefit of others.

Anonymous: Based on a prayer of the Society of St Luke the Painter

3.6.13
For Artists

O You who are the all-pervading glory of the world, we bless You for the power
of beauty to gladden our hearts. We praise You that even the least of us may
feel a thrill of your creative joy when we give form and substance to our
thoughts and, beholding our handiwork, find it good and fair.

We praise You for our brothers and sisters who master form and colour and sound and who have the power to unlock for us the vaster spaces of emotion and to lead us by their hand into the reaches of nobler passions. We rejoice in their gifts and pray You to save them from the temptations which beset their powers. Kindle in their hearts a passionate pity for the joyless lives of the people, and make them rejoice if they are found worthy to hold the cup of beauty to lips that are athirst. Make them reverent interpreters of God to man, who see thy face and hear thy voice in all things, that so they may unveil for us the beauties of nature which we have passed unseeing, and the sadness and sweetness of humanity to which our selfishness has made us blind.

Walter Rauschenbusch

3.6.14
Unemployment

The day is there.
There is the sun.
Ships are in the harbour,
But is there work for me?
The others have friends.
They also have money.
They have given a dash of whisky.
And I stand aside
    and have no work.
Can't you make work for me
    in the harbour,
    dear Lord,
    so that I can share money
    with my wife and children?
Then, on Sunday,
I can put something in the plate.
Please let me have work.
Dear Lord Jesus,
    we praise you.

Prayer from West Africa

3.6.15
Daily Work

The time of business does not with me differ from the time of prayer, and in the noise and clatter of my kitchen, while several persons are at the same time calling for different things, I possess God in as great tranquillity as if I were upon my knees at the blessed sacrament.

Brother Lawrence

3.6.16
The Famous Stone

Teach me, my God and King,
In all things thee to see;
And what I do in anything
To do it as for thee!...

All may of thee partake;
Nothing can be so mean
Which with this tincture, 'for thy sake',
Will not grow bright and clean.

A servant with this clause
Makes drudgery divine;
Who sweeps a room, as for thy laws,
Makes that and the action fine.

This is the famous stone
That turneth all to gold;
For that which God doth touch and own
Cannot for less be told.

George Herbert

3.6.17
More Thankful

Lord, make us more thankful for what we have received;
make us more content with what we have;
and make us more mindful of other people in need.

Based on a prayer by Simon H. Baynes

3.6.18
Work

Work soulfully. Lo, you will not be able to find any differences between heaven and earth
There are two kinds of work. In the ordinary kind of work, you do something and then you look for the result. Then when you get the result, you say, "Perhaps I could have got a better result." There is no end to it. If you want real joy, you will not get it by fulfilling a desire for a particular result. In the second kind of work, you do not care for the result. Only by having the right attitude will you become a happy person. If you do the work with a divine attitude, then it will not be the result which gives you joy, but the very act.
There is no such thing
As insignificant work.
Therefore,
We must need do everything

> With our heart's love
> And our life's respect.

Sri Chinmoy

3.6.19
The Fire Fighter's Prayer

Whenever we are called to serve you, Lord,
wherever fires rage, or folk are trapped,
give us strength to save a life, whoever it may be.
Help us to rescue a little child before it is too late,
or to save an older person too frail to escape.
Enable us to be alert and hear the weakest cry
or quickly and efficiently put fires out.
We want to fulfill our calling, Lord,
to serve our neighbours in their need.
If one of us should fall and lose our life,
then bless with your all-embracing love
those who are dearest to us.
We ask all this trusting in Jesus Christ.

Anonymous

3.6.20
High Flight (For Airmen)

Oh! I have slipped the surly bonds of earth
And danced the skies on laughter-silvered wings;
Sunward I've climbed, and joined the tumbling mirth
Of sun-split clouds... and done a hundred things
You have not dreamed of... wheeled and soared and swung
High in the sunlit silence. Hov'ring there
I've chased the shouting wind along, and flung
My eager craft through footless hall of air.

Up, up the long, delirious, burning blue
I've topped the wind-swept heights with easy grace
Where never lark, nor even eagle flew...
And, while with silent lifting mind I've trod
The high untrespassed sanctity of space,
Put out my hand and touched the face of God.

John Gillespie Magee Jr.

Born of missionary parents, he enlisted in the Spitfire Squadron of the Royal Canadian Air Force, but died on active service on 11.12.1941. This sonnet, composed three months before his death, was scribbled on the back of a letter to his mother.

3.6.21
Judges/Magistrates

Heavenly Father, at whose hand the weak shall suffer no wrong nor the mighty escape just judgement: pour your grace upon your servants our judges and magistrates, that by their true, faithful and diligent execution of justice and equity to all men equally, you may be glorified, the commonwealth daily promoted and increased and we all live in peace and quietness, godliness and virtue, through Jesus Christ.

Thomas Cranmer

3.6.22
For Magistrates and Judges

O God, mighty and merciful, the Judge of all: grant to those who minister justice the spirit of wisdom and discernment; and that they may be strong and patient, upright and compassionate. Fill them, we beseech thee, with the spirit of holy fear. Amen

J. Armitage Robinson

3.6.23
On Going to Work

Give me, dear Lord, a pure heart and a wise mind, that I may carry out my work according to your will. Save me from all false desires, from pride, greed, envy and anger, and let me accept joyfully every task you set before me. Let me seek to serve the poor, the sad and those unable to work. Help me to discern honestly my own gifts that I may do the things of which I am capable, and happily and humbly leave the rest to others. Above all, remind me constantly that I have nothing except what you give me, and can do nothing except what you enable me to do.

Jacob Boehme

3.6.24
For Research Scientists and Inventors

We praise You, O Lord, for that mysterious spark of light within us, the intellect of men and women, which You kindled in the beginning by the breath of Your Spirit and which has grown to a flaming power in our time.
We rejoice in the men of genius and intellectual vision who discern the undiscovered applications of your laws and dig deeper springs through which the hidden forces of your world may well up to the light of day. May all their discoveries be to Your glory and the welfare of other people.

Based on a prayer by Walter Rauschenbusch

3.6.25
Too Busy

How is it, my God, that you have given me this hectic busy life when I have so little time to enjoy your presence. Throughout the day people are waiting to speak with me, and even at meals I have to continue talking to people about their needs and problems. During sleep itself I am still thinking and dreaming about the multitude of concerns that surround me. I do all this not for my own sake, but for yours. To me my present pattern of life is a torment; I only hope that for you it is truly a sacrifice of love. I know that you are constantly beside me, yet I am usually so busy that I ignore you. If you want me to remain so busy, please force me to think about and love you even in the midst of such hectic activity. If you do not want me so busy, please release me from it by, showing how others can take over my responsibilities.

Teresa of Avila

3.6.26
International Sporting Events

Dear God: invisible One of all names known;
The all-powerful former of the swirl of limitless galaxies:
We thank you for our body forms:
For joy in skilled use of brain, muscle and bone.

Please spread throughout this vast gathering
The simple joy of Being: through prayers and
Tight-packed watchers in tiered stands;
Through bright screens and through excited commentators.
Let both winners and losers know true Sportsmanship
In the ancient spirit of all games played before:
This in your sacred name, O God...

Eric Gladwin

3.6.27
For Professional Sports Men and Women

Lord, help all engaged in professional sport to see their work as part of a wider life and to remember that their talent is your gift to them. Strengthen them, we pray, to withstand the many pressures of so public a life. May they set for themselves the highest standards of personal and professional behaviour, both on the field and off, and provide a good example to their supporters.

Marcus Braybrooke

3.6.28
I Think Today

I think today ...
Of truck drivers with their heavy load
How they must concentrate on the road.

I think today of the lonely old
With no one to speak to, to trust, to hold.

The couple whose marriage is falling apart –
The secret tears, the pain in the heart.

I think of the young who know nothing of You
Who cannot distinguish the false from the true.

I think of the teachers who want to teach
But the children just laugh and play and screech.

I think of the rich, the selfish and greedy
Who have no time for the poor and needy.

I think of the many who do not pray
What do they think? What can they say?

I think of those who hurt and hate
How empty their lives! How sad their fate!

Of all these I think and pray
I give you each of them today.

Roger Lesser

3.6.29
For Scientists

O Holy Wisdom of God, enlighten all scientists who search out the secrets of the world, that they may be reverent towards nature, compassionate to the animal creation and humble in their discoveries. Save us from misusing their labours so that the forces they set free may enrich all life rather than be abused for the enrichment of the few and the destruction of the environment. Grant that both in the search for truth and in the use of power we may act responsibly and seek your glory.

Marcus Braybrooke

3.6.30
For Miners

Almighty God, who art present in the highest heaven and in the deep places of the earth: Let thy protecting care be over all who work in the mines of our land, that they may be preserved in safety and in health; and grant that, knowing the dangers that beset them, they may ever take thought one for another and be sustained by a sure trust in thee.

Adapted from the Canadian Prayer Book

3.6.31
Seafarers

O Eternal Lord God, who alone spreadest out the heavens, and rulest the raging of the sea: Be pleased to receive into thy protection all those who go down to the sea in ships, and occupy their business in great waters. Preserve them both in body and soul; prosper their labours with good success; in all time of danger be their defence, and bring them to the haven where they would be.

From the 1928 Book of Common Prayer

3.6.32
The Harvest of the Waters

O Almighty God, who hast made the sea and all that moveth therein: bestow thy blessing on the harvest of the waters, that it may be abundant in its season, and on our fishermen and mariners, that they may be safe in every peril of the deep; so that we all with thankful hearts may acknowledge thee who art the Lord of the sea and of the dry land.

From the 1928 Book of Common Prayer

3.6.33
Peril on the Sea

> Eternal Father, strong to save,
> Whose arm doth bind the restless wave,
> Who bidd'st the mighty ocean deep
> Its own appointed limits keep:
> *O hear us when we cry to thee*
> *For those in peril on the sea...*

William Whiting, (1825-78)

3.6.34
For Farmers and Workers in Industry.

> Loving Father, you promise to supply all our needs
> out of your abundant store:
> prosper the labours of those who enable us
> to enjoy the resources of nature,
> whether by farming or industrial work
> or by transporting their products.
> May we be grateful to them
> and remember to give thanks to you.

P. R. Akehurst and A. J. Bishop

3.6.35
Social Workers

O God, we ask you to strengthen all social workers as they try to bring comfort, help and support to those in distress or special need. We pray for those who work with children and their parents, with the elderly and those who are ill and for those who work with people who have broken the law and who feel alienated from society. May their care express your compassion for all in need.

Marcus Braybrooke

3.6.36
Poets

In the poet's heart lie ancient strengths
Drawn from the streaming glitter of galaxies
And his own wonder
At the creation of eternity

We cry, fighting for the damaged beauty of this world
For those who read of spring but do not know her heart,
Who seek the nature of Power and not the power of Nature
...Unable, now, to even know pure Love.

We write for the innocent, the trampled, or ignored,
For the sweeping harmony of music that is truth
And graceful form that holds the sculptor's magic Being;
For dance that takes the soul beyond all seeing.

From this, the over-brimming of a heart
... Borne on the lilting swing of uttered sound...
Flow bright ripples which hope may pulse with you:
Quiet leaders of great tides that will overwhelm
With freshness any wrong that men may do.

Eric Gladwin

 3.7 Illness and Worry

3.7.1
You Are the Healer

O Lord of humankind, send suffering away and restore health. You are the healer. There is no healing other than the healing You would bless someone with, a healing which would leave no trace of sickness behind.

Bukhari

3.7.2

(Three poems by Brenda Dawson, a primary school headmistress, who was admitted to St Christopher's Hospice on March 6th 1986.)

Be Not Dismayed

'Be not dismayed', the psalmist said.
easier said than done.
I am dismayed, deep into my mind,
I'm frightened, I'm nervous,
my heart's all aflutter,
the future looks bleak and forlorn.
what sort of life can it possibly hold
dependent on others for all that I need?

My life is reduced in quantity,
or is this illusion and lies?
It's changed so much I just can't adjust
To no work, no flat, no legs that walk.
And how do I measure quality?
Is that as it was before?
Can you measure your life by what you do?
No, that is an illusion, it cannot be true.

'Be not dismayed', the psalmist said.
Life just goes on, day follows day
transformed it may be, narrow and tight,
but its depth never varies
and its height is all right.
So what must I do to find value in life?
Attend to the Lord, he will show me the way.
Attend to the Lord, all the live-long day.

Brenda Dawson, April 16th 1986

3.7.3
Had a Good Day?

What is enjoyment in this cell-like situation?
Is it appreciation of each small glory?
The flash of sunlight on a flower.
The song on the lips of a nurse.
The letter from a friend, telephone calls.
A sudden, joyful synchronicity of thoughts or
A glimpse of a child playing,
Absorbed in its fantasy,
A bird singing outside in the garden.
All show forth the Glory of God
And in gratitude I can respond in thankfulness.
But first I have to learn
To recognise the moment of enjoyment.

Brenda Dawson, May 4th 1986

3.7.4
Through a Glass Darkly

It's lucky our eyes look outward
We can't see how we look
Without mirrors.
As our bodies diminish
Or lose their shape
It's others who see it.
We feel its limitations.
How do we look in their eyes?
Does it hurt our family and friends
To see us changed so much?
As we move lifewards
So we become transformed.
Through our dark internal glass we see clearly
But the eyes of our friends cloud over.
In their concern they recall us
As we used to be, loving and alive.
But they seem unable to see the new life
Rising within us.

Brenda Dawson, July 26th 1986

3.7.5
Alzheimer's Disease

Cordial.
How do they keep on smiling?
Mattie Mae and Eydie walk together
as if the cold corridor

were a path in a flowering park.
They nod to me and the word cordial
explodes like springtime in my mind.
By their smiles they
defy the institution every day.
How do they manage to accept,
and further, find contentment,
where others rail and wail?

They put down their shields
and give up their masks,
with the ease of those
at either end of life's circle.
    Oh yes
they say to me with their eyes,
     we are indeed human beings.
At the cusp they embrace
their dear vulnerability.
Eydie and Mattie Mae.
Their smiles enchant us
out of our despair.

Sue Silvermarie

3.7.6
Not to Look Away

Suffering
In the eyes
My job not to look away.

Sue Silvermarie (From 'Bewildered')

Both are from *Tales from My Teachers on the Alzheimer's Unit.*

3.7.7
One and Infinite

Step into the Sunlight
Feel the pain wash away
Enter in the Soul-light
Just BE in today. Forget all emotion
Put your trust in the day
Let the past rush on by you
Put your Self in THE WAY.

Lynne Milum

3.7

3.7.8
Let Go

Do everything with a mind that lets go.
Do not expect any praise or reward.
If you let go a little, you will have a little peace.
If you let go a lot, you will have a lot of peace.
If you let go completely, you will know complete peace and freedom.
Your struggles with the world
will have come to an end.

Insight Meditation – Achaan Chah

3.7.9
You Are My Healing

Thy name is my healing, O my God,
and remembrance of Thee is my remedy.
Nearness to Thee is my hope,
and love for Thee is my companion.
Thy mercy to me is my healing and my succour
in both this world and the world to come.
Thou, verily, art the All-Bountiful,
the All-Knowing,
the All-Wise.

Bahá'u'lláh

3.7.10
We Discover Dharma

Assailed by afflictions, we discover Dharma
And find the way to liberation. Thank you, evil forces!

When sorrows invade the mind, we discover Dharma
And find lasting happiness. Thank you, sorrows!

Through harm caused by spirits we discover Dharma
And find fearlessness. Thank you, ghosts and demons!

Through people's hate we discover Dharma
And find benefits and happiness. Thank you, those who hate us!

Through cruel adversity, we discover Dharma
And find the unchanging way. Thank you, adversity!

Through being impelled to by others, we discover Dharma
And find the essential meaning. Thank you, all who drive us on!

We dedicate our merit to you all, to repay your kindness.

Tibetan: Words of my Perfect Teacher – Gyalwa Longchenpa

3.7.11
If It's Better For Me

Pray to put an end to hope and fear:
If it's better for me to be ill,
I pray for the blessing of illness.
If it's better for me to recover,
I pray for the blessing of recovery.
If it's better for me to die,
I pray for the blessing of death.

Tibetan: Jamgon Kongtrul Rinpoche

3.7.12
Have Patience

Have patience with everything unresolved in your heart
and try to love the questions themselves...
Don't search for the answers,
which could not be given to you now,
because you would not be able to live them.
And the point is, to live everything.
Live the questions now.
Perhaps then, someday far in the future,
you will gradually, without even noticing it,
live your way into the answer.

Rainer Maria Rilke

3.7.13
Mastectomy

(On contemplating mastectomy after breast cancer diagnosis.)

Shock me
Rock me
Mutilate me
Heal me
If You must
So that I
Your once beautiful
Now maimed
Half-woman
Will yet dare
To love You
Twice as much

Kathy Keay

3.7.14
Beatitudes for Disabled People

Blessed are you who take time
to listen to defective speech,
for you help us to know that
if we persevere, we can be
understood.

Blessed are you who walk with
us in public places and ignore
the stares of strangers, for in
your companionship we find
havens of relaxation

Blessed are you that never bids
us 'hurry up' and more blessed
are you that do not snatch our tasks
from our hands to do them for us,
for often we need time rather than help.

Blessed are you who stand beside
us as we enter new ventures, for
our failures will be outweighed
by times we surprise
ourselves and you.

Blessed are you who ask for
our help, for our greatest need
is to be needed.

Blessed are you when by all these
things you assure us that the
thing that makes us individuals
is not our peculiar muscles,
nor our wounded nervous system
but is the God-given self
that no infirmity can
confine.

Marjorie Chappell

3.7.15
Exhausted

That man is perfect in faith who can come to God in the utter dearth of his feelings and desires, without a glow or an aspiration, with the weight of low thoughts, failures, neglects and wandering forgetfulness, and say to him, 'You are my refuge'.

George Macdonald

3.7.16
Callipers

The gifts of science can be the gifts of strengthening.
Thank you Lord for the men and women whose pioneer work
made these callipers possible,
and help me in their use
to know and feel the strength of your love
through inventors that care.

Giles Harcourt

3.7.17
Colostomy

Father it seems so idiotic to be praying about my colostomy when I should be praying about my fear. I am afraid of the bag, afraid of its position, fearful of collision, fearful of others handling me. (And there is my fear of being more abnormal than ever.)

Father you sent your Son to show a way through fear. Now you send skilled doctors and nurses. Let me trust in you and respond to your messengers.

Giles Harcourt (adapted)

3.7.18
For Parents of Organ Donors

If eyes can see anew,
If kidneys and liver can save lives,
If healthy organs can live on in others,
then take my dead child's body
and make out of my nothing
something more, dear Lord,
something good by which he (she) can be remembered,
and an aspect of resurrection through giving,
in the example of your only Son, who is life beyond death.

Giles Harcourt

3.7.19
Pain, the Sister of Joy

I thank Thee for Pain,
the sister of Joy.
I thank Thee for Sorrow,
the twin of Happiness

Pain, Joy, Sorrow, Happiness.
Four angels at work on the well of Love.

Pain and Sorrow dig it deep with aches.
Joy and Happiness fill it up with tears
that come with smiles.

For the seasons of emotion in my heart,
I thank you, O Lord.

Chandran Devanasen

3.7.20
'Give Me Your Weariness'

Lord,
You said so gently,
So persistently
'Give me your weariness
And I'll give you my rest.'
I did – finally.
You did – immediately
Then. Lord, I marvelled
That I had waited so long.

Ruth Harms Calkin

3.7.21
Help My Unbelief

Lord, I believe; help with my unbelief
For I believe in your deep love and mercy,
In your forgiving understanding
Of the human heart.
Through lonely watches of the spirit's night
Within the narrow tunnel of my grief,
I know a quiet dawn will come.
Tortured alone in the creeping loathsome dark
And dragged along a labyrinthine maze,
I still believe your healing sun
Will bring the birth of some new day
To break the iron gates of pain,

To bring again life where hopes, broken, lie
Crippled among her ancient battlements;
Lord, I believe that there will surely be
Light, after the midnight turns to death.

Randle Manwaring

3.7.22
Deliver Us From Fear

O Lord, we beseech you to deliver us from the fear of the unknown future, from fear of failure, from fear of poverty, from fear of sickness and pain, from fear of age, and fear of death. Help us, O Father, by your grace to love and fear you only. Fill our hearts with cheerful courage and loving trust in you.

African: Akanu Ibaim from Nigeria

3.7.23
May No Clouds Hide Your Light

Most loving Father,
Preserve us from faithless fears and worldly anxieties
and grant that no clouds of this mortal life
May hide from us the light of that love which is immortal
And which you have manifested unto us in your Son.

William Bright

3.7.24
Your Hand in the Darkness

As the rain hides the stars, as the autumn mist hides the hills, as the clouds veil the blue of the sky, so the dark happenings of my lot hide the shining of your face from me. Yet, if I may hold your hand in the darkness, it is enough. Since I know that, though I may stumble in my going, you do not fall

A Celtic prayer

3.7.25
The Spirit of Healing

Grant, O Lord, to all those who are bearing pain
    your spirit of healing,
    your spirit of peace and hope
    of courage and endurance,
Cast out from them the spirit of anxiety and fear;
grant them perfect confidence and trust in thee,
    that in your light they may see light;
    through Jesus Christ our Lord.

George Appleton

3.7

3.7.26
I Feel Only Weakness

My strength fails; I feel only weakness, irritation and depression. I am tempted to complain and to despair. What has become of the courage I was so proud of and that gave me so much self-confidence? In addition to my pain, I have to bear the shame of my fretful feebleness. Lord, destroy my pride; leave it no resource. How happy I shall be if you can teach me by these terrible trials that I am nothing, that I can do nothing and that you are all.

François Fénelon

3.7.27
Times of Trial

I asked the Lord
for a bunch of fresh flowers
but instead he gave me an ugly cactus with many thorns.
I asked the Lord
for some beautiful butterflies
but instead he gave me
many ugly and dreadful worms.
I was threatened,
I was disappointed,
I mourned.
But after many days,
suddenly, I saw the cactus bloom
with many beautiful flowers,
and those worms became
beautiful butterflies
flying in the spring wind.
God's way is the best way.

Chun-Ming Kao, written from prison

3.7.28
We Cannot Measure How You Heal

We cannot measure how you heal
    Or answer every sufferer's prayer,
Yet we believe your grace responds
    Where faith and doubt unite to care.

Your hands though bloodied on the cross,
    Survive to hold and heal and warn,
To carry all through death to life
    and cradle children yet unborn.

The pain that will not go away
    The guilt that clings to things long past

The fear of what the future holds
    Are present as if meant to last.

Be present, too, in love which tends
    the hurt we never hoped to find
The private agonies inside
    The memories that haunt the mind.

Some have come who need your help
    And some have come to make amends
As hands which shaped and saved the world
    Are present in the touch of friends.

Lord let your Spirit meet us here
    To mend the body, mind and soul,
To disentangle peace from pain
    And make your broken people whole.

A hymn sung at a memorial service following the Dunblane massacre John L. Bell and Graham Maule, 1989.

3.7.29
Shingles

Dear Lord Jesus,
The pain is so great,
So overwhelming that I want to scream.
Forgive me that I have become self absorbed.
So many suffer more;
I cannot begin to imagine your own suffering on the Cross.
Yet I ask for relief;
And I ask for strength and courage
To bear the pain
And to use it positively
Not with the negativity that I feel.

Mary Braybrooke

3.7.30
Bareness

Lord,
The landscape of my days
Has changed dramatically;
I am a shrunken man.
Once there was variety and spice
To my life –
Now I know only tedium
And hour following hour

Full of scheduled monotony.

Once I was active and alert;
Now I lie back
And the seconds seem empty
As the city flows past me
In an orgy of hurry
And time-tornness.

A spectator now
How can I continue to walk
The littered streets
Of the consumer age
And pray?
How can I find
In the anonymity
With which the city
Cloaks our lives
Any meaning and significance?

Lord,
I am a man lost and bewildered
At our disregard
For those who suffer
And make up the anguish of urban life.
Give me the power
To meditate on the bareness
Of Your life in Bethlehem.

Brian Frost

She wrapped him in cloths and placed him in a manger, because there was no room for them in the inn (Luke 2:7b).

3.7.31
Chalice of Grief

Drink deep of the chalice of grief and sorrow,
held out to you
by your dark angel of Gethsemane:
the angel is not your enemy,
the drink, though sharp, is nourishing,
by which you may come to a deeper peace
than if you pass it by.

Steve Smith

In the Garden of Gethsemane, on the night before he was put to death, Jesus prayed that the cup of suffering might be taken away, adding 'but not my will, but Yours be done, O Lord.'

3.7.32
Sick Child

O God, you are great,
You are the one who created me,
I have no other.
God, you are in the heavens,
You are the only one:
Now my child is sick,
And you will grant me my desire.

African: A Prayer of the Anuak people of Sudan

3.7.33
Be Patient

Let nothing disturb you, nothing alarm you:
while all things fade away
God is unchanging.
Be patient
and you will gain everything:
for with God in your heart
nothing is lacking,
God meets your every need.

St Teresa of Avila

3.7.34
Carers

The more hopeless the disease,
The more splendid the devotion
And unselfish the charity
Of those who strive to alleviate it.

St Bonaventure

3.7.35
Do Not Despair

No need for fear
or deep despair
Seekers of God
Receive his care.
No need for fear
or deep despair

We are at home
And God is there.

St Teresa of Avila

3.7.36
Sorrow, Love's Companion

Life is ours in vain
Lacking love, which never
Counts the loss or gain.
But remember; ever
Love is linked with pain.

Light and sister shade
Shape each mortal morrow
Seek not to evade
Love's companion, Sorrow,
And be not dismayed.

Grief is not in vain,
It's for our completeness.
If the fates ordain
Love to bring life's sweetness'
Welcome too its pain.

Oodgeroo of the tribe Noonuccal

3.7.37
My Heart Was Free

Distracted,
too passionate
dumb about
the way things work
I was stung and tossed
by memories
haunted, you could say
I went on like this,
wandering for seven years
Thin, pale, desperate
Nothing to hold me
taking a rope
I went to the woods
Hanging is better
than this low life.
The noose was strong

I tied it to the branch of a tree
flung it round my neck
when suddenly – look–
it snapped!
Not my neck
my *heart* was free.

Siha, a Therigata nun

© Shambhala Publications from *Songs of the Sons and Daughters of Buddha*

3.7.38
A Doctor's Dedication

Your eternal providence has appointed me to watch over the life and health of Your creatures. May the love for my art actuate me at all times; may neither avarice nor miserliness, nor the thirst for glory or for a great reputation engage my mind, for the enemies of truth and philanthropy could easily deceive me and make me forgetful of my lofty aim of doing good to Your children. May I never see in a patient anything but a fellow creature in pain. Grant me strength, time and opportunity always to correct what I have acquired, always to extend its domain, for knowledge is immense and the spirit of man can extend indefinitely to enrich itself daily with new requirements. Today he can discover his errors of yesterday and tomorrow he may obtain new light on what he thinks himself sure of today.

O God, You have appointed me to watch over the life and death of Your creatures. Here I am, ready for my vocation.

Maimonides

3.7.39
The Physician's Prayer

From inability to let well alone, from too much zeal for the new and contempt for what is old, from putting knowledge before wisdom, science before art and cleverness before common sense, from treating patients as cases and from making the cure of the disease more grievous than the endurance of the same, good Lord deliver us.

Sir Robert Hutchinson (1871-1960)

He was a President of the Royal College of Physicians.

3.7.40
Suffering and Joy

Lord, let me welcome all the pain and suffering that comes to me, for pain and suffering are sent by you. Ever since you enlightened me, thirty-six years ago, I have sought to suffer, both spiritually and physically. And yet because I have desired suffering, all suffering has seemed sweet and pleasant, knowing that you are its source. Now that I am near to doubt, and my whole body is in agony from head to toe, I find myself wondering if I can endure this final encounter with pain. I know that you rule over my pain, and will bring relief when I am ready to be received into your heavenly kingdom. So even in the midst of this agony, I cannot really say that I am suffering. You make all things bearable, filling my heart with inexpressible joy.

St Catherine of Genoa

 3.8 Sufferers

3.8.1
A Sufficient Prayer

Lord, he whom you love is sick.
Do for him according to his need, dear Lord.

Based on John 8:3

3.8.2
Love Held Him There

Nails would not have held God-and-Man fastened to the Cross
had Love not held Him there.

St Catherine of Siena

3.8.3
I Was In Prison

When Christ said, 'I was in prison and you visited me',
He did not draw a distinction between the guilty and the innocent.

Pope John Paul II

3.8.4
Prisoners

O Father of All, may I feel that even he who does me mortal injury is my brother,
made in Thine image, and existing only temporarily in darkness. Banish from my
mind the vengeful "tit-for-tat" spirit.

Let my sympathy go out to all, including those whom society, to protect itself,
has imprisoned. Teach me to desire eagerly their redemption and solace in Thee.

May I not increase the ignorance of wrong-doers by my intolerance or
vindictiveness. Inspire me to help them by my forgiveness, prayers, and tears of
gentle love.

Paramahansa Yogananda

3.8.5
The Joys and Sorrows of Others

When a person responds to the joys and sorrows of others
as if they were his own,
he has attained the highest state of spiritual union.

Hindu: Sri Krishna: the Bhagavad Gita 6:32

3.8.6
Victims of Injustice

O God, we pray for all those in our world
who are suffering from injustice:
For those who are discriminated against
because of their race, colour or religion;
For those imprisoned
for working for the relief of oppression;
For those who are hounded
for speaking the inconvenient truth;
For those tempted to violence
as a cry against overwhelming hardship;
For those deprived of reasonable health and education;
For those suffering from hunger and famine;
For those too weak to help themselves
and who have no one else to help them;
For the unemployed who cry out
for work but do not find it.
We pray for anyone of our acquaintance
who is personally affected by injustice.
Forgive us, Lord, if we unwittingly share in the conditions
or in a system that perpetuates injustice.
Show us how we can serve your children
and make your love practical by washing their feet.

Mother Teresa

3.8.7
Prison

Show me the person
Show me the gaol
Show me the prisoner
Whose life has gone stale
And I'll show you a young man
With so many reasons why
There but for fortune
Go you or I
You or I.

Phil Ochs

3.8.8
Tightly Bound

Although they have tightly bound my arms and legs,
All over the mountains I hear the song of birds,
And the forest is filled
With the perfume of spring flowers.

Who can prevent me from enjoying these
Which take from the long journey
A little of its loneliness?

Ho Chi Minh (1890-1969) On the Road from Prison Diary

3.8.9
Invisible Chains

Who can boast of being free?
Who has not got secret prisons,
invisible chains, all the more constricting
the less they are apparent?

Dom Helder Camara

3.8.10
Prisoners of Conscience

As we closed our doors this morning and walked freely through the church door, other doors slammed behind other people, and they do not know if or when they will open again: doors in prison cells and torture chambers; doors separating families, doors in labour camp units. Let us ask Christ, who came to set all people free, to enable us to experience his freedom and to bring freedom to others.

Pax Christi

3.8.11
The Poor

Here is thy footstool and there rest thy feet where live the poorest and lowliest and lost.
When I try to bow to thee, my obeisance cannot reach down to the depth where thy feet rest among the poorest and lowliest and lost.
Pride can never approach to where thou walkest in the clothes of the humble among the poorest and lowliest and lost.
My heart can never find its way to where thou keepest company with the companionless among the poorest, the lowliest and the lost.

Rabindranath Tagore

3.8.12
Suffering

We bring before you, O Lord, the troubles and perils of people and nations, the sighing of prisoners and captives, the sorrows of the bereaved, the necessities of strangers, the helplessness of the weak, the despondency of the weary, the failing powers of the aged. O Lord, draw near to each, for the sake of Christ our Lord.

St Anselm

3.8.13
Someone is Thinking of Me

Believe me, it was often thus
In solitary cells, on winter nights
A sudden sense of joy and warmth
And a resounding note of love,
And then, unsleeping, I would know
A-huddle by an icy wall
Someone is thinking of me now
Petitioning the Lord for me.
My dear ones, thank you all
Who did not falter, who believed in us!
In the most fearful prison hour
We probably would not have passed
Through everything – from start to end –
Our heads held high, unbowed,
Without your valiant hearts
To light our paths.

Irina Ratushinskaya

For those who prayed for her and campaigned for her release and that of fellow prisoners in the Soviet Union.

3.8.14
Aids

Loving God, you show yourself to those who are vulnerable and make your home with the poor and weak of this world;
Warm our hearts with the fire of your Spirit. Help us to accept the challenge of AIDS.
Protect the healthy, we pray, calm the frightened, give courage to those in pain, comfort the dying and give to the dead eternal life.
Console the bereaved, we beg you, and strengthen those who care for the sick.
May we, your people, using all our energy and imagination, and trusting in your steadfast love, be united with one another in conquering all disease and fear.

Anonymous; from an Interfaith group

3.8.15
Last Letter from Prison

These few words are being set down here as they come from my mind and my heart. And if I must write them with my hands in chains, I find that much better than if my will were in chains...

For us men there are only two possibilities in this world; there is simply no such thing as standing still. Yes, even for those who have worked hard to come close to God, there can be many reverses, just as an army advancing towards its victory does not win all its battles but must endure defeats. Nevertheless, this does not mean that the struggle should be given up as hopeless; instead one must pick oneself up with renewed strength and strive on again towards the desired goals...

Many actually believe quite simply that things have to be the way they are. If this should happen to mean that they are obliged to commit injustice, then they believe that others are responsible. The oath would not be a lie for someone who believes he can go along and is willing to do so. But if I know in advance that I cannot accept and obey everything I would promise under that oath, then I would be guilty of a lie. For this reason I am convinced that it is still best that I speak the truth, even if it costs me my life. For you will not find it written in any of the commandments of God or of the Church, that a man is obliged under pain of sin to take an oath committing him to obey whatever might be commanded of him by his secular ruler...

Dear wife, forgive me everything by which I have grieved or offended you. For my part, I have forgiven everything. Ask all those in Radegund whom I have ever injured or offended to forgive me too.

Franz Jagerstatter

This was his last letter from prison, written in August 1943. Jagerstatter, an Austrian farmer, was conscripted into Hitler's army in February 1943, refused to take the military oath of obedience and was beheaded in Berlin on 9th August 1943.

3.8.16
Strength to Bear My Joys and Sorrows

This is my prayer to thee, my lord – strike, strike at the root of penury
in my heart.
Give me the strength lightly to bear my joys and sorrows.
Give me the strength to make my love fruitful in service.
Give me the strength never to disown the poor or bend my knee before insolent might.
Give me the strength to raise my mind high above daily trifles.
And give me the strength to surrender my strength to thy will with love.

Rabindranath Tagore

3.8.17
A Thirsty Traveller

I heard not thy steps as thou camest.
Thine eyes were sad when they fell on me;
Thy voice was tired as thou spokest low –
"Ah, I am a thirsty traveller."
I started up from my day-dreams
And poured water from my jar on thy joined palms.

Rabindranath Tagore

3.8

3.8.18
A Cup of Water

Whosoever shall give you a cup of water to drink in my name... verily I say unto you, he shall not lose his reward.

Bible: Mark 9:41

3.8.19
The Ambulance

Lord, I hear the sound of the ambulance siren again.
Someone is ill, others will be worrying
Or possibly a new life is coming into the world
And there will be rejoicing after pain.

I pray for the person in the ambulance
For those who are near to him or her
For those looking after him or her.
May Your Presence calm and soothe the way.

Mary Braybrooke

3.8.20
Love's Transforming Power

Through love bitter things seem sweet
Through love bits of copper are made gold
Through love pains are as healing balms
Through love thorns become roses
Through love vinegar becomes sweet wine
Through love the stake becomes a throne
Through love prison seems a rose bower
Through love stones become soft as butter
Through love soft wax becomes hard iron
Through love grief is a joy
Through love stings are as honey
Through love lions are as harmless as mice
Through love sickness is health
Through love the dead rise to life
Through love the king becomes a slave.

Jalal al-Din Rumi

3.8.21
Orphans

Did he not find thee an orphan and sheltered thee?
Find thee wandering and led thee?
Find thee needy and sufficed thee?

Then do not oppress the orphan,

Nor repel the suppliant.
The grace of your Lord - let that be your theme.

Qur'an: 5:6-8

3.8.22
Disability

Father, we lift up to you all who are disabled -
  in hearing, in sight, in limb or in mind.
Save them from bitterness and frustration
  and give them joy in the midst of their limitations.
May they find peace and fulfilment in knowing you
  and discovering your will for their lives.
We pray for special grace for those who care for them.
Give them your love and kindness and understanding
  of the real needs of those they look after. For Jesus' sake.

Mary Batchelor

3.8.23
For Sufferers

Relieve thou, O God, each one
In suffering on land or sea,
In grief or wounded or weeping,
And lead them to the house of thy peace
This night.

A Celtic prayer

3.8.24
Sufferers

Comfort, O merciful Father, by thy Word and Holy Spirit, all who are afflicted or distressed, and so turn their hearts unto thee, that they may serve thee in truth and bring forth fruit to thy glory. Be thou, O Lord, their succour and defence, through Jesus Christ our Lord.

Melanchthon

3.8.25
Lonely

Father, we pray for all lonely people, especially those who coming home to an empty house stand at the door hesitant and afraid to enter. May all who stand on any doorway with fear in their hearts, like the two on the Emmaus road, ask the Living One in. Then, by his grace, may they find that in loneliness they are never alone and that he peoples empty rooms with his presence.

E. M. Farr

3.8.26
In Disaster (Shelter Prayer)

Increase, O God, the spirit of neighbourliness among us, that in peril we may uphold one another, in calamity serve one another, in suffering tend one another, and in homelessness and loneliness of exile befriend one another. Grant us brave and enduring hearts that we may strengthen one another, till the disciplines and testing of these days be ended and You again give peace in our time.

Anonymous

A Prayer used in English air-raid shelters during the Second World War.

3.8.27
Prayer of a Prisoner with a Life-sentence

Dear God,
I hold up all my weakness to your strength,
My failure to your faithfulness,
My sinfulness to your perfection,
My loneliness to your compassion,
My small pain to your agony on the cross. Amen.

Anonymous

3.8.28
Prayer of a Young Offender

Dear God,
Help me to take the right path in life and
Help me to know right from wrong.
Show me a way to get through life and its problems
No matter how hard they are.
Help me to build a life I can be proud of and
Show me the way to make a happy life.
I put my trust in You and You are a God who loves
Us all no matter who we are.

Anonymous

3.8.29
Natural Disasters

When cataclysm strikes, the spirit is tested.
 The Earth has turned in its sleep.
People have been crushed, killed, wounded.
 Let us pray for the survivors,
 that their lives may be rebuilt.

When cataclysm strikes, the spirit is tested,
 wakes from its dream of immortality.

Yet the spirit cannot be crushed, killed, wounded.
Let us pray that everyone who has suffered
    finds strength in the spirit.

Anonymous: A modern prayer from Gujarat, India

3.8.30
The Despised

Today we come to you, Lord, we the despised. We are not a sorry procession, but
a repugnant one. We do not even arouse compassion or hatred, tenderness or
sympathy. We are simply despised; we disgust people. The leper arouses
compassion. The fiercest criminal stirs up hatred or terror. The mentally ill or the
retarded inspire pity or protectiveness. But there is no place reserved for us in the
catalogue of the works of mercy...

We aren't trying to hide or make excuses for the sins that have caused us to be
cast off by society. We only hope that perhaps you, who not only forgive but also
excuse, will be able to avoid humiliating us further and to tell us, as once you
told the man possessed by the devil, that saving us will let others see your glory
and mercy in us. Remember, you said you came to save what was lost. And who is
more lost than we who do not even arouse pity? Sometimes a ray of hope lets us
dream for a moment that perhaps you may bring yourself to love even us.

Juan Arias

3.8.31
For a Brother in Despair

O God, you rule over your creation with tenderness, offering fresh hope in the
midst of the most terrible misery. We pray for our brother whose soul is
blackened by despair, infusing him with the pure light of your love. As he curses
the day he was born and yearns for oblivion, reveal to him the miracle of new
birth which shall prepare him for the joys of heaven.

Dimma

Sister can be substituted for *brother.*

3.8.32
The Sick in Mind

O Holy Spirit who delves into all things,
even the deep things of God
and the deep things of human beings,
we pray you to penetrate the springs of personality
of all who are sick in mind,
to bring them cleansing, healing, and unity.
Sanctify all memory, dispel all fear,
Bring them to love thee

With all their mind and will,
That they may be made whole
And glorify you for ever.

George Appleton

3.9 Care for Others, Love and Forgiveness

3.9.1
May I Abide to Dispel the Misery of the World

For as long as space endures
And for as long as living beings remain
Until then may I too abide
To dispel the misery of the world.

Buddhist: From the Bodhicaryavatara of Shantideva

3.9.2
Forgive

If I have wounded any soul today,
If I have caused one foot to go astray,
If I have walked in my own wilful way –
Good Lord, forgive!
If I have uttered idle words or vain,
If I have turned aside from want or pain,
Lest I myself should suffer through the strain –
Good Lord, forgive!
If I have craved for joys that are not mine,
If I have let my wayward heart repine,
Dwelling on things of earth, not things divine –
Good Lord, forgive!
If I have been perverse, or hard, or cold,
If I have longed for shelter in Thy fold,
When Thou has given me some part to hold –
Good Lord, forgive.
Forgive the sins I have confessed to Thee,
Forgive the secret sins I do not see,
That which I know not, Father, teach Thou me –
Help me to live.

Charles H. Gabriel

3.9.3
Thy Servant

O Lord and Master of my life,
take from me the spirit of sloth, despondency,
lust of power, and idle talk;
But grant rather
the spirit of chastity, humility, patience, and love
to thy servant.
Yea, O Lord and King,
grant me to see my own transgressions,

and not to judge my brother;
for blessed art Thou unto the ages of ages.

St Ephrem, the Syrian

3.9.4
May I Forgive

May I forgive (first inwardly, then outwardly) those who have most deeply injured me. I would return love for hatred, sweet praise for sour complaints, and good for evil.

Paramahansa Yogananda

3.9.5
Kiss Your Attacker

If he strikes you, take it;
Don't dare strike him back.
Kiss his feet and thank him
For that unearned attack.

Baba Farid

3.9.6
Love is Glad

Love is glad when you are glad
Is sad when you are sad
Is hurt when you are.
Love is never so wrapped in himself
He can't listen to you,
And hear you.
Love accepts you exactly as you are –
Is happy for your strengths
Is sorry for you in your weakness,
(However unacceptable it may appear)
Stands beside you in your struggle.
Love knows no time
And is always available.
Love may criticise what you do
But never you,
And looks with you
For the right path, for you.
Love makes no judgements
And has a deep respect for you:
Love shares his all with you
His time, his possessions, his talents.
Love grows by sharing himself;
Love drives out fear;
Love is eternal and never dies;

Love cares.

Ken Walsh

3.9.7
A prayer for Helpers and Carers

May the One who blessed our ancestors be present to those who provide help for the ill and troubled among us. May they be filled with fortitude and courage, endowed with sympathy and compassion, as they give strength to those at their side. May they fight against despair, and continue to find within themselves the will to reach out to those in need. And in their love of others, may they know the blessing of community, and the blessing of renewed faith.

Marcia Plumb

3.9.8
The Hearts of Those Who Wound Us

Lord, teach us to forgive:
to look deep into the hearts
of those who wound us,
so that we may glimpse, in that dark, still water,
not just the reflection
of our own face
but yours as well.

Sheila Cassidy

3.9.9
Make Us Merciful

Father of all mercy make us merciful as you are merciful
Father of all forgiveness make us forgiving as you have forgiven us.

Anonymous

3.9.10
Prayer of a Dying Man

And though I behold a man hate me,
I will love him.
O God, Father, help me, Father!
O God, Creator, help me, Father!
And even though I behold a man hate me,
I will love him.

African: A Dinka Prayer from Sudan

3.9.11
Accepting Forgiveness

Give us grace, dear Lord, to receive forgiveness from others when we have wronged them. Take away our pride and resentment and give us humility and courage to accept fully and freely the forgiveness that they offer to us. For Jesus' sake.
I offer also for all those whom I have in any way grieved, vexed, oppressed and scandalised by word and deed, knowingly or unknowingly, that thou mayest equally forgive us all our sins, and all our offences against others

Thomas More

3.9.12
Also Those of Ill Will

O Lord remember not only the men and women of good will, but also those of ill will. But do not remember all the suffering they have inflicted on us; remember the fruits we have bought, thanks to this suffering – our comradeship, our loyalty, our courage, our generosity, the greatness of heart which has grown out of all this, and when they come to judgement let all the fruits which we have borne be their forgiveness.

Anonymous

Prayer written by an unknown prisoner in Ravensbruck concentration camp and left by the body of a dead child.

3.9.13
Do Not Judge

You cannot weigh the faults of others unless you have learned the art of weighing your own teeming faults.

We will own peace only after we have totally stopped finding fault with others. When we observe other's mistakes, we enter into their imperfections. This does not help us in the least. Strangely enough, the deeper we plunge, the clearer it becomes that the imperfections of others are our own imperfections, but in different bodies and minds.

> When you speak ill of others,
> You have already exposed
> Your own inner weakness
> To the outer world.

Sri Chinmoy

3.9.14
Long Wait

This is a long wait at the bus stop:
It is quite late – we must get home.

Here it comes,
It didn't stop – it just went by;
It seemed all filled up.
It just went past without stopping;
We are still waiting to get on.

We're thinking,
Oftentimes we pass by others

Others who are waiting, eagerly waiting,
    Waiting to get on
    Waiting to have a word,
    Waiting to be heard,
    Waiting for a kindly gesture,
    Waiting for a smile, a kind look
    – we've passed by.
Why, Lord, do we pass by?
Like the bus we are filled up, too;
We are filled up with ourselves,
our worries – our joys,
our hates – our loves,
our fears – our hopes,
    our failures – our victories,
    our wants – our riches,
We are filled up with ourselves.
we are filled up,
and we pass by.

M. A. Thomas

3.9.15
The Telephone

I have just hung up; why did he telephone?
I don't know... Oh! I get it...
I talked a lot and listened very little.

Forgive me, Lord, it was a monologue and not a dialogue.
I explained my idea and did not get his;
Since I didn't listen, I learned nothing,
Since I didn't listen, I didn't help,
Since I didn't listen, we didn't communicate.

Forgive me, Lord, for we were connected,
And now we are cut off.

Michel Quoist

3.9.16
I Share Your Anguish

I share with you the agony of your grief
The anguish of your heart finds echo in my own.
I know I cannot enter all you feel
Nor bear with you the burden of your pain,
I can but offer what my love does give
The strength of caring
The warmth of one who seeks to understand
The silent storm-swept barrenness of so great a loss.
This I do in quiet ways
That on your lonely path
You may not walk alone.

H.Thurman

3.9.17
Forgiving Others

The more he strives to injure me
    The greater is my clemency
So when the wick is cut, its light
    Shines all the clearer through the night

al-Hallaj

3.9.18
An Instrument of Peace

Lord make me an instrument of your peace;
Where there is hatred, let me sow love,
Where there is injury, pardon;
Where there is doubt, faith;
Where there is despair, hope;
Where there is darkness, light;
Where there is sadness, joy.
O divine Master, grant that I may not so much seek
To be consoled, as to console,
To be understood, as to understand,
To be loved, as to love;
For it is in giving that we receive;
It is in pardoning that we are pardoned;
It is in dying that we are born to eternal life.

Attributed to St Francis

3.9.19
There is Nothing That Cannot Be Redeemed

No one can put together what has crumbled into dust,
but you can restore a conscience turned to ashes;
you can restore to its former beauty a soul lost and without hope.
With you there is nothing that cannot be redeemed;
you are love, you are Creator and Redeemer;
we praise you singing: Alleluia.

Gregory Petrov

3.9.20
Strength to Persevere

Give us grace and strength
to forbear and to persevere.
Give us courage and gaiety
and the quiet mind.
Spare to us our friends,
Soften to us our enemies.
Bless us if it may be
in all our innocent endeavours,
if it may not, give us strength
to encounter that which is to come,
that we may be brave in peril,
constant in tribulation, temperate in wrath.
And in all changes of fortune
And down to the gates of death
Loyal and loving
To one another.

Robert Louis Stevenson

3.9.21
Trusting in God

God has created me to do Him some definite service; He has committed some work to me which He has not committed to another. I have my mission – I may never know it in this life, but I shall be told it in the next.

I am a link in a chain, a bond of connection between persons. He has not created me for naught. I shall do good, I shall do his work. I shall be an angel of peace, a preacher of truth in my own place while not intending it – if I do but keep His Commandments.

Therefore, I will trust Him. Whatever, wherever I am, I can never be thrown away. If I am in sickness, my sickness may serve Him; in perplexity, my perplexity may serve Him; if I am in sorrow, my sorrow may serve Him. He does nothing in vain. He knows what he is about. He may take away my friends, He may throw me among strangers. He may make me feel desolate, make my spirits sink, hide my future from me - still He knows what he is about.

John Henry Newman

3.9.22
I'll Keep My Heart Open

When storm winds blow
And windows close
I'll keep my heart open.

When things go wrong
And harsh words hurt –
I'll keep my heart open.

When enemies strike
And friends don't help –
I'll keep my heart open.

When all I've aimed at –
My life's work crashes –
I'll keep my heart open.

When goodness faints
And evil flows –
I'll keep my heart open.

When joys taste bitter
And sadness grows –
I'll keep my heart open.

When I am weak
And near despair –
I'll keep my heart open.

For your great gifts –
Strength, joy and love
I open my heart for You.

Roger Lesser

3.9.23
Be Friendly to All

Be friendly to all and a burden to no one.
Let your manner be courteous,
Your forgiveness willing,
Your promises true,
And your speech wise.

An Amish proverb

3.9.24
Burn up Desire and Pride

O Lord! Make me always to have love for all beings, pleasure in the company of good and learned people, unstinted sympathy for those in pain, and tolerance towards those perversely inclined.

O Lord! May my mind, losing all sense of attachment, always be balanced and peaceful, in pleasure and pain, among friends and foes, in gain and loss, at home and in the forest.

I seek shelter in that Supreme Lord, having seen whom all the universe becomes clearly and distinctly visible and separate, who is pure, Blissful and all-Tranquility, who is without beginning and without end.

I seek shelter in that supreme Lord, who has annihilated desire, pride, delusion, anguish, sleep, fear, sorrow and anxiety, just as a jungle is burned up by the wild fire.

A Jain prayer

3.9.25
Renew the Strength to Serve

Whatever words and deed are noblest, best,
Teach me, O Mazda, and make my life express them;
Through love of fellow beings, through search for Truth,
And the yearnings and prayers of my heart;
Renew, Ahura, through the strength to serve,
My life, and make it as you wish.

Zoroastrian prayer: Yasna 34.15

Ahura Mazda means The Wise Lord and is the usual Zoroastrian name for God.

3.9.26
Make Us Useful in This World

O God! We are weak; give us strength. We are poor; bestow upon us Thine illimitable treasures. We are sick; grant us Thy divine healing. We are powerless;

give us of Thy heavenly power. O Lord! Make us useful in this world; free us from the condition of self and desire. O Lord! Make us firm in Thy love and cause us to be loving toward the whole of mankind. Confirm us in service to the world of humanity, so that we may become servants of Thy servants, that we may love all Thy creatures and become compassionate to all Thy people. O Lord! Thou art the Almighty! Thou art the merciful! Thou art the Forgiver! Thou art the Omnipotent.

'Abdu'l-Bah?

3.10 Old Age

3.10.1
I am Getting Older

Lord, you know better than I know myself that I am getting older and will some day be old. Keep me from the fatal habit of thinking I must say something on every subject and on every occasion. Release me from craving to straighten out everybody's affairs. Make me thoughtful but not moody: helpful but not bossy. With my vast store of wisdom it seems a pity not to use it all, but you know, Lord, that I want a few friends at the end.

Keep my mind free from the recital of endless details, give me wings to get to the point. Seal my lips on my aches and pains. They are increasing and love of rehearsing them is becoming sweeter as the years go by. I dare not ask for grace enough to enjoy the tales of others' pains, but help me to endure them with patience.

I dare not ask for improved memory, but for a growing humility and a lessening cocksureness when my memory seems to clash with the memories of others. Teach me the glorious lesson that occasionally I may be mistaken.

Keep me reasonably sweet; I do not want to be a saint – some of them are so hard to live with – but a sour old person is one of the crowning works of the devil.

Give me the ability to see good things in unexpected places, and talents in unexpected people. And give me, Lord, the grace to tell them so. Amen.

Anonymous: Attributed to a seventeenth-century nun

3.10.2
Then

And someday I won't be tired
Not ever, any more,
Someday I'll be calm and free
And walk by the seashore;
It'll all be over
The thing will be done –
The fight will be won or lost.

Then shall I see more clearly
Then shall I really know,
How you have always loved me;
How you have always been here
Standing by my side.

I'll see how I needn't have worried
And tossed and turned about so,
I'll see that it all had a purpose
A way that it had to go;
I'll see that there was direction
Though at times I didn't think so –
And I'll be quiet

Ken Walsh

3.10.3
Old Age

I have scaled the peak, and found no shelter in fame's bleak and barren height. Lead me, my Guide, before the light fades, into the valley of quiet where life's harvest mellows into golden wisdom.

Rabindranath Tagore

3.10.4
The Years That Are Left

Grant, O Lord, that the years that are left may be the holiest, the most loving, the most mature. I thank you for the past and especially that you have kept the good wine until now. Help me to accept diminishing powers as the opportunity to prepare my soul for the full and free life to come in the state prepared by your Son, Jesus Christ.

George Appleton

3.10.5
Beatitudes From an Old Person

Blessed are they who understand
my faltering steps and palsied hand.

Blessed are they who know my ears today
must strain to catch the things they say.

Blessed are they who seem to know
that my eyes are dim and wits are slow.

Blessed are they who looked away
when coffee spilled at the table today.

Blessed are they who never say,
'You've told that story twice today'.

Blessed are they who know the way
to bring back memories of yesterday.

Blessed are they who know I'm at a loss
to find the strength to carry the cross.

Blessed are they who ease the days
on my journey home in loving ways.

Anonymous

3.10.6

A Psalm at Signs of Ageing

I see you,
    time's messenger of maturing,
    a hair grown grey.
You signal the ending
    of my season of youthfulness.

I'm tempted to tone you
    back to the original shade.
    or to silence your prophecy
    by pulling you out.
But I know you too well
    that you are only the first
    of many grey messengers to come.

I sadly receive the turning of the seasons
    and tend to reject the painful truth
    that time is taking its toll!
Quietly, I rage within,
    that my skin, with age,
begins to fold and crease,
    no longer resilient or tight
    or as elastic with the yeast of youth.

I shall hold a wake, yes, and lament,
    weeping within my heart at the passing
    of the springtime and the summer of my short life,
    so that I may embrace the autumn of age.

O Ever-youthful God,
    make clear to me the ancient truth
    that like the billion-year-old universe
    I too grow younger each day as I grow older.
Within me, that which is beyond
    the corroding clock of time –

at the core of my being – can implode,
travelling backwards to the beginning,
to the inner space that's forever young.

Edward Hays

3.10.7
Old Age

We are born gentle and weak.
At death we are hard and stiff.
Green plants are tender and filled
with sap. When they die they are
withered and dry. Therefore the
stiff and unbending are the disciples
of death. The gentle and yielding
are the disciples of life.

Lao Tsu from the Tao Te Ching

3.10.8
Abide With Us

Abide with us, O Lord, for it is toward evening and the day is far spent; abide
with us, and with your whole church. Abide with us in the evening of the day, in
the evening of life, in the evening of the world. Abide with us and with all your
faithful ones, O Lord, in time and in eternity.

Lutheran Manual of Prayer

3.10.9
Old Age

Lord, our God, we are in the shadow of your wings. Protect us and bear us up.
You will care for us as if we were little children, even to our old age. When you
are our strength we are strong, but when we are our own strength we are weak.
Our good always lives in your presence, and we suffer when we turn our faces
away from you. We now return to you, O Lord, that we may never turn away
again.

St Augustine of Hippo, as he contemplated his old age

3.10.10
The Kindness of Others

Lord, thank you that in your love you have taken from me all earthly riches and
that you now clothe me and feed me through the kindness of others. Lord, thank
you that since you have taken from me my sight, you serve me now with the
eyes of others.

Anonymous

3.10.11
You Part the Fibres of My Being

When the signs of age begin to mark my body and still more when they touch my mind; when the illness that is to diminish me or carry me off strikes from without or is born within me; when the painful moment comes in which I suddenly awaken to the fact that I am ill or growing old; in all those dark moments, O God, grant that I may understand that it is you, provided only my faith is strong enough, who are painfully parting the fibres of my being in order to penetrate to the very marrow of my substance and bear me away within yourself.

Teilhard de Chardin

3.10.12
Questions

When I was young I always asked –
When and how and what and why?
How many stars? Why skylarks sing?
How far away the sky?

When I grew up I did not like
The questions youth asked me:
How can I know the truth of God?
How solve his mystery?

When will the world have justice?
When will the world see peace?
How can a loving God allow
Cruelty to increase?

Now I am old; my hair is white;
I totter on the brink.
No questions come to taunt me now.
I only have to think....

Where will I go, when I go?
What will happen to me?
What is salvation, nirvana, moksha?
What then will I see?

A voice comes through the cloud ahead –
A voice so clear and true –
'Relax, my friend, my dear old friend,
I will take care of you.'

So now I do not ask or wonder,
I do not even think.
I just relax in his dear arms,
From his sweet peace I drink.

Fr Roger Lesser

Nirvana in Buddhism is the cessation of all desires; *moksha* in Hinduism is release from the cycle of rebirth.

3.10.13
Growing Old

Lord, I am growing old. I am slower than I used to be. My memory is not so good. The disabilities and irritations of old age come upon me. I find myself telling the same old jokes. Loved ones and friends pass on across the frontier of this life and the next. Lord God, I dare to ask if in prayer I may keep in touch with them and they with me. May your beloved Son, who brings love to us, take our love to them, for he still spans this world of creation and the world of full life.

George Appleton

3.10.14
A Never Changing Clime

My summer has an end
And mourning I might spend
My autumn days; but happily I know
Beyond this vale of time
A never changing clime
No autumn there, no winter storms blow

An Amish hymn

3.10.15
At Day's End

I love to steal awhile away
From every cumb'ring care
And spend the hours of setting day
In humble grateful prayer.

Thus when life's toilsome day is o'er
May its departing ray
Be calm as this impressive hour
And lead to endless song.

A Mennonite Song

3.11 Death

3.11.1
Death of a Child

O God, he is your servant and the son of your servant. You did create him and sustain him and bring him to death and You will give him life. O God, make him for his parents an anticipation, riches sent on before, a reward which precedes... Let neither us nor them be seduced by temptation after his departure and give him in exchange for his earthly home a better dwelling place.

Muslim Devotions

3.11.2
Death of a Child

O merciful God, Your Son Jesus Christ took children in his arms and blessed them, we commit this child *(name)* to your care. We ask you to surround his/her parents with your love so that they are not overwhelmed by grief, but, supported by their family and friends, they may in due course rediscover meaning and hope. Amen.

Marcus Braybrooke

3.11.3
Finding It Heaven

Oh! Think of stepping ashore,
And finding it heaven;
To clasp a hand outstretched,
And to find it God's hand!
To breathe new air
And find that celestial air;
To feel refreshed,
And find it immortality;
Oh! To think to step from storm and stress
to one unbroken calm;
To awake and find it home.

Anonymous

3.11.4
We are Dying

We are dying, we are dying, so all we can do
is now to be willing to die and build the ship
of death to carry the soul on the longest journey.

A little ship, with oars and food and little dishes, and all accoutrements
fitting and ready for the departing soul.

Now launch the small ship, now the body dies
and life departs, launch out, the fragile soul
in the fragile ship of courage, the ark of faith
with its store of food and little cooking pans
and change of clothes,
upon the flood's black waste
upon the waters of the end.

D. H. Lawrence

3.11.5
She Died

(A poem about Susan by her mother, Norah Leney. At eighteen Susan was given
six months to live. She lived for four and a half years and her faith and courage
inspired others and she made many friends.)

She died
    so peacefully and beautifully
she moved beyond our reach -
Beyond the gate we'd talked about,
    Into that brilliant light,
To peace and wholeness once again.

But we who stayed behind are quietened
    by her passing
and pause on tip-toe
    Listening for her voice to join
    the angels who rejoice
as they adore Him
    Lord of all,
Who in his mercy
    Took her by the hand and led her home.

Norah Leney

3.11.6
Ultimate Reality

When my time has come
and impermanence and death have caught up with me,
When the breath ceases, and the body and mind go their separate ways,
May I not experience delusion, attachment, and clinging,
But remain in the natural state of ultimate reality.

Tibetan Nyingma master - Longchenpa Rabjampa

3.11.7
Abandoning All Attachment

Now when the state of dying (bardo) dawns upon me,
I will abandon all grasping, yearning and attachment,
Enter undistracted into a clear awareness of the teaching,
And eject my consciousness into the space of unborn awareness;
As I leave this compound body of flesh and blood
I will know it to be a transitory illusion.

Tibetan Book of the Dead - Padmasambhava

In Tibetan Buddhism the state after death and before rebirth is called the bardo.

3.11.8
Do Not Weep

Do not stand at my grave and weep
I am not there. I do not sleep
I am a thousand winds that blow
I am the diamond glints on snow
I am the sunlight on ripened grain
I am the gentle autumn rain.
When you awaken in the morning's hush
I am the swift uplifting rush
Of quiet birds in circled flight
I am the soft stars that shine at night
Do not stand at my grave and cry
I am not there. I did not die.

Anonymous

3.11.9
Death's Reply

Thine astral airplane of earthly parting came to take my soul away. I wondered
through what starry vaults I was to soar, to what strange lands I was to travel.
I questioned the mystic emissary of cosmic law. Soundlessly he answered:
"I am the pilot of ever evolving life – often mistakenly called terrible Death. I am
thy brother, uplifter, redeemer, friend – unloader of thy gross burden of body
troubles. I come to fetch thee away from the valley of thy broken dreams to a
wondrous highland of light, to which poison vapours of sorrow cannot climb.

I have removed thy soul bird from the cage of flesh attachment. Long
imprisonment behind bars of bones madest thee used to the cage, but
unwillingly, thou didst always yearn for liberty. Now, cast away fear; thou hast
won thine astral freedom!
O transitory visitor to earth, re-enter the beauteous skies! Explore once more
thine ethereal home!"

Paramahansa Yogananda

3.11.10
Next Spring

'Come next spring,' said David,
'We'll climb those hills together –'
He was my friend, and
Those were his last words to me.
Next spring came, but not David;
He was killed in a car accident.

Too often, we wait for spring.

Ken Walsh

3.11.11
May We Die Peacefully

Let us behave gently,
that we may die peacefully;
That our children may stretch out their hands
upon us in burial.

A prayer of the Yoruba People of Nigeria

3.11.12
Cleanse What I Cannot Cleanse

Before the beginning Thou hast foreknown the end,
Before the birthday the death-bed was seen by Thee:
Cleanse what I cannot cleanse, mend what I cannot mend
O Lord all Merciful, be merciful to me.

While the end is drawing near I know not mine end:
Birth I recall not, my death I cannot foresee:
O God, arise to defend, arise to befriend,
O Lord All merciful, be merciful to me.

Christina Rossetti

3.11.13
Be A Shelter to Me

As a banyan spreads her branches to give shelter to the traveller, so be thou a
shelter to me; and when my journey is over, take me home to my native place –
which is with you in heaven.

Anonymous: A prayer from India

3.11.14
I Commend My Spirit

Father into your hands I commend my spirit.

Bible: Luke 23:46

Words said by Jesus while he was on the cross.

3.11.15
I Have Fought a Good Fight

For I am now ready to be offered, and the time of my departure is at hand.
I have fought a good fight, I have finished my course, I have kept the faith:
Henceforth there is laid up for me a crown of righteousness, which the Lord, the
righteous judge, shall give me at that day: and not to me only but unto all them
also that love his appearing...
The Lord will preserve me unto his heavenly kingdom: to whom be glory for ever
and ever.

Bible: St Paul, 2 Timothy 4:6-8, 18

3.11.16
Today You Will Be With Me

(Jesus said to the penitent thief:)
Today you will be with me in Paradise

Bible: Luke 23:43

3.11.17
Last Lines

No coward soul is mine,
No trembler in the world's storm-troubled sphere:
I see heaven's glories shine,
And faith shines equal, arming me from fear.

O God within my breast,
Almighty, ever-present Deity!
Life – that in me has rest,
As I – undying Life – have power in Thee!

Vain are the thousand creeds
That move men's hearts; unutterably vain;
Worthless as withered weeds
Or idlest froth amid the boundless main.

To waken doubt in one
Holding so fast by Thine infinity;
So surely anchored on
The steadfast rock of immortality.

With wide-embracing love
Thy spirit animates eternal years,
Pervades and broods above,
Changes, sustains, dissolves, creates and rears.

Though earth and man were gone,

And suns and universe ceased to be,
And Thou wert left alone,
Every existence would exist in Thee.

There is not room for Death,
Nor atom that his might could render void:
Thou – THOU art Being and Breath,
And what THOU art may never be destroyed.

Emily Bronte

A note by Charlotte Bronte says, 'The last lines my sister Emily ever wrote.'

3.11.18
Forgiveness

When Al Hallaj was brought to be crucified and saw the cross and the nails, he turned to the people and uttered a prayer, ending with the words:

And these your servants who are gathered to slay me, in zeal for your religion and in desire to win your favour, forgive them, O Lord, and have mercy upon them; for verily if you had revealed to them what you have revealed to me, they would not have done what they have done; and if you had hidden from me what you have hidden from them, I should not have suffered this tribulation. Glory unto you in whatever you do and glory unto you in whatever you will.

al-Hallaj, crucified 922

3.11.19
Forgive Them

Father forgive them; for they know not what they do.

Bible: Luke 23:34

Words said by Jesus while he was on the cross.

3.11.20
Lay Not This Sin to Their Charge

When St Stephen was stoned, he cried out:

Lord Jesus, receive my spirit...
Lay not this sin to their charge.

Bible: St Stephen, the first Christian martyr: The Acts of the Apostles 7:59-60

3.11.21
All That I Have is Yours

The life that I have is
all that I have,
And the life that I have
is yours.
The love that I have
of the life that I have
is yours and yours
and yours.
A sleep I shall have
A rest I shall have,
Yet death will be
but a pause.
For the peace of my years
in the long green grass
will be yours and yours
and yours.

Leo Marks

3.11.22
He Will Raise Me Up

For such is time, that takes in trust
Our youth, our joys, our all we have,
And pays us but with earth and dust;
Who in the dark and silent grave,
When we have wandered all our ways,
Shuts up the story of our days;
But from this earth, this grave, this dust
My God shall raise me up, I trust.

Sir Walter Raleigh, written on the eve of his execution

3.11.23
Find God Now

O friend, hope for God whilst you live, know whilst you live, understand whilst
you live: for in life deliverance abides.
If your bonds be not broken whilst living, what hope of deliverance in death?
    If God is found now, God is found then.

Kabir

3.11.24
One Day You Shall See

Lamps burn in every house, O blind one! And you cannot see them.
One day your eyes shall suddenly be opened, and you shall see:
and the fetters of death will fall from you.

There is nothing to say or to hear,
there is nothing to do:
it is God who is living, yet dead, who shall never die again.

Kabir

3.11.25
My Endless Life

Through birth and death in this world or in others, wherever thou leadest me it is
thou, the same, the one companion of my endless life who ever linkest my heart
with bonds of joy to the unfamiliar.

Rabindranath Tagore

3.11.26
A Psalm for the Dying

Relatives and friends, I am about to leave;
    my last breath does not say "goodbye",
    for my love for you is truly timeless,
    beyond the touch of boney death.
I leave myself not to the undertaker,
    for decoration in his house of the dead,
    but to your memory, with love.

I leave my thoughts, my laughter, my dreams
    to you whom I have treasured
    beyond gold and precious gems.
I give you what no thief can steal,
    the memories of our times together:
    the tender, love-filled moments,
    the successes we have shared,
    the hard times that brought us closer together
    and the roads we have walked side by side.

I also leave you a solemn promise
    that after I am home in the bosom of God,
    I will still be present,
    whenever and wherever you call on me.
My energy will be drawn to you
    by the magnet of our love.
Whenever you are in need, call me;
    I will come to you,
    with my arms full of wisdom and light
to open up your blocked paths,
    and to untangle your knots
    and to be your avenue to God.

And all I take with me as I leave
    is your love and the millions of memories
    of all that we have shared.
So I truly enter my new life
    as a millionaire.

Fear not nor grieve at my departure,
    you whom I have loved so much,
    for my roots and yours
    are forever intertwined.

Edward Hays

3.11.27
Death

Oh, only for so short a while
have you loaned us to each other.
Because we take form in your act of drawing us,
and we breathe in your singing of us.
But only for a short while
have you loaned us to each other.
Because even a drawing cut in
crystalline obsidian fades
and the green feathers, the crown feathers,
of the Quetzal bird lose their colour,
and even the sounds of the waterfall
die out in the dry season.
So, we too, because only for a short while
have you loaned us to each other

An Aztec prayer

3.11.28
Give Him Rest

O God, give him rest with the devout and the just,
In the place of the pasture of rest
And of refreshment, of waters in the paradise
Of delight, whence grief and pain and sighing
Have fled away.
Holy, holy, holy, Lord God of hosts
Heaven and earth are full of your holy glory.

An early Egyptian commendation

3.11.29
Sorrow's Springs Are the Same

Margaret
are you grieving
Over Goldengrove unleafing?
Ah! As the heart grows older
It will come to such sights colder
By and by, nor spare a sigh
Tho' world of wanwood leafmeal lie;
And yet you will weep and know why:
Now no matter, child, the name:
Sorrow's springs are the same.
Nor mouth had, no, nor mind expressed,
What heart heard of, ghost guess'd:
It is the blight man was born for;
It is Margaret you mourn for.

Gerald Manley Hopkins

3.11.30

We Would Ask of Death
Then Amitra spoke, saying, We would ask now of Death.
And he said:
You would know the secret of death.
But how shall you find it unless you seek it in the heart of life?
The owl whose night-bound eyes are blind unto the day cannot unveil
    the mystery of light.
If you would indeed behold the spirit of death, open your heart wide
    unto the body of life.
For life and death are one, even as the river and the sea are one.

In the depth of your hopes and desires lies your silent knowledge of the beyond;
And like seeds dreaming beneath the snow your heart dreams of spring.
Trust the dreams, for in them is hidden the gate to eternity.
Your fear of death is but the trembling of the shepherd when he stands before
the king
    whose hand is to be laid upon him in honour.
Is the shepherd not joyful beneath his trembling, that he shall wear the mark of
the king?
Yet is he not more mindful of his trembling?

For what is it to die but to stand naked in the wind and to melt into the sun?
And what is it to cease breathing but to free the breath from its restless tides,
that it may rise and expand and seek God unencumbered?

Only when you drink from the river of silence shall you indeed sing.

3.11

And when you have reached the mountain top, then you shall begin to climb.
And when the earth shall claim your limbs, then shall you truly dance.

Kahlil Gibran

3.11.31
True Love is Never Lost

Master, what is the best way to meet the loss of someone we love?
By knowing that when we truly love, it is never lost. It is only after death that the depth of the bond is truly felt and our loved one becomes more a part of us than was possible in life.

Anonymous: an Oriental saying

3.11.32
Before Death

O Father of heaven, O Son of God, redeemer of the world, O Holy Ghost, three persons and one God, have mercy upon me, most wretched caitiff and miserable sinner. I have offended both against heaven and earth more than my tongue can express. Whither, then, I'll keep my heart open. may I go, or wither shall I flee? To heaven I may be ashamed to lift up my eyes, and in earth I find no place of refuge or succour. To thee, therefore, O Lord, do I run...

Thomas Cranmer: his last words before going to the stake, 21 March 1556

3.11.33
A Land of Pure Delight

> There is a land of pure delight,
> Where Saints immortal reign;
> Infinite day excludes the night,
> And pleasures banish pain.
>
> There everlasting spring abides,
> And never-withering flowers;
> Death, like a narrow sea, divides,
> This heavenly land from ours.
>
> Sweet fields beyond the swelling flood
> Stand dressed in living green;
> So to the Jews old Canaan stood,
> While Jordan rolled between.
>
> But timorous mortals start and shrink
> To cross his narrow sea,
> And linger shivering on the brink,
> And fear to launch away.
>
> O could we make our doubts remove,

These gloomy doubts that rise,
And see the Canaan that we love
With unbeclouded eyes!

Could we but climb where Moses stood,
And view the landscape o'er,
Not Jordan's stream, nor death's cold flood,
Should fright us from the shore!

Isaac Watts

Isaac Watts wrote this hymn near Southampton looking across to the Isle of Wight. The references are to the Israelites preparing to cross the river Jordan into the Promised Land. Moses was not allowed to enter the land, but was taken to the top of a high mountain where God showed him the land that the Israelites would occupy.

3.11.34
Death: The Buddha's Law Among the Birds

Alas the flowers last year so beautiful - next year to be destroyed by frost;
so, too, will disappear the transient interlude, a mere illusion.
the rainbow, so beautiful in all its hues, fades away to nothingness;
so, too, will disappear these festive robes
for all their finery.
However clear the voice and strong its echo,
it cannot last;
so, too, the mighty of this earth for all their greatness.
Those who visit fairs and markets soon disperse again;
so too our families, friends, and companions
for all their number.

The Buddha

3.11.35
The Mother and Her Dead Sons

I do not grudge them: Lord, I do not grudge
My two strong sons that I have seen go out
To break their strength and die, they and a few,
In bloody protest for a glorious thing;
They shall be spoken of among their people,
The generations shall remember them,
And call them blessed;
But I will speak their names to my own heart
In the long nights;
The little names that were familiar once
Round my dead hearth.
Lord, Thou art hard on mothers;

We suffer in their coming and their going;
And though I grudge them not, I weary, weary
Of the long sorrow - and yet I have my joy:
My sons were faithful, and they fought.

Padraic Pearse

3.11.36
I Am of the Nature to Die

I am of the nature to grow old.
There is no way to escape growing old.

I am of the nature to have ill-health.
There is no way to escape having ill-health.

I am of the nature to die.
There is no way to escape death.

All that is dear to me and everyone I love
     are of the nature to change.
There is no way to escape being separated from them.

My actions are my only true belongings.
I cannot escape the consequences of my actions.
My actions are the ground on which I stand.

The Buddha

3.11.37
Light the Long Way Before Me

From one darkness
Into another darkness
I soon must go.
Light the long way before me,
Moon on the mountain rim.

Lady Izumi Shikibu

3.11.38
The Road that Leads To God

Where will I go?
Where will I go?

To the road, to the road
That leads to God.

King Nezahualcoyotl of Texcoco

3.11.39
May Your Soul Be Serene

Death
May your soul be serene.
May your soul be joyful as you return to the Lord.
May your soul be pleasing in his sight.

Qur'an: 89:15-30

3.11.40
The Just Shall Shine

But the souls of the just are in the hand of God,
and the torment of death shall not touch them.
In the sight of the unwise they seemed to die:
and their departure was taken for misery:
And their going away from us, for utter destruction:
but they are in peace.
And though in the sight of men they suffered torments,
their hope is full of immortality.
Afflicted in few things, in many they shall be well rewarded:
because God hath tried them, and found them worthy of himself.
As gold in the furnace he hath proved them,
and as a victim of a holocaust he has received them,
and in time there shall respect be had to them.
The just shall shine, and shall run to and fro
like sparks among the reeds.
They that trust in him, shall understand the truth:
and they that are faithful in love
shall rest in him.

Bible: Book of Wisdom 3:1-7,9

3.11.41
A Time to be Born and a Time to Die
For everything there is a season, and a time
for every matter under heaven:
            a time to be born, and a time to die;
            a time to plant, and a time to pluck up what is planted;
            a time to kill, and a time to heal;
            a time to break down, and a time to build up;
            a time to weep, and a time to laugh;
            a time to mourn, and a time to dance;
            a time to throw away stones, and a time to gather stones together;
            a time to embrace, and a time to refrain from embracing;
            a time to seek, a time to lose;
            a time to keep, and a time to throw away;
            a time to tear, and a time to sew;

a time to keep silence, and a time to speak;
a time to love, and a time to hate;
a time for war, and a time for peace.

Bible: The Book of Ecclesiastes 3:1-8

3.11.42
No Grief is Necessary

You grieve where no grief is necessary.
The wise-hearted mourn neither for the living
Nor for the dead.
You and I and all who have
Come to be here have always been
And will never cease to be.

Beyond birth and death are the spirit.
Death does not touch it,
Though the house of the spirit seems to die.

The end of birth is death;
The end of death is birth.
As it is so ordained,
What is there to bring sorrow?

From a traditional Hindu story

3.11.43
My Best Acts

O Lord may the end of my life be the best of it, may my closing acts be my best acts, and make the best of days the day when I shall meet You.

Muslim Devotions

3.11.44
I Shall Go To Him

King David said, 'While the child was still alive, I fasted and wept; for I said, 'Who knows? The Lord may be gracious to me, and the child may live. But now he is dead; why should I fast? Can I bring him back again? I shall go to him, but he will not return to me.'

Bible: 2 Samuel 12:23

3.11.45
Give Rest, O Lord

In the light of thy countenance,
And in the sweetness of thy beauty
Give rest unto him who thou hast chosen...

From an Orthodox Christian Prayer

3.11.46
Light Perpetual

Rest eternal grant unto her, O Lord
And let light perpetual shine upon her.

Anonymous: Traditional Christian Bidding

3.11.47
The Freeing of the Soul

When you bear my burial litter
On the day of my death,
Do not fancy that my heart
Stays here in this world.

Do not cry for me, saying,
'How sad, how sad!'
That's falling in with the devil
And that would be truly sad.

Seeing me, readied to be buried
Don't wail, 'He's gone!'
Lowering my body into the grave
Don't say your good-byes.

The tomb is only a veil covering
The union of paradise;
You've witnessed my descent
Now see me arise.

Are the sun and moon
Injured as they set?
My death appears to you
As a setting; it is, rather, the dawn.

Do you think the tomb
Is a prison?
It is the freeing
Of the soul.

Has there been a seed
Sown in the earth
That has not one day
Come to flower?

Jalal al-Din Rumi

3.11.48
The Ferryboat

You shall cross in the ferryboat and
Shall not turn back.
You shall sail on the flood waters and
Your life shall start afresh.

Your Ba, your living soul
Shall not depart from your body and
Your Ba shall become divine
With the blessed dead.

Your Ba shall take shape
As a heron or a swallow,
A falcon or a bittern
Whichever pleases you.

Your own true heart
Shall be with you.
You shall penetrate the netherworld and
You shall go up to the sky.

Ancient Egyptian Prayer

The *Ba* is the living soul.

3.11.49
The Spirit... Bright and Illustrious

All that lives comes to die, and dying, the soul returns to the earth. Hidden below, the flesh and bones decompose and form the earth of the fields.

But the spirit emerges magnificently bright and illustrious. The airs surrounding death which engender feelings of sadness are but the subtle manifestation of the essential spirit of our ancestors and all things.

Confucius

3.11.50
Taking the Next Step

As a man passes from dream to wakefulness,
so does he from this life to the next.

Even as a caterpillar, on reaching the tip of a blade of grass, in taking the next step, draws itself up toward itself, so does this self, having cast off this body and having dissolved its ignorance, in taking the next step, draw itself together.

As a goldsmith, taking a piece of gold, transforms it into another newer and more beautiful form, even so this self, casting off this body and dissolving its ignorance, makes for itself another newer and more beautiful form.

Hindu Sayings

3.11.51
The Living Self

The living self is the image of the Supreme Being.
It is neither old nor a child;
Neither it suffers pain, nor in death's snare is caught;
It is not shattered nor dies;
In all time it is pervasive.
It feels not heat nor cold;
Neither has it friend nor foe;
It feels not joy nor sorrow:
All its own; to it belongs all might.
It has neither father nor mother;
Beyond the limits of matter has it ever existed,
Of sin and goodness it feels not the touch -
Within the heart of each being it is ever awake.

O Lord, Thou art the glory of all kings,
The flag bearer of true faith,
Beyond grief and sorrow,
Thou dost adorn and sustain the universe.

A Sikh prayer

3.11.52
Love Your Life

Live your life that the fear of death can never enter your heart.
Love your life, perfect your life, beautify all things in your life.
Seek to make your life long and of service to your people.
Prepare a noble death song for the day when you go over the great divide.
When you arise in the morning, give thanks
    for the light, for your life, for your strength.
Give thanks for your food and for the joy of living.
If you see no reason to give thanks, the fault lies in yourself.
When your time comes to die, be not like those
    whose hearts are filled with fear of death,
    so that when their time comes they weep and pray
    for a little more time to live their lives over again in a different way.
Sing your death song, and die like a hero going home.

Native American: Chief Tecumseh

3.11.53

We Can Never be Separated From God

God is sitting inside you,
Nearer than your hands and feet.
The distance between you and God
Is as thin as an insect's wing.
We can never be separated from God,
Neither at birth nor at death.

A Sikh prayer

3.11.54

They Are Not Dead

Those who are dead are never gone.
They are in the breast of the woman.
They are in the child who is wailing,
And in the firebrand that flames,
The dead are not under the earth.
They are in the fire that is dying.
They are in the grasses that weep.
They are in the plaintive rocks.
They are in the forest and they are in the house.
The dead are not dead.

Traditional African song

3.11.55

Nothing Can Separate Us From the Love of God

Who shall separate us from the love of Christ? Shall tribulation, or distress, or persecution, or famine, or nakedness, or peril, or sword... ?
Nay in all these things we are more than conquerors through him that loved us.
For I am persuaded that neither death, nor life, nor angels, nor principalities, nor powers, nor things present, nor things to come,
Nor height, nor depth, nor any other creature, shall be able to separate us from the love of God, which is in Christ Jesus Our Lord.

Bible: St Paul, Romans 8:35-39

3.11.56

Out of the Depths

Out of the depths have I cried unto thee, O Lord.
O Lord, hear my voice: let thine ears be attentive to the voice of my supplications.
If thou, Lord, shouldest mark iniquities, O Lord, who shall stand?
But there is forgiveness with thee, that thou mayest be feared.
I wait for the Lord, my soul doth wait, and in his words do I hope.
My soul waiteth for the Lord more than they watch for the morning: I say more than they watch for the morning.

Let Israel hope in the Lord: for with the Lord there is mercy, and with him is
plenteous redemption.
And He shall redeem Israel from all His iniquities.

Bible: Psalm 130

3.11.57
The Last Journey

Go forth upon thy journey from this world, O Christian soul,
In the peace of him in whom thou hast believed,
In the name of God the Father, who created thee,
In the name of Jesus Christ, who suffered for thee,
In the name of the Holy Ghost, who strengthened thee.
May angels and archangels, and all the armies of the heavenly host, come to
meet thee,
May all the saints of God welcome thee,
May thy portion this day be in gladness and peace and thy dwelling in Paradise.
Go forth upon thy journey, O Christian soul.

Anonymous: Traditional Christian prayer

3.11.58
God Be In My Head

God be in my head,
    And in my understanding:

God be in my eyes,
    And in my looking:

God be in my mouth,
And in my speaking:

God be in my heart,
    And in my thinking:

God be at mine end,
    And at my departing.

Pynson's Horae (1514)

3.11.59
God Gives Life and Death

Say, 'It is God who
Gives you life, then
Gives you death; then
He will gather you together
For the Day of Judgment.'

Qur'an: 45:26

3.11.60
The Death Dirge

Thou goest home this night to thy home of winter,
To thy home of autumn, of spring, and of summer;
Thou goest home this night to thy perpetual home,
To thine eternal bed, to thine eternal slumber.

Sleep, thou, sleep, and away with thy sorrow,
Sleep, thou, sleep, and away with thy sorrow,
Sleep, thou, sleep, and away with thy sorrow;
Sleep, thou beloved, in the Rock of the fold.

Sleep this night in the breast of thy Mother,
Sleep, thou beloved, while she herself soothes thee;
Sleep thou this night on the Virgin's arm,
Sleep, thou beloved, while she herself kisses thee.

The great sleep of Jesus, the surpassing sleep of Jesus,
The sleep of Jesus' wound, the sleep of Jesus' grief,
The young sleep of Jesus, the restoring sleep of Jesus,
The sleep of the kiss of Jesus of peace and of glory.

The sleep of the seven lights be thine, beloved,
The sleep of the seven joys be thine, beloved,
The sleep of the seven slumbers be thine, beloved,
On the arm of the Jesus of blessings, the Christ of grace.

The shade of death lies upon thy face, beloved,
But the Jesus of grace has His hand round about thee;
In nearness to the Trinity farewell to thy pains,
Christ stands before thee and peace is in His mind.

Sleep, O sleep in the calm of all calm,
Sleep, O sleep in the guidance of guidance,
Sleep, O sleep in the love of all loves;
Sleep, O sleep in the love of all loves;
Sleep, O beloved, in the Lord of life,
Sleep, O beloved, in the God of life!

The Celtic Vision

3.11.61
The Clasp of Love

May the Father take you
    In His fragrant clasp of love,
When you go across the flooding streams
    And the black river of death.

The Celtic Vision

3.11.62
Pilgrim's Progress

Then said he, 'I am going to my Father's: and though with great difficulty I am
got hither, yet now I do not repent me of all the trouble I have been at to arrive
where I am. My sword I give to him that shall succeed me in the pilgrimage, and
my courage and skill to him that can get it. My marks and scars I carry with me
to be a witness for me, that I have fought his battles who now will be my
rewarder.' When the day that he must go hence was come, many accompanied
him to the river side, into which as he went he said, 'Death, where is thy sting?'
So he passed over and all the trumpets sounded for him on the other side.

John Bunyan

3.11.63
Where God Awaits Us

There in that other world, what waits for me?
What shall I find after that other birth?
No stormy, tossing, foaming, smiling sea,
But a new earth.

No sun to mark the changing of the days,
No slow, soft falling of the alternate night,
No moon, no star, no light upon my ways,
Only the Light.

No grey cathedral, wide and wondrous fair,
That I may tread where all my fathers trod.
Nay, nay, my soul, no house of God is there,
But only God.

Mary Coleridge

3.11.64
Go Running Home

(For a burial)
Into the darkness and warmth of the earth
    We lay you down
Into the sadness and smiles of our memories
We lay you down

Into the cycle of living and dying and rising again,
We lay you down
May you rest in peace, in fulfilment, in loving
May you run straight home into God's embrace.
(For a cremation)
Into the freedom of wind and sunshine
We let you go
Into the dance of the stars and the planets
We let you go
Into the wind's breath and the hands of the star maker
We let you go
We love you, we miss you, we want you to be happy
Go safely, go dancing, go running home.

Ruth Burgess

3.11.65
Safe in God's Hands

All our laughter, all our sadness,
    Safe now in God's hands.

All our anger, all our gladness,
    Safe now in God's hands

All our stories, all our memories,
    Safe now in God's hands.

Those we remember, those we love,
    Safe now in God's hands.

Ruth Burgess

3.11.66
A Memorial Service for a Stillborn Child or a Miscarriage

O Eternal – I keep asking you why you allowed this to happen.
You know my anger against you.
I am confused, bitter and upset.
I cannot help it,
I am blaming you.
Why should this have happened to me?
Yet – I need you now more than ever before.
I need the comfort of knowing that, even when I cannot understand,
You still care.
Eternal, help me to trust in your love. Amen.

(Psalms 121 and 23 are read.)

O God,
all I feel is pain
where my baby used to be.
It was a collection of cells,
already my child, with a secret name and a secret voice.
The baby has gone and pain has settled in its place.
My hopes bled away in the night
and I am left with the pain
where my baby used to be.

Sylvia Rothschild

3.11.67
The Healing Song

From deep within the home of my soul. Now let the healing, the healing begin...
Heal our bodies, open our hearts, awaken our minds.
O Lord our God,
    for a time you gave us the hope of a new life,
    placed in us the expectation of a new awakening.
Now, in your wisdom,
You have taken that hope from us,
    have delayed for reasons known only to you,
    the arrival of that new soul into our world.
Lord, we thank you still
    for the hope you gave us.
And pray that you may renew in us that hope in time to come;
    though the pain of our disappointment is real and deep,
    we acknowledge still that you are our God;
You renew Life beyond Death,
You give, and take away,
You hold all souls in the palm of your hand.
May it be your will to give us, once more,
    the chance to share with you
    in the bringing of new life to this our world;
May it be your will that we shall be strengthened both by our hopes and by our
    disappointments
    and learn to love, the more deeply, that which we have.
Blessed are you, Lord, who shares the sorrow of your creation

Walter Rothschild

3.11.68
Tell it Again and Again

This has happened to us, we tell it again and again.
We pour out our hearts, full of grief.
You who are in heaven hear our prayer.
You, O Eternal, are a God of mercy and compassion.

Forms of Prayer for Jewish Worship

3.11.69
God Full of Compassion

God full of compassion whose presence is over us, grant perfect rest beneath the shelter of your presence with the holy and pure on high who shine as the lights of heaven, to our loved and dear ones who have gone to their everlasting home. Source of mercy, cover them in the shelter of your wings for ever and bind their soul into the gathering of life. It is God who is their heritage. May they be at peace in their place of rest. Amen.

Sylvia Rothschild

3.11.70
What is Dying?

What is dying? I am standing on the sea-shore. A ship sails to the morning breeze and starts for the ocean. She is an object of beauty and I stand watching her till at last she fades on the horizon, and someone at my side says, 'She is gone.' Gone where? Gone from my sight, that is all; she is just as large in the masts, hull and spars as she was when I saw her, and just as able to bear her load of living freight to its destination.

The diminished size and total loss of sight is in me, not in her; and just at the moment when someone at my side says, 'She is gone,' there are others who are watching her coming, and other voices take up a glad shout, 'There she comes' – and that is dying.

Bishop Brent

3.11.71
Friendship After Death

Since no one, Lord, can desire more for another person than he wishes for himself,
I ask you not to separate me when I am dead from those who were so dear to me while I lived. I beg that where I am, they too may be with me. As I have not been able to see much of them here on earth, let me enjoy their company in heaven for ever. I beseech you, God most high, to grant a speedy resurrection to these children whom I love so much.

St Ambrose of Milan

3.11.72
You will Attain the Supreme Goal

Remembering me at the time of death, close down the doors of the senses and place the mind in the heart. Then, while absorbed in meditation, focus all energy upward towards the head. Repeating in this state the divine Name, the syllable OM that represents the changeless Brahman, you will go forth from the body and attain the supreme goal.

Hindu scriptures: Bhagavad Gita 8: 12-13

3.11.73
Truth Shall Prevail

After you depart this life, God shall demand a reckoning of your deeds
That in his ledger are recorded ...
Says Nanak, Falsehood must be destroyed;
Truth in the end shall prevail.

Sikh scriptures: Adi Granth

3.11.74
The Indestructible Spirit

May your eyesight return to the sun, your breath to the winds; may your water
mingle with the ocean and your earthly part become one with the earth. The
indestructible spirit passes on into another body according to the actions
performed in this life

Hindu scriptures: Rig Veda

A Hindu text that may be recited as the funeral pyre is lit and the dead body is
cremated.

3.11.75
Peace be to this Spirit

O Effulgent God! You are the Dispenser of Justice; You recompense everyone
according to his or her deeds. Peace be to the spirit of this dead body in the
westward direction. May there be peace to this spirit also in the east, the north
and the south and all other directions. Oh, All-knowing and All-illuminating God,
You are the Creator, the Sustainer and the Destroyer of the Universe. May you
bestow a worthy abode on this soul

Atharva Veda

A Hindu text that may be recited as the funeral pyre is lit and the dead body is
cremated.

3.11.76
On This Happy Day

On this truly happy day of my life, as I am at the point of death, I write this to
you. The disease in my bladder and stomach are pursuing their course, lacking
nothing of their natural severity; but against all this is the joy in my heart at the
recollection of my conversations with you.

A letter written to a friend by Epicurus on his deathbed

3.11.77
Every National Will Bow the Knee

To God belongs
The dominion of the heavens
And the earth, and

The Day that the Hour
Of Judgement is established.
That Day will the followers
Of Falsehood perish!

And thou wilt see
Every nation bowing the knee:
Every national will be called
To its Record: 'This Day
Shall ye be recompensed
For all that ye did!

This Our Record speaks
About you with truth:
For we put on record
All that ye did.

Then, as to those who
Believed and did righteous
Deeds, their Lord will
Admit them to His Mercy:
That will be the manifest triumph.

The Qu'ran, 45:27-30

3.11.78
Open the Gates of Compassion and Light

O Lord, who is full of compassion, who dwells on high, God of forgiveness, who is merciful, slow to anger and abounding in loving kindness, grant pardon of transgressions, nearness of salvation, and perfect rest beneath the shadow of your divine presence, in the exalted places among the holy and pure, who shine as the brightness of the firmament, to N who has gone to his eternal home. We beseech you, O Lord of compassion, remember unto him for good all the meritorious and pious deeds which he has wrought while on earth. Open unto him the gates of righteousness and light, the gates of pity and grace. O shelter him for evermore under the cover of your wings; and let his soul be bound up in the bond of eternal life. The Lord is his eternal inheritance; may he rest in peace. And let us say Amen.

A Jewish Burial prayer

3.11.79
Kaddish

Glorified and sanctified be God's great name throughout the world which he has created according to his will. May he establish his kingdom in your lifetime and during your days, and within the life of the entire house of Israel, speedily and soon; and say *Amen.*

May his great name be blessed forever and to all eternity.
Blessed and praised, glorified and exalted, extolled and honoured, adored and
lauded be the name of the Holy One,
Blessed be he, beyond all the blessings and hymns, praises and consolation that
are ever spoken in the world; and say *Amen.*
May there be abundant peace from heaven, and life, for us and for all Israel; and
say *Amen*
He who creates peace in his celestial heights, may he create peace for us and for
all Israel; and say *Amen.*

One of the best known Jewish prayers

Although originally used for different purposes, the 'Mourners Kaddish' is recited
in Aramaic by mourners in the synagogue. It is neither a prayer for the dead or
to the dead, but a powerful assertion of faith in the God of Life.

3.11.80
Be Comforted, Be at Peace

Be comforted. Be comforted, dear ones;
There is eternal life for all souls who love God, Who is love; and where there is
love there can be no separation. Your loved one is by your side. Death cannot
separate you. Be comforted and at peace.

A Saying of White Eagle

4 The World and Society

4.1 A Fellowship of Faiths

4.1.1
Unity

Let there be many windows in your soul that all the glory
    of the universe may beautify it.
Not the narrow pane of one poor creed can catch the radiant rays
    that shine from countless sources.
Tear away the blinds of superstition; let the light pour through
    fair windows, broad as truth itself and high as heaven...
Tune your ear to all the wordless music of the stars
And to the voice of nature,
And your heart shall turn to truth and goodness
As the plant turns to the sun.
A thousand unseen hands reach down to help you to their peace –
Crowned heights, and all the forces of the firmament shall fortify your strength .
Be not afraid to thrust aside half-truths and grasp the whole.

Ralph Waldo Trine

4.1.2
Every Name

O God, I beseech Thee by every Name of Thine by which Thou hast named Thyself
or which Thou hast sent down in Thy book or taught to any of Thy creatures or
made Thine own in the unseen world.

Muslim Devotions

4.1.3
Religions Are Converging Roads

Religions are different roads converging upon the same point.
What does it matter that we take different roads
so long as we reach the same goal.

Mahatma Gandhi

4.1.4
Time to Meet

Lord of all creation,
we stand in awe before you,
impelled by the visions of the harmony of all people.
We are children of many traditions –
inheritors of shared wisdom and tragic misunderstandings,
of proud hopes and humble successes.
Now it is time for us to meet –

in memory and truth,
in courage and trust,
in love and promise.

In that which we share,
let us see the common prayer of humanity;
in that in which we differ,
let us wonder at the freedom of men and women;
in our unity and our differences,
let us know the uniqueness that is God.

Forms of Prayer for Jewish Worship

4.1.5
All Names Are To Be Adored

O Gods!
All your names and forms are to be
revered, saluted and adored.

Hindu Scriptures: Rig Veda 10, 63, 2

4.1.6
A Church in the Heart

Surely the Lord is in this place. This is
none other but the house of God

Who builds a church within his heart
And takes it with him everywhere
Is holier far than he whose church
Is but a one-day house of prayer.

Morris Abel Beer: based on Genesis 28:16

4.1.7
I Belong to the Beloved

Not Christian or Jew or
Muslim, not Hindu,
Buddhist, Sufi, or Zen.
Not any religion or cultural system.
I am not from the east
or the west,
not out of the ocean or up from the ground,
not natural or ethereal,
not composed of elements at all.
I do not exist, am not an entity in this
world or the next,
did not descend from
Adam and Eve or any origin story.

My place is the placeless,
a trace of the traceless.
Neither body or soul.
I belong to the beloved,
have seen the two worlds as one
and that one
call to and know, first, last, outer, inner,
only that breath breathing human being.

Jalal al-Din Rumi

4.1.8

I belong to the Great Church which holds the world in its starlight aisles;
That claims the great and good of every race and clime;
That finds with joy the grain of gold in every creed;
And floods with light and love the germs of good in every soul.

Robert G. Ingersoll

4.1.9
Thou Hast Many Names

I say my prayers on beads of love, strung together with everlasting threads of devotion. I hold to no single Name – God, Spirit, Brahma, Allah, Heavenly Father, Divine Mother – for All are Thine.

I invoke Thee sometimes as Christ, Krishna, Shankaracharya, Mohammed, Buddha, Moses, and other prophets; for I know Thou hast delighted, and wilt ever delight, in revealing Thyself in different forms.

In Thy cosmic play on the stage of the centuries, in Thy myriad appearances, Thou didst take many Names, but Thou hast only one Nature: Perennial Joy.

Paramahansa Yogananda

4.1.10
Branches of One Tree

The diverse religions are branches of Thy one immeasurable tree of truth. May we enjoy the luscious fruits of soul realisation that hang from the boughs of scriptures of every clime and time.

Teach us to chant in harmony the countless expressions of our supreme devotion. In Thy temple of earth, in a chorus of many-accented voices, we are singing only to Thee.

O Divine Mother, lift us on Thy lap of universal love. Break Thy vow of silence and sing us the heart-melting melody of human brotherhood.

Paramahansa Yogananda

4.1.11
In All Shrines

O Spirit, I worship Thee in all shrines. Into the temple of peace come Thou, O Lord of Joy! Enter my shrine of meditation, O Bliss God, Sanctify me with Thy presence.

Eternal Allah, hover over the lone minaret of my holy aspiration. The mosque of my mind exudes a frankincense of stillness.

On the altar of my inner vihara I place flowers of desirelessness. Their chaste beauty is Thine, O Spirit!

In a tabernacle not made with hands, I bow before the sacred ark and vow to keep Thy commandments.

Heavenly Father, in an invisible church built of devotion granite, receive Thou my humble heart offerings, daily renewed by prayer.

Paramahansa Yogananda

4.1.12
By Routes Diverse

By routes diverse men may the mountain climb
Each path presenting different views sublime
But when to the proud summit they do rise
The self-same smiling Moon doth greet all eyes.

A Shinto prayer

4.1.13
A Prayer for all Humankind

Great Central Light
Long reverenced
Of many hundred names.
Maker of the old, kind, Laws.
Focus, since Mystery first began,
Of our inner minds
Seeking,
Trusted,
Fought over,
Thanked,
Praised or even cursed,
By all skin colours
Of woman, man or child
Through the joy, sadness, plenty and hardship
Of long calendars of Time.

You!
Excuse for offering or sacrifice,
Murder and glory,
Sometimes...
Simple greed with ego intertwined.
Allied to high pride
Even arrogance
In confidence
Of bestowal of one unique and Divine Right...

Excuse
For loving Blessing,
Humble sacrifice,
Simplicity,
Chaste poverty or
Relieving of suffering
Of those trapped in a harsh brash world.
Dear God!
All of whose Laws derive from gentleness
For so long:
Sunrise; sunset;
Crescent moon
With full flood following.
For so long
Have the fragments:
Splintered fragments of your Truths
Lain shattered in our monopolistic minds.
Lain in disarray across the majestic sweep of Earth
Smothering the infinite wholeness of a Universal Love.

Until this Day and Age
When frantic desperation grips material Display:
For, born of the teeming realms of Thought;
Unity, like some mighty, swinging, magnet
Points a lasered arrow
Towards the golden beauty of its Pole
So that new guardians
Of the ancient reverenced pantheons
Borne on new shimmering waves of electronic speed
Join in one re-discovered Interfaith
Of Joy
Of Love...

Sacred Light!
Of perfection

Infinite in compassion;
Let us still try
Late though our wisdom is:
If we have erred with misplaced certainty
Lead us, please, to Peace.
Forgive... remove...
Division of the Race of Men...

Eric Gladwin: written for the World Congress of Faiths 50th Anniversary, 1986

4.1.14
A Prayer Visualising the Healing of the World

(Picture the world as seen from space and imagine that you are holding the world in the palm of your hands.)

Holy Lord
Reverenced and loved
Divine and of the Sacred ways.
Of this world its Light:
    I visualise.
    I caress and heal.
    I now hold beauty.
Then it travels on a lit Path
To the flawless radiance at your feet;
Bearing my prayer for your Blessing
And returned to palms and finger tips
Cupped, protective, as a chalice filled with Peace...

Eric Gladwin

4.1.15
The Pilgrims Hymn for Peace, Truth and Unity

We ask that we live and labour in peace, in peace
Each man shall be our neighbour in peace, in peace
Distrust and hatred will turn to love,
All the prisoners freed,
And our only war will be the one
Against all human need.

We work for the end of disunion in truth, in truth
That all may be one communion in truth, in truth
We choose the road of peace and prayer
Countless pilgrims trod.
So that Hindu, Muslim, Christian, Jew
We all can worship one God.

We call to our friends and brothers, unite, unite
That all may live for others, unite, unite!
And so the nations will be as one,
One the flag unfurled,
One law, one faith, one hope, one truth,
One people and one world.

Donald Swann

4.1.16
Mirrors of Sadness

(Beirut Scene, April 1989)

Some used the name of Allah.
"In His name we kill," they said.
Man, woman, child or baby
Prove our God-love when they're dead.
So the Muezzin called his Blessing
And sang praises to the skies
Amidst the rotting corpse-strewn street;
The buzzing sweat of flies...

But others called on Jesus Christ
Amidst the shattered blocks.
At fourteen years they waved black guns:
Pouring bullets, flame and shrapnel
Into blood-soaked family homes.
Whilst the priest sat on the balcony
A Bible in his hands
And blessed these others;
Killing in the sacred name of God.

Eric Gladwin

4.1.17
True Religion

Fools laud and magnify the mosque
While they oppress the holy ones of heart.
But the former is mere form; the latter, spirit and truth.
The only true mosque
Is the one in the hearts of saints.

Jalal al-Din Rumi

4.1.18
The Needs of All People

O Lord, baptise our hearts into a sense
of the conditions and needs of all people.

George Fox

4.1.19
One God

Some remember God as Ram;
    some call him Khuda;
Some use the name Gosain;
    some worship him as Allah.
Gracious Lord Almighty,
    you are the source and cause of everything,
O Lord, Compassionate One,
    Shower your grace on all.
Some bathe at Hindu holy places;
    some go to perform the Hajj;
Some engage in Puja;
    some bow their heads in prayer;
Some study Vedas;
    some read the Bible or Qur'an.
Some dress in blue;
    some wear white;
Some call themselves Muslims;
    some are called Hindus,
Some desire to go to heaven;
    some long for paradise.
But whoever does the will of God,
To him all things are revealed.

Guru Arjan

4.1.20
The Breath of All Breath

O servant, where dost thou seek Me?
Lo! I am beside thee.
I am neither in temple nor in mosque:
    I am neither in Kaaba nor in Kailash:
Neither am I in rites and ceremonies,
    nor in Yoga and renunciation.
If thou art a true seeker, thou shalt at once see me:
    thou shalt meet Me in a moment of time.
Kabir says, 'O sadhu! God is the breath of all breath.'

Kabir

4.1.21
All Creatures As His Own Self

O Brother, when I was forgetful, my true Guru showed me the Way.
Then I left off all rites and ceremonies...
The man who is kind and who practises righteousness, who remains passive
amidst the affairs of the world, who considers all creatures on earth as his own
self,
He attains the Immortal being, the true God is ever with him.

Kabir

4.1.22
All Are One

Recognize all people as one.

Guru Gobind Singh

4.1.23
Truth Is One

Truth is one: sages call it by various names.

Hindu Scriptures

4.1.24
Many Paths to God

The paths to God are more in number that the breathings of created beings.

Zoroastrian

4.1.25
The Sacred Hoop

I was seeing in a sacred manner
the shapes of all
things in the spirit,
and the shape of all shapes as they must live
together like one being.
And I saw that the sacred hoop of my people
was one of many hoops that made one circle,
wide as daylight and as starlight,
and in the centre grew one mighty flowering tree
to shelter all the children of
one mother and one father.
And I saw that it was holy.

Black Elk

4.1.26
No Temple

In the eternal life there is no longer any place for religions; the pilgrim has no need of a way after he has finally arrived. In St John's vision of the heavenly city at the end of the Christian scriptures it is said that there is no temple – no Christian church or chapel, no Jewish synagogue, no Hindu or Buddhist temple, no Muslim mosque, no Sikh gurdwara... For all these exist in time, as ways through time to eternity.

John Hick

4.1.27
Wash Yourself of Distinctions

Love is not concerned
With caste or creed or race.
Wash yourself of such distinctions
Then your Love you will face.

Baba Farid

4.1.28
God of Many Names

O God of many names,
give peace in our hearts,
in our homes,
in our world,
in our universe,
the peace of our need,
the peace of your will.

George Appleton

4.1.29
In Every Religion

I worship you in every religion that teaches your laws and praises your glory.
I worship you in every plant whose beauty reflects your beauty.
I worship you in every event which is caused by your goodness and kindness.
I worship you in every place where you dwell.
And I worship you in every man and woman who seeks to follow your way of righteousness.

Zoroaster

4.1.30
Gather Us In

Gather us in, thou love that fillest all;
    Gather our rival faiths within thy fold.
Rend each man's temple-veil and bid it fall,
    that we may know that thou hast been of old;

4.1

Gather us in.

Gather us in: we worship only thee;
In varied names we stretch a common hand;
In diverse forms a common soul we see;
In many ships we seek one spirit-land;
Gather us in.

Each sees one colour of thy rainbow-light,
Each looks upon one tint and calls it heaven;
Thou art the fullness of our partial sight;
We are not perfect till we find the seven;
Gather us in.

Some seek a Father in the heavens above,
Some ask a human image to adore,
Some crave a Spirit vast as life and love;
Within thy mansions we have all and more;
Gather us in.

George Matheson

4.1.31
We Come Together

We come together from different communities in the world,
from different places and different cultures,
to share our faith and to learn from one another.
We come in hope.

We come together in gratitude for all that we have received,
for family and friends, for food and shelter,
and for the traditions and disciplines which sustain our faith.
We come in gratitude.

We come confessing that often we have failed to live by the teachings of
our traditions which urge care of the earth, respect for others,
and justice for all.
We come in confession.

We come together with awareness of the harsh conflicts in the world,
of the religious hatred that scars the hearts of many,
and of the suffering of those who are less fortunate than we.
We come in awareness.

We come together with respect for our differences,
with an open mind to beliefs and practices that we do not share,

and with a desire to listen and to understand.
We come in respect

We come together to find ways of encouraging greater co-operation among
    members of different religious communities
    and to be strengthened in our own efforts to reconcile those who are
divided.
We come in hope.

We come together in friendship, as we all seek to deepen our faith
    and our commitment to the truth of our traditions.
We come in hope.

*Prayers used at the Opening Ceremony of the international interfaith
gathering, Sarva-Dharma-Sammelana, held at Bangalore in 1993*

4.1.32
Unite Our Hearts

O My God! O My God! Unite the hearts of thy servants,
    and reveal to them Thy great purpose.
May they follow Thy commandments and abide in Thy law.
Help them, O God, in their endeavour, and grant them strength to serve Thee,
    O God!
Leave them not to themselves, but guide their steps by the light of knowledge,
    and cheer their hearts by Thy love. Verily, Thou art their Helper
    and their Lord.

Baha'u'llah

4.1.33
Cement Our Hearts Together

O Thou Kind Lord! Thou hast created all humanity from the same stock.
Thou hast decreed that all shall belong to the same household.
In Thy Holy Presence they are all Thy servants and are sheltered beneath
Thy
    tabernacle;
all have gathered together at Thy Table of Bounty;
all are illumined through the light of Thy Providence.

O God! Thou art kind to all, Thou hast provided for all, dost shelter all,
    conferest life upon all. Thou hast endowed each and all with talents
    and faculties, and all are submerged in the Ocean of Thy Mercy.

O Thou kind Lord! Unite all. Let the religions agree and make the nations one,
    so that they may see each other as one family and the whole earth as one
home. May they all live together in perfect harmony. O God!
Raise aloft the banner of the oneness of all mankind.

O God! Establish the most great peace.
Cement Thou, O God, the hearts together.

O Thou kind Father, God! Gladden our hearts through the fragrance of Thy love.
Brighten our eyes through the Light of Thy Guidance.
Delight our ears with the melody of Thy Word and shelter us all in the Stronghold of Thy
    providence.

Thou art Mighty and Powerful. Thou art the Forgiving and thou art the
One who overlooketh the shortcomings of all mankind.

'Abdu'l Baha

4.1.34
Loving and Tender Hearts

O God, my God! Aid Thou Thy trusted servants to have loving and tender hearts.
Help them to spread, amongst all the nations of the earth,
the light of guidance that cometh from the Company on high.
Verily, Thou art the Strong, the Powerful, the Mighty, the All-Subduing, the Ever-Giving.
Verily, Thou art the Generous, the Gentle, the Tender, the Most Bountiful.

'Abdu'l Baha

4.1.35
All People Bless the Creator

From the East to the West,
    From the North and the South,
All nations and peoples
    Bless the creator of creatures with a new blessing;
    For God made the light of the sun rise today over the world...

From the Sunrise Office of the Armenian Church

4.2 Human Unity

4.2.1
A Reflection

When I look at you,
I'm looking into a still blue lake
Seeing a reflection
Not identical to me
Yet, underneath,
The meaning is still the same.
When I look at you,
I'm looking in a mirror,
Or just wishing
That we were more alike.
The words you speak
Are the words I write.
When I look at you,
I see a river
A flowing that never ceases
Spreading love in many branches.
Your silence, your actions,
Have strong undercurrents.

Lynne Milum

4.2.2
All Souls Are One Soul

You and I are One
All of You and Us are One.
All The Souls are One Soul
All The Lights are One Light.

The Messenger of Unity

4.2.3
Prosperity for All

May the whole world enjoy
good health,
long life,
prosperity,
happiness and peace.
Om, shanti, shanti, shanti.

Vethathiri Maharishi

4.2.4
The True Conception of Brotherhood

Divine Mother, give us a new, true conception of brotherhood. May we forsake wars and heal the wounds of all nations with the salve of Christ-love and the lasting balm of sympathetic understanding.

Cosmic Mother, awaken in us Thine impartial love for all; bless us that we be free from the sway of greed and delusion. Inspire us to build a new world – one in which famine, disease and ignorance will be only memories of a dismal past. Creative Mother, arouse us to knowledge of Thy plan, when Thou didst form the cosmos and people it with rational creatures. Let us be ashamed to act like savage animals, devoid of reason, settling their differences only by might. Help us to solve all problems not by jungle logic but by reason and unfaltering trust in Thee. O Mother of All, teach us to call each man by his rightful name of Brother.

Paramahansa Yogananda

4.2.5
My Neighbour

I am glad you made my neighbour different from me;
a different coloured skin, a different shaped face;
a different response to you.
I need my neighbour to teach me about you:
She knows all the things I don't know.

Monica Furlong

4.2.6
As Love Would Make it

Give us, O God, a vision of your world as your love would make it;
a world where the weak are protected and none go hungry;
a world whose benefits are shared,
so that everyone can enjoy them;
a world whose different people and cultures
live with tolerance and mutual respect;
a world where peace is built with justice,
and justice is fired with love.

Anonymous

4.2.7
God of All

Source and goal
of community,
whose will it is that all
your people enjoy
fullness of life:
may we be builders

of community,
caring for your
good earth
here and world-wide
and as partners with the poor,
signs of your
ever friendly love;
that we may delight in diversity
and choose solidarity
for you are in
community with us
our God for ever.

Anonymous

4.2.8
We Did Not Introduce You

Lord today you have made us known to friends we did not know,
And you have given us seats in homes which are not our own.
You have brought the distant near,
and made a brother of a stranger,
Forgive us Lord...
We did not introduce you.

A Polynesian prayer

4.2.9
The Eyes of a Friend

O Lord give me strength that the whole world look to me with the eyes of a friend. Let us ever examine each other with the eyes of a friend.

Hindu: Yajurveda

4.2.10
The Joy of Love

The greatest joy is that of love –
Loving life,
Loving others,
Loving yourself,
Loving your work.
The next greatest joy is the freedom to serve

Ben Okri

4.2.11
When is it Day?

(There is an old story about the rabbi who asked his disciples how they knew that night had ended and the day was on its way back. 'Could it be,' asked one, 'when you can see an animal in the distance and tell whether it is a sheep or a dog?'

'No,' the rabbi replied. 'Could it be,' asked a second, 'when you can look at a tree in the distance, and tell whether it is a fig or an olive tree?' 'No,' replied the rabbi. 'Well then, when is it?' the disciples pressed. 'It is when you look on the face of any man or woman and see that he or she is your brother or sister because if you cannot do this, no matter what time it is, it is still night.')

O God, today and every day, help me to see all human beings as my brothers and sisters made in your image, and so may I always live in and by that light.

John Carden

4.2.12
All Makes Me Think of You

The milk-float,
The poor man begging,
the staircase and the lift,
the railway lines, the furrows of the sea,
the pedigree dog and the ownerless dog,
the pregnant woman,
the paper-boy
the man who sweeps the streets,
the church, the school,
the office and the factory,
streets being widened,
hills being laid low,
the outward and the homeward road,
the key I use to open my front door;
whether sleeping or waking –
all, all, all
makes me think of You.
What can I give to the Lord
for all He has given to me?

Archbishop Dom Helder Camara of Brazil

4.2.13
Learn to Love One more Human Being

It is not so important to love all people today
as it is that each day
you learn to love one more human being

The Urantia Book p. 1098

4.2.14
Children Meet

On the seashore of endless worlds
children meet with shouts and dances

Rabindranath Tagore

4.2.15
Repentance

Grandfather: Look at our brokenness.
We know that in all creation
Only the human family
Has strayed from the Sacred Way.
We know that we are the ones
Who are divided
And we are the ones
Who must come back together
to walk in the Sacred Way.
Grandfather,
Sacred One,
teach us love, compassion and honour,
That we may heal the earth
And heal each other.

Native American: An Objibway prayer

4.2.16
Unity

O God, Let us be united
Let us speak in harmony...
Common be our prayer;
Common be the end of our assembly;
Alike be our feelings;
Unified be our hearts;
Common be our intentions;
Perfect be our unity.

The Hindu Scriptures: The Rig Veda

4.2.17
Action

What profit is there in agreeing that universal friendship is good,
and talking of the solidarity of the human race as a grand ideal?
Unless these thoughts are translated into the world of action,
they are useless.
The wrong in the world continues to exist just because
people talk only of their ideals,
and do not strive to put them into practice.
If actions took the place of words, the world's misery
would soon be changed into comfort.

'Abdu'l Baha

4.2.18
Walk Cheerfully

Be patterns, be examples in all countries, places, islands, nations, wherever you come, that your carriage and life may preach among all sorts of people, and to them; then you will come to walk cheerfully over the world, answering that of God in every one.

George Fox

4.2.19
For Tolerance

Father of all, free us from every prejudice born of hate and fear and kept alive by ignorance and pride. Open our hearts and minds to new friendships and new contributions of the spirit from races and cultures, religions and classes other than our own.
Enrich us by the great thoughts and experiences of all peoples and countries.
With all thy children on earth make us sharers of thine abundant life and workers together in thy kingdom of love and peace.

G. A. Cleveland Shrigley

4.2.20
Walls

I want to break down walls, Lord
I want to break down walls,
Between the rich and the poor, Lord
Between the young and the old;
Between the white and black, Lord
O help me break down walls.

I want to break down walls, Lord
I want to break down walls,
Between progressive youth, Lord
And old conservatives;
Between the simple and the wise, Lord
O help me break down walls.

I want to break down walls, Lord
I want to break down walls,
Between Muhammad's sons, Lord
And worshippers of Shiva,
Between low caste and high, Lord
O help me break down walls.

I want to break down walls, Lord
I want to break down walls,
Between your friends and foes, Lord
Between the good and bad,
Between East and West, Lord
O help me break down walls.

I want to break down walls, Lord
I want to break down walls,
Between the communists, Lord
And rightists of all hues,
Between the Arabs and the Jews, Lord
O help me break down walls.

I want to break down walls, Lord
I want to break down walls,
Between the great religions, Lord
The Churches and the Church,
The Christians who dispute, Lord
O help me break down walls.

Roger Lesser

Shiva is a major Hindu deity.

4.2.21
Neighbours

Lord,
I see people of all races
In this city,
Struggling for existence,
Crying out for justice;
I see a city of broken hearts
And comfortless lives
As the lonely hug their pain
And cry out for solace
And for companionship.

Lord,
Grant us the power
To be neighbours
For those whose lives
Intertwine with ours;

Grant us the power to celebrate
With those who celebrate
And weep with those who weep.

May we find You at work
In the ambiguities of all our lives
As we live, and love and die.

Brian Frost

4.2.22
The Sun of Truth

O peoples of the world! The Sun of Truth hath risen to illumine the whole earth, and to spiritualize the community of man. Laudable are the results and the fruits thereof, abundant the holy evidences deriving from this grace. This is mercy unalloyed and purest bounty; it is light for the world and all its peoples; it is harmony and fellowship, and love and solidarity; indeed it is compassion and unity, and the end of foreignness; it is the being at one, in complete dignity and freedom, with all on earth.

The Blessed Beauty saith: 'Ye are all the fruits of one tree, the leaves of one branch.' Thus hath He likened this world of being to a single tree, and all its peoples to the leaves thereof, and the blossoms and fruits. It is needful for the bough to blossom, and leaf and fruit to flourish, and upon the interconnection of all parts of the world-tree, dependeth the flourishing of leaf and blossom, and the sweetness of the fruit.

For this reason must all human beings powerfully sustain one another and seek for everlasting life; and for this reason must the lovers of God in this contingent world become the mercies and the blessings sent forth by that clement King of the seen and unseen realms. Let them purify their sight and behold all humankind as leaves and blossoms and fruits of the tree of being. Let them at all times concern themselves with doing a kindly thing for one of their fellows, offering to someone love, consideration, thoughtful help. Let them see no one as their enemy, or as wishing them ill, but think of all humankind as their friends; regarding the alien as an intimate, the stranger as a companion, staying free of prejudice...

O Thou kind Father, God! Gladden our hearts through the fragrance of Thy love. Brighten our eyes through the Light of Thy Guidance. Delight our ears with the melody of Thy Word, and shelter us all in the Stronghold of Thy Providence.

Thou art the Mighty and Powerful, Thou art the Forgiving and Thou art
the One Who overlooketh the shortcomings of all mankind.

'Abdu'l Bahá

4.2.23
Witness-bearers for Justice

O God, we seek your forgiveness for the numerous injustices around us,
  for our inability to create a world of equality.
We pray for a deepening of our commitment to justice,
  for the ability to reflect on the many ways in which
  we offend people of other creeds, of the opposite sex, of other nations.
Above all we ask for the courage to stand up as witness-bearers for justice,
  though this may be against ourselves.

A Unitarian Universalist prayer

4.2.24
Universal Peace

These are the days of seed sowing. These are the days of tree planting.
The bountiful bestowals of God are successive.
He who sows a seed in this day will behold his reward in the fruits and harvest of
the
  heavenly Kingdom.
This timely seed, when planted in the hearts of the beloved of God,
  will be watered by showers of divine mercy and warmed by
  the sunshine of divine love.
Its fruitage and flower shall be the solidarity of mankind,
  the perfection of justice and the praiseworthy
  attributes of heaven manifest in humanity.
All who sow such a seed and plant such a tree according to the teachings of
Bahá'u'lláh
  shall surely witness this divine outcome in the degrees of its perfection and
will
  attain unto the good pleasure of the Merciful One.

Today the nations of the world are self-engaged, occupied with mortal and
  transitory accomplishments, consumed by the fires of passion and self.
Self is dominant; enmity and animosity prevail. Nations and peoples are thinking
  only of their worldly interests and outcomes.
The clash of war and din of strife are heard among them.
But the friends of the Blessed Perfection have no thoughts save the thoughts of
heaven
  and the love of God.

Therefore, you must without delay employ your powers in spreading the effulgent glow of

the love of God and so order your lives that you may be known and seen as examples of its radiance.

You must deal with all in loving-kindness in order that this precious seed entrusted to

your planting may continue to grow and bring forth its perfect fruit.

The love and mercy of God will accomplish this through you if

you have love in your own heart.

'Abdu'l Bahá

4.3 God in the Poor – Service

4.3.1
Help the World Progress

So may we be like those making
the world progress toward perfection;
May Mazda and the Divine Spirits help us
and guide our efforts through Truth;
For a thinking man is where Wisdom is at home.

Zoroastrian prayer – Yasna 30:9

4.3.2
May I be Happy

May I be filled with loving kindness.
May I be well.
May I be peaceful and at ease.
May I be happy.

Ancient Tibetan Buddhist Meditation

4.3.3
To Arrive At the End

Living beings are without number;
I vow to row them to the other shore.

Defilements are without number;
I vow to remove them from myself.

The teachings are immeasurable;
I vow to study and practise them.

The way is very long;
I vow to arrive at the end.

Buddhist: Four vows of the Bodhisattva

4.3.4
The Loveable Bee

May I never use cruel sarcasm, which, like flies, alights on the open wounds of
man and thus swells his troubles.

I would emulate Thy loveable bee, attracted by the nectar of sweetness in the
heart hives of others.

Paramahansa Yogananda

4.3.5
Lighting a Candle is a Prayer

Lighting a candle is a Prayer,
When we have gone, it stays alight,
kindling in the hearts and minds
of others the prayers we have
already offered for them
and for others, for the sad,
the sick, and the suffering –
the prayers of thankfulness too.

Lighting a candle is a parable:
burning itself out, it gives light to others.
Christ gave himself for others.
he calls us to give ourselves.

Lighting a candle is a symbol:
of love and hope,
of light and warmth.
Our world needs them all

Anonymous

4.3.6
Can You Hear the World Crying?

Busy, normal people: the world is here.
Can you hear it wailing, crying, whispering?
Listen: the world is here.
Don't you hear it.
Praying and sighing and groaning for wholeness?
Sighing and whispering: wholeness,
wholeness, wholeness?
An arduous, tiresome, difficult journey
towards wholeness...
The cry for bodily health and spiritual
strength is echoed from person to
person, from patient to doctor...
Our spirits cry out for the well-being of
the whole human family...
the beggars and the mad people in our streets:
– Where are their relatives?
Who is their father? Where is their mother?
We cry for the wholeness of humanity.

From an African Call for Life

4.3.7
Waiting for You

Waiting for you
reminds me
of all the other people in the world
waiting:
Those in prison
confined, shut off
waiting for time to pass
or death
to bring release:
Those in pain
maimed by accidents of a physical kind
waiting to be healed back to an active life.
And those with accidents
of another kind:
divorce, unemployment, schizophrenia
the old, the ugly, the lonely
those on the margins
sitting uncomfortably
waiting
for love, for work, for sanity,
for respect, for healing
for someone or something to fill the gaps
and soothe the pain
reinforced by time.

I look at the gate now mended
and firmly closed.
You do not come.
I turn from emptiness to emptiness
O God
yet wonder if You are also waiting
in the shadows?

Anonymous: Waiting Woman's Prayer

4.3.8
Any Good I Can Do

Dear Lord,
I expect to pass through this world but once;
and any good thing, therefore, that I can do
or any kindness that I can show to any fellow creature,
let me do it now;
let me not defer or neglect it,
for I shall not pass this way again.

Stephen Grellet

4.3.9
A Beggar Woman's Prayer

Lord, I thank you that since with your love you have taken from me all earthly riches, you now clothe and feed me out of the goodness of others, for all that clothes my heart in the desire of possessions has become foreign to me.
Lord, I thank you that since you have taken from me the power of my eyes, you now serve me through the eyes of others.
Lord I thank you that since you have taken from me the power of my hands...
Lord, I thank you that since you have taken from me the power of my heart, you now serve me with the hands and hearts of others.
Lord, I ask you to reward them here on earth with your divine love, so that they might beseech and serve you with all virtues until they come to a holy end.

Mechtild of Magdeburg

4.3.10
Your Kingdom

Our Father
Who is in us here on earth, Holy is your name
In the hungry who share their bread and their song.
Your Kingdom come,
A generous land where confidence and truth reign.
Let us do your will, Bring a cool breeze for those who sweat.
You are giving us our daily bread
When we manage to get back our lands
Or to get a fairer wage.
Forgive us
For keeping silent in the face of injustice
And for burying our dreams.
Don't let us fall into the temptation
Of taking up the same arms as our enemy,
But deliver us from evil which disunites us.
And we shall have believed in humanity and life
And we shall have known your Kingdom
Which is being built for ever and ever.

Anonymous: A Prayer From Central America

4.3.11
Cambodia

The suffering of Cambodia has been deep.
From this suffering comes great compassion.
Great compassion makes a peaceful heart.
A peaceful heart makes a peaceful person.
A peaceful person makes a peaceful family.
A peaceful family makes a peaceful community.
A peaceful community makes a peaceful nation.

And a peaceful nation makes a peaceful world.

May all beings live in peace and happiness.

Samdech Preah Maha Ghosananda

4.3.12
Enjoy the World

O God of all beauty, whose will it is that all creatures enjoy the world and the life you have given us, we know that many are unable to do this, through hunger, poverty, disease, oppression, ignorance, or sin. Let me never rest content in your joys until I have done everything in my power and in your grace to help others to share them also, O God of all goodness and willer of abundant life.

George Appleton

4.3.13
The Long Travail

Grant us to look with your eyes of compassion,
O merciful God, at the long travail of humankind:
the wars, the hungry millions,
the countless refugees,
the natural disasters,
the cruel and needless deaths,
our inhumanity to one another,
the heartbreak and hopelessness of so many lives.
Hasten the coming of the messianic age
when the nations shall be at peace,
and men and women shall live free from fear and free from want
and there shall be no more pain or tears,
in the security of your will
and the assurance of your love,
shown us in Jesus the Christ.

George Appleton

4.3.14
Free Me To Love and Serve

Lord my thoughts turn in upon myself. Turn them upward to you and outward to your other children, that I may forget myself and lose all fear and anxiety, all self-seeking and self-consciousness, in worship of you and in love of others. O save me from myself to worship, love and serve in perfect freedom.

George Appleton

4.3.15
When to Start

How wonderful it is that nobody need wait a single moment before beginning to improve the world.

Anne Frank, aged 14 just before being dragged to her death in 1944

4.3.16
To a Bosnian Orphan

There is something of magic in a little child
In his laughter and trust and his winsome smile
There is something so tragic in this little child
In his unnamed fears and suspicious guile.

Where is your mother and where is your dad?
Where are the toys you play with, my son?
Where is the joy that other boys had?
You have learned to limp before you can run.

Where are you going to? What is your fate?
What can you hope for now you are five?
Have you a birthday to celebrate?
How long do you hope to stay alive?

What comfort, what help, what joy can I bring you?
Alone, without friends, with no one to care?
What else can I say? What song can I sing you?
If I had loved more, your pain I would share.

Roger Lesser

4.3.17
A Spirit of Compassion

Go out in a spirit of compassion,
And take to the others the benefits which you have received.
Teach the Way, which is glorious at the beginning, in the middle, and at the end.
Urge people to live lives of perfect holiness.
There are many people whose souls are covered only by a few specks of dust.
If the Way is not preached to them, they cannot be saved;
But if they hear about the Way, they will follow it.

Buddhist: Mahavagga 1,1

4.3.18
Live on Spiritual Bliss

Let us live joyfully.
Let us form a community which possesses nothing.
Let us live on spiritual bliss, radiating spiritual light.

Buddhist: Dhammapada 197-201

4.3.19
Open Thy Eyes

Leave this chanting and singing and telling of beads!
Whom dost thou worship in this lonely dark corner of a temple with doors all

shut?
Open thine eyes and see thy God is not before thee!
He is where the tiller is tilling the hard ground and where the path maker is
breaking stones... Put off thy holy mantle and even like him come down on the
dusty soil!
Meet him and stand by him in toil and in sweat of thy brow.

Rabindranath Tagore

4.3.20
Lord, Teach us to Hate our Poverty of Spirit

Poverty is
– a knee-level view from your bit of pavement;
a battered, upturned cooking pot and countable ribs,
coughing from your steel-banded lungs, alone, with your face to the wall;
shrunken breasts and a three year old who cannot stand;
the ringed fingers, the eyes averted and a five-paise piece in your palm;
smoking the babus' cigarette butts to quieten the fiend in your belly;
a husband without a job, without a square meal a day, without energy, without
hope;
being at the mercy of everyone further up the ladder because you are a threat to
their self-respect;
a hut of tins and rags and plastic bags, in a warren of huts you cannot stand up
in, where
your neighbours live at one arm's length across the lane;
a man who cries out in silence;
nobody listening, for everyone's talking;
the prayer withheld
the heart withheld
the hand withheld; yours and mine.

Anonymous: Litany from Calcutta

4.3.21
Service

Make us worthy, Lord, to serve our fellow human beings throughout the world
who live and die in poverty and hunger.
Through our hands, grant them this day their daily bread; and by our
understanding love, give them peace and joy.

Daily prayer of the co-workers of Mother Teresa of Calcutta

4.3.22
Every Cry of Pain

May my heart lend its ear to every cry of pain.

The Buddha

4.3.23
To Serve Thy Glory

Make us, Lord,
to see and serve thy glory,
in seeing
and salving
the pain of the world.

Kenneth Cragg

4.3.24
Parable of Sheep and Goats

As a shepherd divideth his sheep from his goats, the King shall set the sheep on his right hand, but the goats on the left.

Then the King shall say unto them on his right hand, Come ye blessed of my father, inherit the kingdom prepared for you from the foundation of the world:

For I was an hungred, and ye gave me meat: I was thirsty and ye gave me drink: I was a stranger and ye took me in:

Naked, and ye clothed me: I was sick, and ye visited me: I was in prison, and ye came unto me.

Then shall the righteous answer him, saying, Lord, when saw we thee an hungred, and fed thee? or thirsty and gave thee drink?

When saw we thee a stranger, and took thee in? or naked, and clothed thee?

When saw we thee sick, or in prison, and came unto thee?

And the King shall answer and say unto them, Verily I say unto you, Inasmuch as ye have done it unto one of the least of these my brethren, ye have done it unto me.

Bible: Matthew 25:33-40

4.3.25
Thou Camest Not

God rebuked Moses, saying, 'I am God, I fell sick; thou camest not.'

Moses said: 'O transcendent One, thou art clear of defect, what mystery is this? Explain, O Lord.'

God said unto him again, 'Wherefore didst thou not kindly ask after me when I was sick?'

He answered, 'O Lord, thou never ailest. My understanding is lost: unfold the meaning of these words.'

God said, 'Yea, a favourite and chosen slave of mine fell sick. I am he. Consider well: his infirmity is my infirmity, his sickness is my sickness.'

Jalal al-Din Rumi

4.3.26
God in Disguise

Treat all people well.
Perhaps to your surprise,
The one whom you are meeting
Is God in some disguise.

Tulsidas

4.3.27
The Steep Path of Virtue

The steep and difficult path of virtue is:
'Freeing the slave,
Giving food in the day of hunger
to the orphan who is near of kin
or to some needy soul in distress.'

Qur'an: 90:13-16

4.3.28
A Single Soul

Our bread and water are of one table.
The progeny of Adam are as a single soul.

Muhammad Iqbal

4.3.29
Understanding

O God, help us not to despise or oppose what we do not understand.

William Penn

4.3.30
Serving Others

Strengthen us, O God, to relieve the oppressed, to hear the groans of poor
prisoners, to reform the abuses of all professions, that many be made not poor to
make a few rich; for Jesus Christ's sake.

Oliver Cromwell

4.3.31
Compassion

Let your soul lend its ear to every cry of pain like as a lotus bares its heart to
drink the morning sun. Let not the fierce sun dry one tear of pain before you
have wiped it from the sufferer's eye. But let each burning human tear fall on
your heart and there remain nor ever brush it off, until the pain that caused it is
removed. These tears, O you of heart most merciful, these are the streams that
irrigate the fields of charity immortal.

Hindu Tradition

4.3.32
It is Not Given

It is not given to us to see the completion of the work,
nor to desist from it either.

Jewish: A Rabbinic saying

4.3.33
Victims of Landmines

Lord, how can I serve you without arms?
How can I walk in your way without feet?
I was collecting sticks for the fire when I lost my arms,
I was taking the goats to water when I lost my feet.
I have a head but my head does not understand why there are landmines in the
grazing land or why there is a tripwire across the dusty road to the market.

My heart is filled with a long ache. I want to share your pain but I cannot.
It is too deep for me. You look at me but I cannot bear your gaze. The arms
factory provides a job for my son and my taxes paid for the development of
smart bombs.
I did not protest when the soldiers planted fear into the earth that
smothers the old people and the anxious mothers and fills the young men with
hate.

Lord, we are all accomplices in the crime of war which is a lust for power at all
costs.
The cost is too much for humanity to bear
Lord give us back our humanity, our ubuntu...
Teach us to serve you without arms.

Archbishop Desmond Tutu

4.3.34
Walk Cheerfully

Walk cheerfully
Be patterns, be examples in all countries, places,
islands, nations, wherever you come,
that your carriage and life may preach
among all sorts of people, and to them;
then you will come to walk
cheerfully over the world,
answering that of God in every one.

George Fox

4.3.35
Doubly At Your Service

Doubly at your service
Doubly at your service, O God. Amen.

One of the prayers used by Muslim pilgrims at Mecca

4.3.36
Hunger

We have squandered the gift of life.
The good life of some is built on the pain of many;
the pleasure of a few on the agony of millions.
To you we lift our outspread hands.
We thirst for you in a thirsty land.
We worship death in our quest to possess ever more things;
we worship death in our hankering after our own security,
our own survival, our own peace, as if life were divisible, as if love were divisible,
as if Christ had not died for all of us.
To you we lift our outspread hands.

*Anonymous: Prayer used at Sixth Assembly of the World Council of Churches
(Vancouver 1983)*

4.3.37
Have Mercy on the Sorrowful

Have mercy, O God, on all who are sorrowful,
those who weep and those in exile.
have pity on the persecuted and the homeless
who are without hope;
those who are scattered in remote corners of this world;
those who are in prison and ruled by tyrants.
Have mercy on them as is written in your holy law, where your compassion is
exalted.

A Jewish prayer

4.3.38
Lord, Open Our Eyes

Lord, open our eyes,
That we may see you in our brothers and sisters.
Lord, open our ears,
That we may hear the cries of the hungry, the cold,
The frightened, the oppressed.
Lord, open our hearts,
That we may love each other as you love us.
Renew in us your spirit
Lord, free us and make us one.

Mother Teresa

 4.4 Peace

4.4.1
For I am Dead
(From Hiroshima)

I come and stand at every door,
But none can hear my silent tread:
I knock, and yet remain unseen,
For I am dead, for I am dead.

I'm only seven, although I died
In Hiroshima long ago;
I'm seven now, as I was then:
When children die, they do not grow.

My hair was scorched with swirling flame,
My eyes grew dim, my eyes grew blind,
It came and burned my bones to dust,
And that was scattered by the wind.

I need no fruit, I need no rice,
I need no sweets or even bread:
I ask for nothing for myself,
For I am dead, for I am dead.

All that I ask is that for peace
You fight today, you fight today
So that the children of this world
May live and grow and laugh and play.

Anonymous

4.4.2
The Resurrection – An Elegy for the Six Million

One day they will assemble in the valley of bones –
Ashes sifted out of furnaces, vapours from Lunenberg,
Parchments from some friend's books, cakes of soap,
half-formed embryos, screams still heard in nightmares.
God will breathe upon them. He will say: be men.

But they will defy Him: We do not hear you. Did you hear us?
There is no resurrection for us. In life it was a wondrous thing
For each of us to be himself, to guide his limbs to do his will.
But the many are now one. Our blood has flowed together,

Our ashes inseparable, our marrow commingled,
Our voices poured together like water of the sea.
We shall not surrender this greater self.
We the Abrahams, Isaacs, Jacobs, Sarahs, Leahs, Rachels,
Are now forever Israel.

Almighty God, raise up a man who will go peddling through the world.
Let him gather us up and go through the world selling us as trinkets.
Let the peddler sell us cheaply. Let him hawk his wares and say:
Who will buy my souvenirs? Little children done in soap,
A rare Germanic parchment of the greatest Jew in Lodz.
Men will buy us and display us and point to us with pride:
A thousand Jews went into this and here is a rare piece
That came all the way from Crakow in a box car,
A great statesman will place a candle at his bedside,
It will burn but never be consumed.
The tallow will drip with the tears we shed.
And it will glow with the souls of our children.
They will put us in the bathrooms of the United Nations
Where diplomats will wash and wash their hands
With Polish Jews and German Jews and Russian Jews,
Let the peddler sell the box of soap that was once buried
With Kaddish and Psalms by our brothers.

Some night the statesman will blow upon the candle
And it will not go out.
The souls of the little children will flicker and flicker
But not expire.
Some day the diplomats will wash their hands and find them stained with blood.
Some day the citizens of the German town
Will awake to find houses reeking
With all the vapours from all the concentration camps,
From Hell itself, and the stench will come from the
Soap box.

Then they will rise up, statesmen, diplomats, citizens
And go hunting for the peddler: You who disturb our rest
And our ablutions, you who haunt us with your souvenirs,
You who prick our conscience, death upon you!

But the peddlers shall never cease from the earth
Until the candles die out and the soap melts away.
David Polish

4.4.3
Peace in the Heart

If there is to be peace in the world,
There must be peace in the nations.
If there is to be peace in the nations,
There must be peace in the cities.
If there is to be peace in the cities,
There must be peace between neighbours.
If there is to be peace between neighbours,
There must be peace in the home.
If there is to be peace in the home,
There must be peace in the heart.

Lao Tsu

4.4.4
Peace Prayer

May Peace Prevail on Earth.

World Peace Prayer – Masahisa Goi – 1955

4.4.5
Africa

God bless Africa,
Guard her children.
Guide her rulers,
And give her peace for Jesus Christ's sake. Amen.

Trevor Huddleston

4.4.6
The News We Are Waiting For

When tomorrow I open my eyes
I should like to hear the news
All the children in the world
Are waiting for:
That peace, the Redeemer, has come.

Vardit Fertouk

A prayer written when he was eight.

4.4.7
The Peace Prayer

Lead us from death to life,
       from falsehood to truth.
Lead us from despair to hope,
       from fear to trust.
Lead us from hate to love,

from war to peace.
Let peace fill our heart, our world, our universe.

Satish Kumar

4.4.8
Litany of Peace

As we are together, praying for Peace, let us be truly with each other.
Let us be at peace within ourselves, our bodies and our minds, our emotions and spirit.
Let us return to ourselves and become wholly ourselves.
Let us be aware of the source of being common to us and to all living things.
Evoking the presence of the Great Compassion, let us open our hearts to receive compassion – for ourselves and for all living beings.
Let us pray that all living beings may realize that they are all brothers and sisters, all nourished from the same source of life.
Let us pray that we ourselves may cease to be the cause of suffering to each other.
Let us pledge ourselves to live in a way which will not deprive other beings of air, water, food, shelter, or the chance to live.
With humility, with awareness of the uniqueness of life, and with compassion for the suffering around us, let us pray for the establishment of peace in our hearts and peace on Earth.

A Buddhist Litany of Peace

4.4.9
Peace Blossoms in Your Heart

Peace wants to blossom inside your heart and nowhere else.

You and I create the world by the vibrations that we offer to the world. If we can invoke peace and then offer it to somebody else, we will see how peace expands from one to two persons, and gradually to the world at large.

> There is no human being on earth
> Who does not have the capacity
> To offer the message of peace
> To the world at large.
> But what is needed now
> Is the soulful willingness.

Sri Chinmoy

4.4.10
Peace in Your Heart

If you do not find peace inside your own heart, then you will not find it anywhere else on earth.

Peace is based first on love and then on non-attachment. No thirst for gain, no fear of loss – lo, Peace is yours. Peace is also based on renunciation. This renunciation is not the renunciation of worldly possessions, but of limitation and ignorance. That peace is true peace which is not affected by the roaring of the world, outer or inner.

Dive deep within:
You are bound to hear
The whispering
Peace-sea-messages.

Sri Chinmoy

4.4.11
Universal Peace

May there be peace in the higher regions;
May there be peace in the firmament;
May there be peace on earth.
May the waters flow peacefully;
May the herbs and plants grow peacefully;
May all the living powers bring unto us peace.
The supreme Lord is peace.
May we all be in peace, peace, and only peace;
And may that peace come unto each of us.
    Shanti, shanti, shanti.

Hindu scriptures: Yajurveda

4.4.12
Love One Another

God our Father, Creator of the world,
please help us to love one another.
Make nations friendly with other nations;
make all of us love one another like brothers and sisters.
Help us to do our part to bring peace in the world
and happiness to all people.

A prayer from Japan

4.4.13
Father Forgive

The hatred which divides nation from nation,
race from race, class from class,
Father, forgive.

4.4

The covetous desires of peoples and nations
to possess what is not their own,
Father, forgive.

The greed which exploits the labours of men and women,
and lays waste the earth
Father, forgive.

Our envy of the welfare and happiness of others,
Father, forgive.

Our indifference to the plight of the homeless and the refugee,
Father, forgive.

The lust which uses for ignoble ends
the bodies of men and women,
Father, forgive.

The pride which leads us to trust in ourselves
and not in God.
Father, forgive.

Anonymous: Prayer on a plaque on the altar of Coventry Cathedral, written in 1964

4.4.14
Look in Compassion

Look in compassion, O heavenly Father, upon this troubled and divided
world.
Though we cannot trace your footsteps or understand your working, give
us
grace to trust you with an undoubting faith; and when your own time is
come,
reveal, O Lord, that new heaven and new earth wherein dwells
righteousness,
where the Prince of Peace rules, your Son our Saviour Jesus Christ.

Charles Vaughan

4.4.15
Keep Them Both Together in Your Hearts

Pray not for Arab or Jew, for Palestinian or Israeli,
But pray rather for yourselves, that you may not divide them in your
prayers
But keep them both together in your hearts.

Anonymous: Christian Aid

4.4.16
From Space

Give us, O God, the vision which can see Thy love in the world in spite of human failure. Give us the faith to trust Thy goodness in spite of our ignorance and weakness. Give us understanding hearts, and to do what each one of us can do to set forward the coming of the day of universal peace.
Amen.

Frank Borman

A prayer offered in space on Christmas Eve 1968 by Apollo VIII's commander.

4.4.17
Called to Work for Peace

You continue to call us to work for peace.
Our world is broken and wounded by injustice, violence and indifference.
Alone, we would be overwhelmed by the challenges that face us.
But together, supported by your Spirit,
We can do more than any of us could dream or imagine.

Written for 50th anniversary of Pax Christi International Movement in 1995

4.4.18
Tibet

May the Spirit of Compassion help us to feel for the sufferings
of the people of Tibet.
May the Spirit of Love melt the cold hearts of those
who trample on human rights
May the Spirit of Beauty move us to preserve the unique splendours
of the land of Tibet.
May the Spirit of Wisdom help us to treasure the mystical insights
of Tibetan religious teachers.
May the Spirit of Patience and Endurance strengthen those who are oppressed
and those who are exiled from their homes.
May the Spirit of Courage strengthen those who speak for those who have no
voice.
May the Spirit of Non-violence bring healing, peace and justice
to all the people of China and Tibet.
May the Spirit of Unity help us to recognise people of every nation as brothers
and sisters.

Marcus Braybrooke

4.4.19
Nuclear Danger

Dear Lord, awaken the people of the earth and their leaders to the realization of the madness of the nuclear arms race. Today we mourn the dead of past wars, but will there be anyone to mourn the dead of the next one? O Lord, turn us away from our foolish race to self-destruction; let us see that more and more weaponry indeed means more of a chance to use it. Please, Lord, let the great talents you have given to your creatures not fall into the hands of the powers and principalities for whom death is the means as well as the goal. Let us see that the resources hidden in your earth are for feeding each other, healing each other, offering shelter to each other, making this world a place where men, women and children of all races and nations can live together in peace.

Give us new prophets who can speak openly, directly, convincingly, and lovingly to kings, presidents, senators, religious leaders and all men and women of good will, prophets who can make us wage peace instead of war. Lord, make haste to help us. Do not come too late!

Henri Nouwen

4.4 20
The Parachute

From the hearts of peaceful souls
    may a flag of peace unfurl
    to fall from the sky
    like a vast parachute
    onto a region of war.

May enmities flounder
    tiring themselves
    to exhaustion beneath the parachute of peace.

A modern prayer from Sarajevo, Bosnia

© Duncan Baird Publishers from Bridge of Stars

4.4.21
May the Houses Become Homes

Once more may the houses become homes,
    not monuments of a way of life abandoned.

Once more may the hospital become preoccupied
    by accidents, tumours and viruses.

Once more may the museum, now a barracks,
    become a museum
      with an annexe on the subject of war,
      in honour of a new and permanent peace.

A modern prayer from Croatia

4.4.22
Friendship to All

I give friendship to all, and enmity to none.
Know that violence is the root-cause of all
    miseries in the world.
Violence, in fact, is the knot of bondage.
"Do not injure any living being"
This is the eternal, perennial, and unalterable
    way of spiritual life.
A weapon, however, powerful it may be,
    can always be superseded by a superior weapon;
    however no weapon can
    be superior to non-violence and love.

A Jain prayer

4.4.23
May Peace Triumph Over Discord

In this place may obedience triumph over disobedience,
Peace over discord, Generosity over niggardliness,
Reverence over contempt,
The true spoken word over the lie,
Truth over falsehood.

Zoroastrian Scriptures: Yasna 60,5

4.4.24
Bless us with the light of Your Countenance

Grant peace, welfare and blessing,
Grace and love and mercy to us,
    to all Israel, and to all people.
Bless us, our Father, one and all, with the light of Your countenance;
for by the light of Your countenance You have revealed to us,
O Lord our God, the Law of life, a love of kindness and righteousness,
blessing and mercy, life and peace.
For it is good in your sight that all people should be blessed with
enduring peace.
We praise You, O Lord, the Source of peace.

A Jewish prayer for peace

4.4.25
The World is On Fire

The world is on fire: O God, Save it in Your mercy.
Through whatever door we come to You,
Save us, we pray.
The True Guru has revealed that the person who reflects on the True Word
Is ever at peace:

And, without the Lord, there is no one else
To Bless us with Forgiveness.

A Sikh prayer for peace: Adi Granth

4.4.26
United in Spirit

Receive our gratefulness for allowing this expression of Global Unity
And for allowing us all to be united in the Spirit.
Just as the birds praise you in the morning; just as the waters and the
murmur of trees exhort your greatness,
Receive from these hearts from different latitudes, different languages,
different cultures, our praise and our gratitude.

A Native Peruvian prayer

This prayer was offered at an international interfaith gathering, Sarva-Dharma-
Sammelana, held in Bangalore in 1993.

4.4.27
For the Peace of the World

For the peace of God and his loving kindness toward humanity, let us
pray to the Lord,
Kyrie, eleison.

For peace in the whole world, for the leaders of our countries and for
their heavenly help and guidance, let us pray to the Lord.
Kyrie, eleison.

For the remission of sins and forgiveness of our offences; for our
deliverance from all affliction, wrath, danger, necessity, and war, let
us pray to the Lord.
Kyrie, eleison.

For our fathers and mothers, brothers and sisters praying with us at
this hour; for our prayer, that it may be heard and well accepted by God and
that his mercies and compassion be sent to us, let us pray to the Lord.
Kyrie, eleison.

From the Liturgy of St James of the Orthodox Christian Church

Kyrie, eleison is an ancient Greek prayer which means Lord, have mercy.

4.4.28
May Barriers Crumble

Grant O Lord that your Holy and Life-giving Spirit may so move every
Human heart, that barriers which divide us may crumble, suspicions disappear
And hatred cease; that our divisions being healed, we may live in justice
And peace...

National Council of Churches in the Philippines

4.4.29
For Peace in the Middle East

O God, creator and sustainer of all things, Lord of infinite love,
Kindness and mercy, guide us to the way of love when hatred and pride appear to
Be the easier and more attractive way.
Kyrie, eleison.

O God, cherisher and sustainer of all beings, sovereign Lord over all
Your creation, in your boundless mercy and care, teach us wisdom and
Compassion
to face this threat of suffering, discord and death. Teach us, our most
holy creator, to love mercy and justice, as you love mercy and justice.
Kyrie, eleison.

O God of all dominion in whose hands is all good, teach our leaders
humility, wisdom and good judgement.
Help us all to defuse every crisis peacefully before it plunges us into a whirlpool
of senseless suffering, bloodshed and war.
Kyrie, eleison.

O God we give thanks to you for giving us this good earth as a sacred
Trust to enjoy and share with all your creatures.
Help us to keep your trust and not destroy it.
Save us, our compassionate Lord, from our folly by your wisdom,
from our arrogance by your forgiving love, from our greed by
your infinite bounty and from our insecurity by your healing power.
Kyrie, eleison.

O God, guide us to your ways, the ways of righteousness and peace.
Grant us peace, O Lord of peace.
Help us to do your will in our lives, in our relationships and in our daily activities.
Forgive us all in your mercy and save us from our own evil.

Anonymous: Prayers written together by a Christian, a Jew and a Muslim

4.4.30
Recommendation

Promise me, promise me this day
While the sun is just overhead
Even as they strike you down
With a mountain of hate and violence,
Remember, brother,
Man is not our enemy.

Just your pity,
Just your hate,
Invincible, limitless,
Hatred will never let you face
The beast in man.
And one day, when you face this
Beast alone, your courage intact,
Your eyes kind,
Out of your smile
Will bloom a flower
And those who love you
Will behold you
Across 10,000 worlds of birth and dying.

Alone again
I'll go on with bent head
But knowing the immortality of love.
And on the long, rough road
Both sun and moon will shine,
Lighting my way.

Thich Nhat Hanh

Reprinted from Being Peace (1987) by Thich Nhat Hanh with permission of
Parallax Press, Berkeley, California

4.4.31
Spirit of Peace

Spirit of peace, come to our waiting world;
Throughout the nations, may your voice be heard.
Unlock the door of hope, for you hold the key;
Spirit of peace, come to our world.

Spirit of love, come to our waiting world;
Throughout the nations, may your voice be heard.
Unlock the door of hope, for you hold the key;
Spirit of love, come to our world.

Spirit of strength, come to or waiting world;
Throughout the nations, may your voice be heard.
Unlock the door of hope, for you hold the key;
Spirit of strength, come to our world.

Spirit of light, come to our waiting world;
Throughout the nations, may your voice be heard.
Unlock the door of hope, for you hold the key;
Spirit of light, come to our world.

Spirit of God, come to our waiting world;
Throughout the nations, may your voice be heard.
Unlock the door of hope, for you hold the key;
Spirit of God, come to our world.
Spirit of God, come to our world.

Geoffrey Gardner

4.4

4.5 Human Rights

4.5.1
Keep the Sputtering Light Burning

Make us keep the sputtering lantern burning
and not to break a wounded reed.
Make us understand
the secret of eternal life
from the pulse of blood in our veins
and realize the worth of a life
from the movement of a warm heart.
Make us not discriminate
the rich and the poor
the high and the low
the learned and the ignorant
those we know well and those we do not know.
Oh!
A human life can't be exchanged for the whole world,
this supreme task of keeping the lives
of sons and daughters of God.
Let us realize how lovely it is
to feel the burdens of responsibility

Anonymous prayer by a worker of Peace Market, Korea, written during study at night in 1977

4.5.2
Prophecy of an Asian Woman

All the broken hearts
shall rejoice;
all those who are heavy laden,
whose eyes are tired
and who do not see,
shall be lifted up
to meet with
the Motherly Healer.
The battered souls and bodies
shall be healed;
the hungry shall be fed;
the imprisoned shall be free;
all earthly children shall regain joy
in the reign
of the just and loving one
coming for you

coming for me
in this time
in this world.

Anonymous

4.5.3
The Power of Hope

Nailed to a cross because you would not
compromise on your convictions.
Nailed to a cross because you would not
bow down before insolent might.
My saviour, you were laughed at,
derided, bullied, and spat upon
but with unbroken spirit,
Liberator God, you died.

Many young lives are sacrificed
because they will not bend;
Many young people are in prison for following your lead.
Daily, you are crucified;
my Saviour, you are sacrificed
in prison cells and torture rooms
of cruel and ruthless powers.

The promise of Resurrection,
the power of hope it holds,
and the vision of a just new order
you proclaimed that first Easter morning.
Therefore, dear Saviour, we can affirm
that although bodies are mutilated and broken,
the Spirit refuses submission.
Your voice will never be silenced,
Great Liberating God.

Aruna Gnanadason

4.5.4
The Future

Lord, we thank You for Your gift of hope, our strength in times of
trouble.
Beyond the injustice of our time, its cruelty and its wars, we look
forward to a world at peace when men and women deal kindly with each other,
and
no one is afraid.
Every bad deed delays its coming, every good one brings it nearer.
May our lives be Your witness, so that future generations bless us. May the day

come, as the prophet taught, when "the sun of righteousness will rise with healing in its wings".
Help us to pray for it, to wait for it, to work for it and to be worthy of it. Blessed are You Lord, the hope of Israel.

Forms of Prayer for Jewish Worship

4.5.5
How to Change the World

Teach us, Lord, that in order to change the world,
We must also change ourselves.
The man whom you strengthen in his service to God will love you.
The way to strengthen him is to love him.

Nachman of Bratzlav

4.5.6
Torture

I don't understand how people do the horrible things to each other which I read about in the newspapers.
I find it hard to believe that they can torture each other the way they seem to, because they have different political views or different religious beliefs. But eye witnesses tell me it
really happens.

Lord, I cry to you to help those who inflict such injuries.
Take hatred from their hearts; give them understanding of the evil they do.

Strengthen the persecuted; give them courage and a firm belief in you.

Give me and all who try to serve you the desire to serve the suffering and fill us with love which will defeat the power of evil in the world.

Michael Hollings

4.5.7
Our Words Will Fly Out

For all those whose tongues are in manacles,
    whose pens are suffering from a drought of ink,
        let us pray.

No virtuous thought may be imprisoned for ever.
    As a dove flies out through prison bars,
    our beautiful words, roosting in their cage,
    will soon fly out and flock around the heads of tyrants,
    masking their sun.

Anonymous modern prayer from Beijing, China
© Duncan Baird Publishers, London, from Bridge of Stars

5 The Natural World

5.1 Animals

5.1.1
No Fearful Evils

No fearful evils
Will ever overtake
Him who protects
All living beings
And is kind to them.
They whose minds
Are filled with kindness
Will never enter
A world dark with woes.

Tiruvalluvar

5.1.2
Prayer for All Beings

May creatures all abound in prosperity and peace.
May all be blessed with peace always;
All creatures weak or strong,
All creatures great and small,
Creatures unseen or seen,
Dwelling afar or near,
Born or awaiting birth,
May all be blessed with peace.

Buddhist Scripture: Sutta-Nipata

5.1.3
Universal Love

Even as a mother at the risk of her life
would watch over her own, her only child,
So let us with boundless mind and goodwill
survey the whole world.

Buddhist Scripture: Sutta-Nipata

5.1.4
God's Care for the Animals

God sendeth the springs into the rivers: which run among the hills.
Beside them shall the fowls of the air have their habitation: and sing among the branches.
He watereth the hills from above: the earth is filled with the fruit of thy works.
He bringeth forth grass for the cattle: and green herb for the service of men;

That he may bring food out of the earth and wine that maketh glad the heart of man:
and oil to make him a cheerful countenance, and bread to strengthen man's heart.
The trees of the Lord are also full of sap: even the cedars of Libanus which he hath planted;
Wherein the birds make their nests: and the fir-trees are a dwelling for the stork.
The high hills are a refuge for the wild goats: and so are the stony rocks for the conies.
He appointed the moon for certain seasons: and the sun knoweth his going down.
Thou makest darkness that it may be night: wherein all the beasts of the forest do move.
The lions roaring after their prey: do seek their meat from God.
The sun ariseth, and they get them away together: and lay down in their dens...
O Lord, how manifold are thy works: in wisdom hast thou made them all; the earth is full of thy riches.
So is the great and wide sea also: wherein are things creeping innumerable, both small and great beasts...
These wait all upon thee: that thou mayest give them meat in due season...
The glorious Majesty of the Lord shall endure for ever: the Lord shall rejoice in his works.

Bible: Psalm 104:10-25, 27, 31

5.1.5
Suffering Animals

Hear our humble prayer, O God, for our friends the animals, especially for animals who are suffering; for all that are overworked and underfed and cruelly treated; for all wistful creatures in captivity that beat against bars; for any that are hunted or lost or deserted or frightened or hungry; for all that are in pain or dying; for all that must be put to death. We entreat for them all mercy and pity, for those who deal with them we ask a heart of compassion and gentle hands and kindly words. Make us ourselves to be true friends to animals and so to share the blessings of the merciful.

A prayer from the Orthodox Church

5.1.6
At Peace

Like a cat asleep in a chair
At peace, in peace
And at one with the master of the house, with the mistress,
At home, at home in the house of the living,
Sleeping on the hearth, and yawning
Before the fire.

D. H. Lawrence

5.1.7
At One With the Living God

All that matters is to be at one with the living God
To be a creature in the house of the God of life.

Anonymous

5.1.8
Driving the Cows

Closed be to you every pit,
Smooth to you be every hill,
Snug to you be every bare spot,
Beside the cold mountains...

The fellowship of Mary Mother be yours,
The fellowship of Brigit of kine be yours,
The fellowship of Michael victorious be yours,
    In nibbling, in chewing, in munching.

A Celtic prayer

Saint Bridget (Brigit) was a very popular Celtic saint and women felt especially
close to her.

5.1.9
A Milking Prayer

Bless, O God, my little cow,
    Bless, O God, my desire;
Bless Thou my partnership,
    And the milking of my hands, O God.

Bless, O God, each teat,
    Bless, O God, each finger;
Bless Thou each drop
    That goes into my pitcher, O God!

A Celtic prayer

5.10
Thanksgiving for a pet who has died

Whenever I turned my key
in the lock
I knew she would be waiting,
Welcoming me home.
Those days when the world
seemed too cruel,
Too hard, too fast, too
lonely,

5.1

She was always kind, easy,
gentle,
The best listener.
She always made us laugh,
Was the source of many
stories:
'Remember the time she did
this ...?'
'Remember the time she did that ...?'
And, though she kept her
not-human mystery,
Eating, sleeping, drifting,
dreaming,
Still we felt she let us know
her well.
And we told each other:
'She likes me doing that!'
'See how she smiles at me!'
'Isn't she sweet! Isn't she
silly!'
Feeling that she knew us
Better almost than we knew
ourselves.
That she taught us something
We were MEANT to learn.
Effortlessly loving, totally
loved.
Now, whenever I turn my
key in the lock,
I shall remember her waiting,
Welcoming me home.

Sheila Yeger

 5.2 God in Nature

5.2.1
I Find You in All Things

I find you, Lord, in all things and in all
my fellow creatures, pulsing with your life;
as a tiny seed you sleep in what is small
and in the vast you vastly yield yourself.

Rainer Marie Rilke

5.2.2
I am So Small

The World is so vast
and I so small
its beauty and grandeur
Overwhelm Me.

Yet every feature
reveals God's Love
The heavens above and
the earth below.

Anonymous

5.2.3
Be Still

    I speak to you.
Be still
Know I am God. I spoke to you when you were born.
Be still
Know I am God. I spoke to you at your first sight.
Be still
Know I am God. I spoke to you at your first word.
Be still
Know I am God. I spoke to you at your first thought.
Be still
Know I am God. I spoke to you at your first love.
Be still
Know I am God. I spoke to you at your first song.
Be still
Know I am God. I speak to you through the grass of the meadows.
Be still
Know I am God. I speak to you through the trees of the forests.
Be still
Know I am God. I speak to you through the valleys and the hills.

Be still
Know I am God. I speak to you through the Holy Mountains.
Be still
Know I am God. I speak to you through the rain and snow.
Be still
Know I am God. I speak to you through the waves of the sea.
Be still
Know I am God. I speak to you through the dew of the morning.
Be still
Know I am God. I speak to you through the peace of the evening.
Be still
Know I am God. I speak to you through the splendour of the sun.
Be still
Know I am God. I speak to you through the brilliant stars.
Be still
Know I am God. I speak to you through the storm and the clouds.
Be still
Know I am God. I speak to you through the thunder and lightening.
Be still
Know I am God. I speak to you through the mysterious rainbow.
Be still
Know I am God. I will speak to you when you are alone.
Be still
Know I am God. I will speak to you through the Wisdom of the Ancients.
Be still
Know I am God. I will speak to you at the end of time.
Be still
Know I am God. I will speak to you when you have seen my Angels.
Be still
Know I am God. I will speak to you throughout Eternity.
Be still
Know I am God. I speak to you.
Be still
Know I am God.

Essene Gospel of Peace

5.2.4
Give Us Happiness

May the winds bring us happiness.
May the rivers carry happiness to us.
May the plants give us happiness.
May night and day yield us happiness.
May the dust of the earth bring us happiness.
May the heavens give us happiness.
May the trees give us happiness.

May the sun pour down happiness.
May the cows yield us happiness.
May my body become pure.
May I be free from impurity and sin.
May I realize myself as the Light divine.
May my mind become pure.
May my self become pure.
May my body become pure.
Salutations to Brahman.
Salutations to the God in the fire.
Salutations to the God in the earth.
Salutations to the God in the plants.
Salutations to the God in speech.
Salutations to the Lord of speech.
I offer my salutations to the
Supreme Being, the all-pervading Spirit.

Hindu Scriptures: Taittirya Aranyaka

5.2.5

The Joy of Elevated Thoughts

I have felt
A presence that disturbs me with the joy
Of elevated thoughts;
A sense sublime
Of something far more deeply interfused,
Whose dwelling is the light of setting suns,
And the round ocean and the living air,
And the blue sky, and in the mind of man.

William Wordsworth

5.2.6

It is God Who Creates

It is God who has created the stars for you, so that they may guide you in the darkness, both on land and at sea.

It is God who created you from one being, and provided you with homes where you can rest.

It is God who sends rain from the sky, bringing forth buds and green leaves on every plant.

Qur'an: 6:95-99

5.2.7
Birdsong

I listen with reverence to the birdsong cascading
At dawn from the oasis, for it seems to me
There is no better evidence for the existence of God
Than in the bird that sings, though it knows not why,
From a spring of untrammelled joy that wells up in its heart.

An Arab Chieftan

5.2.8
God is Everywhere

God is in the water, God is in the dry land, God is in the heart.
God is in the forest. God is in the mountains, God is in the cave.
God is in the earth, God is in heaven...
You are in the tree, You are in its leaves.
You are in the earth, you are in the firmament.

Gobind Singh

5.2.9
To Love All Things

Love will teach us all things; but we must learn how to win love; it is got with
difficulty... Love all God's creation, both the whole and every grain of sand. Love
every leaf, every ray of light. Love the animals, love the plants, love each separate
thing. If thou lovest each thing thou wilt perceive the mystery of God in all: and
when once thou perceivest this, thou wilt henceforward grow every day to a
fuller understanding of it: until thou come at last to love the whole world with a
love that will then be all-embracing and universal.

Dostoevsky

5.2.10
Love the World

O Lord, let me feel this world
As your love taking form,
Then my love will help it.

Rabindranath Tagore

5.2.11
To be Beautiful

Beloved God of the woods and streams,
grant us to be beautiful inwardly,
and all that we have of outer things
to be at peace with those within.
Counting only the wise to be truly rich,
increase to all who here abide
their stores of gold.

Plato

5.2.12
We Praise You

O God...
We praise you for the arching sky and the blessed winds
For the driving clouds, and the constellations on high.
We praise thee for the salt sea and the running water,
For the everlasting hills, for the trees
And for the grass under our feet.
We thank you for our senses by which we can see the splendour of the morning
And hear the jubilant songs of love
And smell the breath of the springtime.
Grant us, we pray you,
A heart wide open to all this joy and beauty,
And save our souls from being so steeped in care
Or so darkened by passion
That we pass heedless and unseeing even when the thornbush
By the wayside is aflame with the glory of God.

Walter Rauschenbusch

5.2.13
To See Thee

Lord grant us eyes to see
Within the seed a tree,
Within the glowing egg a bird,
Within the shroud a butterfly:
Till taught by such, we see
Beyond all such creatures thee,
And hearken for thy tender word
And hear it, 'Fear not: it is I!'

Christina Rossetti

5.2.14
Open My Eyes to See the Beauty

You, O God, are the Lord of the mountains and the valleys. As I travel over
mountains and through valleys, I am beneath your feet. You surround me with
every kind of creature. Peacocks, pheasants, and wild boars cross my path. Open
my eyes to see their beauty, that I may perceive them as the work of your hands.
In your power, in your thought, all things are abundant.

Native American: A Sioux Indian prayer

5.2.15
Come Down To Me

You are like a honey-comb on the branch of a tree:
I can see the sweet honey, but the branch is too high for me to climb.
You are like a goldfish swimming in a pond,

Only an arm's length from the bank; yet if I try to catch you in my hand
You slip from my grasp.

You are like a snake
Your skin dazzling in its bright colours,
Yet your tongue able to destroy a man with a single prick.

Be merciful to me, O Lord. Give me life, not death.
Reach out to me and hold me in your arms.
Come down to me, and lift me up to heaven.
Sustain my feeble soul with your power.

Manikka Vasahar

5.2.16
All Creation Praises God

The breath of life in every creature shall bless You, Lord our God, and the spirit of all flesh ever recalls Your beauty and Your greatness. From everlasting to everlasting You are God. Besides You we have no king who rescues and saves us, frees and delivers us, and answers and cares for us. At all times of trouble and distress there is no king who can help and support us but You.

God of the first and last ages, God of all creatures, Lord of history, adored in worship – He guides His universe with love, and His creatures with mercy. The Lord neither slumbers nor sleeps. He wakes the sleepers, and rouses the uncaring. He gives life beyond death, He heals the sick, He gives sight to the blind and raises up those bent low. To you alone we declare our gratitude.

Forms of Prayer for Jewish Worship

5.2.17
Mountains

God, the mountains point to your glory. Their vastness and wildness remind me of your power and my weakness. I trust in your protection and your guidance. Your love reaches unto the skies.

Marcus Braybrooke

5.2.18
Enjoy

God, let me remain peacefully here and enjoy this landscape.
Help me to let go my worries
And to rest in You and in Your beauty.

Marcus Braybrooke

5.2.19
The Circle of Trees

How lovely are thy holy groves
God of heaven and earth.
My soul longs and faints
for the circle of thy trees.
My heart and my flesh
sing with joy to thee
O God of life.

May all things move and be moved in me
all know and be known in me.
May all creation
Dance for joy within me.

Native American: Chinook prayer

5.2.20
The Sun,

Hail to thee, thou sun of the seasons,
    As thou traversest the skies aloft;
Thy steps are strong on the wing of the heavens,
Thou art glorious mother of the stars.

Thou liest down in the destructive ocean
    Without impairment and without fear;
Thou risest upon the peaceful wave-crest
    Like a queenly maiden in bloom

A Celtic prayer

5.2.21
Like A Wild Flower

Lord, you are like a wild flower. You spring up in places where we least expect
you. The bright colour of your grace dazzles us. When we reach down to pluck
you, hoping to possess you for our own, you blow away in the wind. And if we
tried to destroy you, by stamping on you and kicking you, you would come back
to life. Lord, may we come to expect you anywhere and everywhere. May we
rejoice in your beauty. Far from trying to possess you, may you possess us. And
may you forgive us for all the times when we have sinned against you.

Henry Suso

5.2.22
The Person

Who looks on the creatures of the Earth,

Big and small,

As his own self,

Comprehends this immense world.

Among the careless,

The person who restrains himself,

Is enlightened.
Manikka Vasahar

5.2.23
To the Breath of Life
Homage to you, Breath of Life, for the whole universe obeys you. You are the ruler of all things on earth, and the foundation of the earth itself.

Homage to you, Breath of Life, in the crashes of thunder and in the flashes of lightning. The rain you send gives food to the plants and drink to the animals.

Homage to you, Breath of Life, in the changing seasons, in the hot dry sunshine and the cold rain. There is comfort and beauty in every kind of weather.

The plants themselves rejoice in your bounty, praising you in the sweet smell of their blossom. The cattle rejoice, praising you in the pure white milk they give.

Homage to you, Breath of life, in our breathing out and breathing in. At every moment, whatever we are doing, we owe you praise and thanksgiving.

Homage to you, Breath of Life, in our birth and in our death. In the whole cycle of life sustain and inspire us.

Homage to you, Breath of Life, in the love and friendship we enjoy. When we love one another, we reflect your infinite love.

Men and women rejoice in your bounty, praising you in poem and song. The little children rejoice, praising you in their innocent shrieks of laughter.

Hindu Scriptures: Atharva Veda

5.2.24
Our Only Home
We seek your forgiveness for our indifference to the numerous signs of your presence around us, for our inability to value the skies and the earth as our only home, for our inability to make the connections between our lives and the earth

from where we emerge and to which we shall proceed. We pray for a profound change in the hearts of all men and women so that we may stop the destruction of the ecological balance, the pollution of our skies and water, the decimation of our forests and the accompanying impoverishment of the human spirit. Our Lord, You have not created this world in vain.

A Unitarian Universalist Prayer

5.2.25
How Grateful We Are

> We lift our eyes in awe,
> toward heaven, soaring above.
> We bow our heads in prayer
> toward earth, rich and deep.
> Living amid such gifts
> Of Kami's great giving,
> How happy and grateful we are!
>
> The Mediation of the Living Spirit
> Does not stop for a single day.
> The protection of the Parent Kami
> Embraces all, far and wide.
>
> The blessings of Kami flow without limit
> Through all generations.
> The ways of Kami are mysterious and wondrous,
> Beyond our understanding.

A Shinto prayer

Kami are the sacred powers venerated by Shinto devotees.

5.2.26
The Life That Nurtures All

The brilliance of heaven, the richness of earth
Time flows without cease, years pass without end
In heaven and earth is the life that nurtures all
In heaven and earth is the Truth that orders all
For this wondrous form
For these wondrous works
Let us praise Tenchi Kane no Kami
Let us praise Kami of heaven and earth.

A Shinto prayer

Kami are the sacred powers venerated by Shinto devotees.

5.3 Mother Nature

5.3.1
Gaian Prayer

Mother,
You are the soul of the Earth.
You are the drops of rain on a Spring Morning.
You are the cold silence of falling snow.
You envelop all life in your Life.

Jason Clark

5.3.2
Peace

Peace She says to me.
Peace to your soul.
I am the beauty in the leaf.
I am the echo in a baby's laugh.
I am your Mother.
I am the joy in the heart that beats.
I am the free woman.
I am the one who breaks the shackles of oppression.
You are my hands and feet.

Jason Clark

5.3.3
Bowing My Head

I am bowing my head
In the eye of the Mother who gave me birth,
In the eye of the Maiden who loves me,
In the eye of the Crone who guides me in wisdom,
In friendship and affection.
Through thy gift of nature, O Goddess,
Bestow upon us fullness in our need.
Love towards the Lady,
The affection of the Lady,
The laughter of the Lady,
The wisdom of the Lady,
The passion of the Lady,
The blessing of the Lady,
And the magic of the Lady ...
Each shade and light,
Each day and night,
Each moment in kindness,
Grant us Thy Sight.

A Celtic prayer

5.3.4
Wilderness

What would the world be, once bereft
Of wet and of wildness? Let them be left,
O let them be left, wildness and wet;
Long live the weeds and the wildness yet.

Gerald Manley Hopkins: 'Inversnaid'

5.3.5
They Shall Not Hurt Nor Destroy in All My Holy Mountain

The wolf also shall lie down with the lamb and the leopard shall lie down with
the kid; and the calf and the young lion and the fatling together; and a little
child shall lead them.

And the cow and the bear shall feed; their young ones shall lie down together;
and the lion shall eat straw like the ox.

And the sucking child shall play on the hole of the asp, and the weaned child
shall put his hand on the cockatrice' den.

They shall not hurt nor destroy in all my holy mountain; for the earth shall be full
of the knowledge of the Lord, as the waters cover the sea.

Bible: Isaiah 11:6-9

5.3.6
My Wish for Our Earth Mother

This is what I want to happen: that our earth mover
May be clothed in ground corn four times over;
That frost flowers cover her over entirely;
That the mountain pines far away over there
May stand close to each other in the cold;
That the weight of snow crack some branches!
In order that the country may be this way
I have made my prayer sticks into something.

Native American: from a Zuni offering prayer

5.3.7
Earth Teach Me

Earth teach me stillness
As the grasses are stilled with light.
Earth teach me suffering
As old stones suffer with memory.
Earth teach me humility
As blossoms are humble with beginning.
Earth teach me caring
As the mother who succours her young.
Earth teach me courage
As the tree which stands alone.

Earth teach me limitation
As the ant which crawls on the ground.
Earth teach me freedom
As the eagle soars in the sky.
Earth teach me regeneration
As the seed which rises in the spring.
Earth teach me to forget myself
As melted snow forgets its life.
Earth teach me to remember kindness
As dry fields weep in the rain.

Native American: A Prayer from Ute people

The Ute are a small, formerly nomadic, tribe living in South-western USA.

5.3.8
I am

I am the wind on the sea.
I am the wave of the sea.
I am the bull of seven battles.
I am the eagle on the rock.
I am a flash from the sun.
I am the most beautiful of plants.
I am a strong wild boar.
I am a salmon in water,
I am a lake in the plain.
I am the word of knowledge.
I am the head of the spear in battle.
I am the God that puts fire in the head.
Who spreads light in the gathering on the hills?
Who can tell the ages of the moon?
Who can tell the place where the sun rests?

Druid Song of Amergin

5.3.9
Thanks to Our Mother

We return thanks to our mother,
the earth, which sustains us.
We return thanks to the rivers and streams
which supply us with water.
We return thanks to all herbs, which furnish medicines
for the cure of our diseases.
We return thanks to the bushes and trees, which provide us with fruit.
We return thanks to the wind,
which, moving the air, has banished diseases.
We return thanks to the moon and stars,

which have given us their light when the sun was gone.
We return thanks to our grandfather
that he has protected his grandchildren from witches and reptiles,
and has given us his rain.
We return thanks to the sun,
that he has looked upon the earth with a beneficent eye.
Lastly, we return thanks to the Great Spirit, in whom is embodied all goodness,
and who directs all things for the good of his children.

Native American: A prayer of the Iroquois people

5.3.10
Sacred Earth

Teach your children what we have taught our children
That the Earth is our Mother
Whatever befalls the Earth, befalls the children of the Earth
God is the God of all people...
And what is man without the beasts...?
All things are connected. This we know,
The Earth does not belong to man, man belongs to the Earth.
This we know.
All things are connected like the blood which unites one family.
All things are connected.

Native American: Words of Chief Sealth of the Suquamish

5.3.11
Earth Awaking

Earth, our mother, breathe forth life
all night sleeping
now awaking
in the east
now see the dawn.

Earth, our mother, breathe and waken
leaves are stirring
all things moving
new day coming
life renewing.

Eagle soaring, see the morning
see the new mysterious morning
something marvellous and sacred
though it happens every day
Dawn the child of God and Darkness.

Native American: Pawnee prayer

5.3

5.3.12
Hymn to the Earth

Earth is the source of food, of rice and barley;
From her derive the five tribes of men.
To rain-steeped Earth, the Rain-giver's wife, be homage...

Nay the Goddess Earth, bearer of many a treasure
And of wealth stored up in diverse hidden places,
The generous sharer of riches, impart to us,
In addition to gold and gems, a special portion of her favour!

May Earth who bears mankind, each different grouping
Maintaining its own customs and its speech,
Yield up for me a thousand streams of treasure,
Like a placid cow that never resists the hand.

Hindu Scriptures: Atharva Veda XII

 # 5.4 Beauty

5.4.1
Centre of Centres

Centre of all centres, core of cores,
almond self-enclosed and growing sweet -
all this universe, to the furthest stars
and beyond them, is your flesh, your fruit.
Now you feel how nothing clings to you;
your vast shell reaches into endless space,
and there the rich, thick fluids rise and flow,
Illuminated in your infinite peace.
A billion stars go spinning through the night,
blazing high above your head.
But in you is the presence that
will be, when all the stars are dead.

Rainer Marie Rilke

5.4.2
A Thing of Beauty

A thing of beauty is a joy for ever:
Its loveliness increases; it will never
Pass into nothingness.

John Keats

5.4.3
To See the World

To see the world in a grain of sand,
And a heaven in a wild flower,
Hold infinity in the palm of your hand,
And eternity in an hour.

William Blake

5.4.4
A Wave of Joy

I am sea foam spumed from the deeps of joy. I am a wave of joy, seeking to dance in all billows of joy, struggling to be the ocean of joy. May the ripples of my laughter spread endlessly, finally subsiding on the bosom of infinite joy.

Paramahansa Yogananda

5.4.5
Love the Birds

Teach us to love the birds and the beasts; the frail wayside flowers and mute grasses, oft crushed by our unheeding feet.

The countless forms in Nature are expressions of Thy versatile genius – originals from Thy ceaselessly vibrating fingers. May we see in all creation Thine inimitable handiwork.

Paramahansa Yogananda

5.4.6
Fire of the Spirit

Fire of the Spirit,
Life of the lives of creatures,
Spiral of sanctity,
Bond of all natures,
Glow of charity,
Lights of clarity,
Taste of sweetness to the fallen,
Be with us and hear us.

Hildegarde of Bingen

5.4.7
May The Winds Blow Sweetness

May the wind blow sweetness,
The rivers flow sweetness,
The herbs grow sweetness,
For the Man of Truth!

Sweet be the night,
Sweet the dawn,
Sweet be earth's fragrance,
Sweet father Heaven!

May the tree afford us sweetness,
The sunshine sweetness
Our cows yield sweetness – milk in plenty
May the wind blow sweetness.

Hindu Scriptures: Rig Veda

5.4.8
The Way

The highest form of goodness is like water:
The goodness of water benefits all peoples
And does not strive:
Water is content with places detested by men.
So is the Way.

Tao Te Ching

5.4.9

The Blessing of the Sea

(A Meditation from an Account)

Please join me and visualise.
Let us journey secretly
To the beauty of experiencing
The Blessing of the Sea.

Walk, slowly,
Past the pebbled beach.
Now, welcoming, is sand
Giving to feet and curling toes;
Here soft and mouldable as snow
These ripple-carved by passing tides.

The seaweed greens and bladder-wrack
Curtain for shrimps their secret pools
And crabs behind sunk beady eyes
Sink through a swirl of watery grains.
The wind picks at the beach and rocks
Bearing far whispers of the waves...

We move towards the spray-lashed rocks'
Rise-fall-retreat of chattering stones.
To see convergent dolphins schools'
Excited ballet-dance on tails.
More whales now blow!
Flying fish and more.
Drawing in hosts of glittering scales...

Then
From massed clouds
Teased by the sun
Shaped by the soft hands of the wind
There comes a shaft
Of purest light
Downward
Directed toward the seas.
Strikes as a blow
Into all Form
Now bathed in Love
In love reborn
And all about bathes in the Power.

The very waves pause stunned
Forming
A Crown of scintillating Light.
No face is there
But beauty...
... With awareness of a Might.

And circling dolphins dance a tribute
As great whale tails thrash and pound
In mute ecstasy of thankfulness
For the Christening of the Sea...

In these moments we all marvel
as a longing fills our hearts;
Stood where fragrant breeze fingers sweep across the golden sand
And the unsaid prayers are answered
For the great Shaft moves to land:
Moves... striking through the Being of us to the waiting Earth below.
So Light and Light's joy fills us
As we turn reluctantly.
Walking:
Across rocks, sand and beach.
Sharing:
With loving humbleness
The Christening of the Sea.

Eric Gladwin

5.4.10
The Sun Was Not Yet Up

The sun wasn't up yet; you could see the morning star through the trees. There was a silence that was really extraordinary. Not the silence between two noises or between two notes, but the silence that has no reason whatsoever – the silence that must have been at the beginning of the world. It filled the whole valley and the hills. The two big owls, calling to each other, never disturbed that silence, and a distant dog barking at the late moon was part of this immensity. The dew was especially heavy, and as the sun came up over the hill it was sparkling with many colours and with the glow that comes with the sun's first rays.

Krishnamurti

5.4.11

Dawn, Daughter of Heaven
See now, the shining Daughter of Heaven approaches,
Dispelling gloom of night that we may see.
The friendly Lady ushers in the light.

The ascending Sun, refulgent star of heaven,
Co-worker with the Dawn, pours down his beams.
O Dawn, at your arising and the Sun's,
Grant us, we pray, our portion in your light.

O Dawn, glorious Daughter of high Heaven,
Promptly we rise and come to welcome you.
Most generous one, granter of all desires,
To worshipers you give both joy and treasure.

O glorious Dawn, you bring the earth to view
And lighten up the lofty vault of heaven.
We yearn to be yours, partaking in your rewards.
Accept our love as that of mother's children.

Bring to us, Dawn, your grace most bountiful,
That shall be celebrated far and wide.
Give us what you possess as nourishment for men,
That we may rejoice therein, O Daughter of Heaven.

Give to our princes wealth and everlasting fame.
To us grant in the contests herds of kine.
O shining Dawn, you who inspire the generous
And are full of grace, drive from us all our foes.

Hindu Scriptures: Rig Veda VII, 81

5.4.12

The Sun's Birthday

I who have died am alive again today,
and this is the sun's birthday; this is the birth
day of life and of love and wings: and of the gay
great happening illimitably earth.

e. e. cummings

5.4.13

Give Sight to Our Eyes

May the Sun guard us
In the highest heaven!
May the breezes protect us
In the airy spaces!
May fire be our guardian
In earthly places!

May the Inspirer, whose glowing flame
Deserves a hundred
Sacrificial offerings,

Be pleased with us!
From lightning flashes
Keep us safe.

May the God of light
Grant to us sight!
May the heavenly peaks
Grant to us sight!
May God the creator
Grant to us sight!

Give sight to our eyes
And sight to our bodies
That we may see.
May we see the world
At a single glance
And in all its details.

Thus, O Sun,
May we gaze on you,
Most fair to behold!
May we see clearly,
With the eyes of Men!

Hindu Scriptures: Rig Veda X, 158

5.4.14
New Moon

Hail to thee, thou new moon,
    Beauteous guidant of the sky;
Hail to thee, thou new moon,
    Beauteous fair one of grace.

Hail to thee, thou new moon,
    Beauteous guidant of the stars;
Hail to thee, thou new moon,
    Beauteous loved one of my heart.

Hail to thee, thou new moon,
Beauteous guidant of the clouds;
Hail to thee, thou new moon,
    Beauteous dear one of the heavens.

A Celtic prayer

To the Celtic people, the moon was a good friend, who guided their course on land and sea. For a seafaring people the light and guidance of the moon could well be a matter of life and death when they had to thread their way through intricate reefs and rocks on a dark night.

5.4.15
Step Outside

Whoever you are: some evening take a step
out of your house, which you know so well.
Enormous space is near, your house lies where it begins,
whoever you are.
Your eyes find it hard to tear themselves from the sloping threshold,
but with your eyes
slowly, slowly, lift one black tree
up, so it stands against the sky: skinny alone.
With that you have made the world. The world is immense
and like a word that is still growing in silence.
In the same moment that you will it,
your eyes, feeling its subtlety, will leave it...

Rainer Maria Rilke

5.4.16
See God Everywhere

Let me be quiet now, and kneel,
    Who never knelt before,
Here, where the leaves paint patterns light
    On a leaf-strewn forest floor;
For I, who saw no God at all
    In sea or earth or air,
Baptised by Beauty, now look up
    To see God everywhere.

Ellen Francis Gilbert

5.4.17
Beauty

Before me, beauty
Behind me, beauty
Below me, beauty
Above me, beauty
Around me, beauty
May I speak beauty
May I walk in beauty always
Beauty I am.
All is restored to beauty
All is restored to beauty
All is restored to beauty
All is restored to beauty

From the Navajo Blessing

Bibliography

A Book of Graces, Carolyn Martin, Hodder and Stoughton, 1980.

A Chain of Love, Mother Teresa and her Suffering Disciples, Kathryn Spink, SPCK, 1984.

A Child's Book of Prayers, Tessa Strickland, Barefoot Books, Bath, 1997.

A Diary of Private Prayer, John Baillie, Oxford University Press, 1936.

African Prayers, Robert Van de Weyer, John Hunt Publishing, 2001.

Alive to God, Kenneth Cragg, Oxford University Press, 1970. (New edition, *Common Prayer*, Oneworld Publications, 1999.)

All Desires Known, Janet Morley, SPCK, London, 1992.

All in Good Faith, Jean Potter and Marcus Braybrooke, World Congress of Faiths, 1997.

All in the End is Harvest, Agnes Whitaker, Darton, Longman and Todd, 1984.

Alternative Service Book of the Church of England, Clowes, SPCK, Cambridge University Press, 1980

An Orthodox Prayer Book, E. Lash, Oxford University Press, 1991.

Another Day, John Carden, SPCK, 1986.

As You Grieve, Aaron Zerah, Sorin Books, Notre Dame. 2000.

Being Peace, Thich Nhat Hahn, Parallax Press, Berkeley, California, 1987.

Beyond all Pain, Cicely Saunders, SPCK, 1983.

Beyond the Horizon, Cicely Saunders, Darton, Longman and Todd, 1990.

Book of a Thousand Prayers, Angela Ashwin, Marshall Pickering 1996.

Book of Alternative Services of the Anglican Church of Canada, Anglican Book Centre, Toronto, 1985.

Book of Common Prayer (1662).

Book of Common Prayer (1928).

Book of God's Love, Muhaiyaddeen M. R. Bawa, Fellowship Press, Philadelphia, 1993.

Breath of God, Roger Lesser, Writers Workshop, Calcutta, 2001.

Bridge of Stars, Marcus Braybrooke, Duncan Baird, 2001.

Celebrating Earth Holy Days, Susan J. Clark, Crossroad, New York, 1992.

Celtic Prayers, Robert Van de Weyer, John Hunt Publishing, 1997.

The Celtic Vision, Esther de Waal, Liguori Publications, Missouri, 2001, first published by Darton, Longman and Todd, 1988. (Selections from *Carmina Gadelica* by Alexander Carmichael.)

Collects with the New Lectionary, P. R. Akehurst and A. J. Bishop, Grove Books.

Common Worship, Church House Publishing, 2000

Compassion for Animals, Andrew Linzey and Tom Regan, SPCK, 1988.

Contemporary Parish Prayers, Frank Colquhoun, Hodder and Stoughton, 1975.

Dawn Through Our Darkness, Giles Harcourt, Collins, 1985.

Down to Earth and Up to Heaven, Sid Hedges, Pilgrim Press, 1964.

Edge of Glory, David Adam, SPCK, 1985.

Eucharistic Prayers and Liturgies, Evelyn Underhill, Mowbrays, 1939.

Every Nation Kneeling, Will Hayes, Order of the Great Companions, 1954.

Everything Starts With Prayer, Mother Teresa, White Cloud Press, Oregon, 1998.

Favourite Prayers, Deborah Cassidi, Continuum, 1998.

Forms of Prayer for Jewish Worship, edited by the Assembly of Rabbis of the Reform Synagogues of Great Britain, The Reform Synagogues of Great Britain, 1977.

Gift of Prayer, Fellowship in Prayer, Princeton, New Jersey, and SCM Press Ltd,1995.

Gitanjali, Rabindranath Tagore, Macmillan, 1913.

God of All Ages, Eric Gladwin, (privately published). 2000.

God and the Universe of Faiths, John Hick, Macmillan, 1973.

Golden Thread, Dorothy Boux, Shepheard-Walwyn and Gateway Books, 1990.

Good Friday People, Sheila Cassidy, Darton, Longman and Todd Ltd, and Orbis 1991

In A Dark Time, Nicholas Humphrey and Robert Jay Lifton, Faber and Faber, 1984.

In His Strength, Thelma Bailey, Bedeguar Books, Warminster, 1994.

Interpreted by Love, Elizabeth Basset, Darton, Longman and Todd, 1994.

It's Me, O Lord, Michael Hollings and Etta Gullick, Hodder and Stoughton, 1972.

Jerusalem Prayers, George Appleton, SPCK, 1974.

Journey of a Soul, George Appleton, Collins, 1974.

Laughter, Shouting and Silence, Kathy Keay, HarperCollins, 1994.

Learning of God, Readings from Amy Carmichael, Stuart and Brenda Blanch, SPCK, 1985.

Lion Prayer Collection, Mary Batchelor, Lion Publishing, 1992.

Liturgies of the Holocaust, Marcia Little, Edwin Mellen Press, 1986.

Lord, I Keep Running Back to You, Ruth Calkin, Tyndale House Publishing, Wheaton Il, c.1979

Lotus Book of Prayer, Satchidananda Ashram, Yogaville, 1986.

Love is My Meaning, Elizabeth Basset, Darton, Longman and Todd, 1975.

Loving God, Baba Virsa Singh, Gobind Sadan Institute for Advanced Studies in Comparative Religion, New Delhi, 1995.

Metaphysical Meditations, Paramahansa Yogananda, Self-realization Fellowship, Los Angeles, California, 1964.

Morning, Noon and Night, John Carden, Church Missionary Society, 1976.

Muslim Devotions, Constance Padwick, SPCK, 1961.

Muslim Prayers, Roger Lesser, Islamic Studies Association, 1990.

New Day Beckons, Sri Chinmoy, Agni Press, Jamaica, NY 11432.

Oxford Book of Prayer, George Appleton, Oxford University Press, 1985.

Parish Prayers, Frank Colquhoun, Hodder and Stoughton, 1967.

Poems of Kabir, English translation, Rabindranath Tagore and Evelyn Underhill, Macmillan, 1962.

Prayer and Meditation, F. C. Happold, Penguin, 1971.

Prayer for Pilgrims, John Johansen-Berg, Darton, Longman and Todd, 1993.

Prayer In A Troubled World, George Appleton, Darton, Longman and Todd, 1988.

Prayer (The Fount Book of), Robert Van de Weyer, HarperCollins, 1993.

Prayers and Meditations from Around the World, Tracy Baumgardner, Jain Publishing, Fremont, California, 1996.

Prayers for A Planetary Pilgrim, Edward Hays, Forest of Peace Publishing, Inc. Leavenworth, KS 66048-0269, 1989.

Prayers for Help and Healing, William Barclay, Collins, 1968.

Prayers for Meditation, Karl Rahner, Burns and Oates and Herder and Herder, 1968. English translation by Rosaleen Brennan.

Prayers for Others, Michael Hollings and Etta Gullick, McCrimmon Publishing, Southend-on Sea, 1977

Prayers of Darkness and Light, Brian Frost, New World Publications, 2001.

Prayers of Life, Michel Quoist, Gill and Son, Dublin 1963, and Sheed and Ward, Kansas City.

Prayers of the Way, John Johansen-Berg, Epworth, 1992.

Present Moment, Wonderful Moment: Mindfulness Verses for Daily Living, Thich Nhat Hanh, Parallax Press, Berkeley, California.

Quiet Mind, White Eagle, The White Eagle Publishing Trust, 1972.

Radiant Prayers, Muhammad Taqi Usmani, Idaratul Ma'arif, Karachi, 1999.

Resources for Multifaith Celebrations, Daniel Faivre, Westminster Interfaith, 1997.

Saints and Sages of India, Roger Lesser, Intercultural Publications, New Delhi, 1992.

Selected Prayers, Jamal A Badawi, Ta-Ha Publishers, 1979.

Short Prayers for the Long Day, Giles Harcourt and Melville Harcourt, Collins, 1978.

Signs and Wonders, Basil Dowling, Caxton Press, New Zealand, 1945.

Sometimes I Weep, Ken Walsh, SCM Press, 1973.

Songs of Solitude, V. F. Vineeth, Dharmaram Publications, Bangalore, 1992.

Songs of the Sons and Daughter of Buddha, E.T. Andrew Schelling and Waldman 1996

Soul's Almanac, Aaron Zerah, Penguin Putnam, New York, 1998.

St Christopher's in Celebration, Cicely Saunders, Hodder and Stoughton, 1988.

Stamper of the Skies, A Bible for Animal Lovers, Will Hayes, Order of the Great Companions, 1938.

Taking Up the Timbrel, Sylvia Rothschild and Sybil Sheridan, SCM Press, 2000.

Tales from My Teachers on the Alzheimer's Unit, Sue Silvermarie, Families International Inc, Milwaukee, WI 53224, 1996.

The Prophet, Kahlil Gibran. William Heinemann Ltd, 1926. (Pan Books edition 1980.)

The Times Prayers and Readings for All Occasions, Owen Collins, HarperCollins, 2001.

Tides and Seasons, David Adam, SPCK, 1989

Transcendence, Daniel Faivre, Westminster Interfaith, 1994.

Universal Wisdom, Bede Griffiths, HarperCollins, 1994.

Urantia Book, Urantia Foundation, Chicago, 1995.

Vedic Experience, Raimundo Panikkar, Darton, Longman and Todd, 1977.

Visions of an Interfaith Future, Celia and David Storey, International Interfaith Centre, Oxford, 1994.

Whispers from Eternity, Paramahansa Yogananda, Self-realization Fellowship, Los Angeles, California, 1949.

Wisdom of the Plain Folk, Songs and Prayers from the Amish and Mennonites, Donna and Robert Leahy, Penguin, 1997.

With One Voice, Sid G. Hedges, The Religious Education Press, 1970.

Women Pray, Monica Furlong, Skylight Paths Publishing, Woodstock, Vermont, 2001.

Wings of Soul: The World and Wisdom of Dadi Janki, Dadi Janki, Brahma Kumaris Information Services, 1998.

World Scriptures, Andrew Wilson, Paragon House, 1991.

WEB SITE

The World Prayers Project: www.worldprayers.org

Notes on Contributors and References

'Abdu'l Baha (1844-1921). Title of Abbas Effendi, eldest son and appointed successor of Baha'u'llah as head of the Baha'i faith: 1.2.31, 1.7.22, 1.8.10, 1.9.2, 3.4.24, 3.4.25, 3.9.26, 4.1.33, 4.1.34, 4.2.17, 4.2.22, 4.2.24.

Abu Bakr (d. 634). Father-in-law of Muhammad: 1.7.10.

Achaan Chah. Contemporary teacher of Insight Meditation: 3.7.8

Adam, David. Priest and contemporary writer of prayers in a Celtic idiom: 1.2.2, 1.3.35, 1.8.38.

African American anthem: 1.8.12.

African prayers: 1.3.12, 1.4.23, 1.5.11, 1.6.8, 1.8.12, 1.8.14, 3.3.1, 3.4.20, 3.6.14, 4.3.6.
Dinka, 2.4.11.
Efe People, 3.1.6.
Ethiopian prayer, 1. 3.10, 2.2.11.
Ghana, 1.5.12, 2.4.20.
Guinea, 1.8.34
Hottentot, 2.3.33.
Kalahari Bushman, 3.1.11.
Kenyan, 1.6.8, 2.4.17, 2.4.27, 3.1.13, 3.3.3, 3.4.20.
Nigeria, 1.8.14, 3.7.22, 3.11.11.
Pygmy, 1.3.12.
Sudan, 3.7.32, 3.9.10.
Ugandan (Christian), 3.3.5.
Ugandan (Nyoro), 3.4.16.

Akhenaton, Pharaoh or Amenhotep IV (d. 1358 BCE). A ruler of Egypt who renounced the old gods and introduced a purified and universalised solar cult: 1.4.22.

al-Hallaj (d.922). One of the most controversial figures in Islam, he taught the path of mystical union with God, but fell foul of the jurists. He was eventually imprisoned and executed in Baghdad: 1.4.25, 3.9.17, 3.11.18.

A Kempis. See Thomas à Kempis.

Akehurst, P. R. Co-author of a book of modern collects: 3.6.34.

Alfred the Great (849-899). King of Wessex and encourager of learning and religion: 1.8.41.

Amar Das, Guru (1479-1574). Third Sikh Guru: 3.4.30.

American Confederate soldier: 1.8.19.

Ambrose, St (c.339-397). Bishop of Milan and one of the four traditional doctors of the Church: 2.4.3, 3.11.71.

Amish prayers. The Amish people are a group of strict Mennonites (see below), who preserve their traditional way of life: 3.9.24, 3.10.14.

Angelus Silesius (1624-1677) (Johannes Scheffler). A Christian mystical writer, who was inspired by Eckhart. He converted from the Lutheran to the Catholic Church: 1.3.33.

Anonymous: 1.2.3, 1.2.4, 1.2.18, 1.3.2, 1.3.32, 1.5.2, 1.5.20, 1.5.22, 1.5.29, 1.5.49, 1.7.25, 1.8.11, 1.8.12, 1.9.18, 2.1.1, 2.1.3, 2.1.7, 2.2.2, 2.2.15, 2.3.17, 2.3.18, 2.3.19, 2.3.23, 2.3.31, 2.3.43, 2.3.50, 3.2.16, 3.2.23, 3.4.9, 3.4.10, 3.6.6, 3.6.12, 3.6.19, 3.8.26, 3.8.27, 3.8.28, 3.8.29, 3.9.9, 3.10.1, 3.10.5, 3.10.10, 3.11.3, 3.11.8, 3.11.13, 3.11.31, 3.11.46, 3.11.57, 4.2.6, 4.2.7, 4.3.5, 4.3.7, 4.3.10, 4.3.20, 4.3.36, 4.4.1, 4.4.13, 4.4.15, 4.4.20, 4.4.21, 4.4.29, 4.5.1, 4.5.2, 4.5.7, 5.1.7, 5.2.2.

Anselm, St (c.1033-1109). Monk and Archbishop of Canterbury. Influential theologian, known especially for *Proslogion* and *Cur Deus Homo*: 1.3.40, 1.5.14, 3.8.12.

Appleton, George Twentieth century Anglican Archbishop in Jerusalem and writer of prayers: 1.2.19, 1.7.7, 1.7.8, 3.1.19, 3.2.25, 3.4.17, 3.7.25, 3.8.32, 3.10.4, 3.10.13, 4.1.28, 4.3.12, 4.3.13, 4.3.14.

Apuleius, Lucius (born c. 125). Roman philosopher and satirist: 1.6.7.

Arias, Juan. Contemporary Spanish Roman Catholic priest: 3.8.30.

Arjan, Guru (1503-1606). Fifth Sikh Guru and first Sikh martyr, who compiled the *Adigranth Sahib*, the first Sikh scripture: 1.3.17, 1.7.28, 4.1.9.

Armenian ancient liturgy: 2.3.29, 4.1.35.

Arnold, Matthew (1822-1888). English poet and writer on culture and morality: 1.2.6, 1.2.11.

Ashwin, Angela. Contemporary writer and compiler of prayers: 2.2.14.

Asoka (3rd century BCE). Indian ruler and Emperor who converted to Buddhism: 3.4.7.

Astley, Lord Jacob (1579-1652). Royalist commander in the English Civil War: 2.2.10.

Augustine of Hippo (354-430). Saint and Doctor of the Church. Born in Algeria of a pagan father and a Christian mother, who prayed constantly for her son, he abandoned his childhood Christian faith but eventually came back to it. He became a bishop in North Africa and one of the most influential early Christian thinkers, best known for his autobiographical *Confessions* and for *City of God*: 1.3.38, 1.9.10, 1.9.15, 1.9.21, 1.9.24, 2.4.25, 3.10.9.

Aurobindo Sri (1872-1950). Influential Hindu teacher best known for his *The Life Divine*: 1.4.8.

Austen, Jane (1775-1817). English novelist: 1.1.7.

Avicenna. See Ibn Said.

Aztec prayer: 3.2.8, 3.11.27.

Baal Shem Tov (1698-1760). Founder of Hasidism, see below: 1.1.36.

Baba Farid (1169-1266). He lived for much of his life at Pakpatan, now in Pakistan, which became a place of pilgrimage. One of the earliest of the great Sufis of India: 1.3.20, 1.3.37, 3.9.5, 4.1.27.

Babylonian fragments: 1.7.18.

Babylonian Talmud. Completed in c. 600 CE, this is a commentary on much of the *Mishnah*, or collection of Jewish oral law: 1.1.28, 1.1.29.

Baha'i prayers: 3.11.72. See also 'Abdu'l Bah'a and Baha'u'llah.

Baha'u'llah. The Arabic title meaning 'the Splendour of God', adopted by Mirza Husayn 'ali Nuri (1817-1892), the Persian prophet-founder of the Baha'i religion. He devoted his final years to his writings, which are regarded by his followers as revelations from God. He died in the vicinity of Akka (Acre) where he had been imprisoned. His remains are buried at the Bahji, which is now a shrine for pilgrims: 1.3.28, 1.8.31, 1.8.42, 2.3.1, 3.7.9, 4.1.32.

Bailey, Thelma. Twentieth-century English author who, despite a serious disability, wrote several books of spiritual poetry and prayers: 1.8.47.

Baillie, John (1886-1960). Scottish theologian, also known for his *A Diary of Private Prayer*, published in 1936: 2.3.49.

Baquie, Lynn. A contemporary American member of 'Fellowship in Prayer': 1.3.29.

Barclay, William (1907-1978). Scottish writer on the Bible: 3.4.23.

Barnabas (1st century CE). Christian apostle. The *Letter of Barnabas* is a first-century Christian Letter ascribed, erroneously, to the Apostle Barnabas: 1.8.35.

Barrowby. Contemporary writer of prayers: 3.1.5.

Basavanna (c. 1106-67). A South Indian religious reformer associated with the founding of Lingayata or Virasaivism. He taught that the body is the true temple of God: 1.3.45.

Basho. Author of Japanese Haiku poems: 2.5.8, 2.5.10, 2.5.12, 2.5.17, 2.5.18.

Basil the Great (330-79). Cappadocian (Christian) Father. His *Rule of Basil* was very influential in the development of Eastern monasticism: 1.8.36.

Batchelor, Mary. Contemporary British writer and compiler of prayers: 3.8.22.

Bawa Muhaiyaddeen, M. R. Twentieth-century Tamil Muslim religious teacher: 1.8.31.

Baynes, Simon H. Contemporary Christian clergyman and author of some prayers: 3.6.17.

Bede, Venerable (c. 673-735). English monk of Jarrow in Northumbria and scholar, known for his *Ecclesiastical History of the English People*: 1.8.46.

Beer, Morris Abel. Unitarian writer: 4.1.6.

Bell, John. Contemporary Hymn Writer: 3.7.28

Bianco da Siena. Mediaeval author of 'Come

Buddha. Title meaning 'the Enlightened one', applied especially to Gotama, who is also known as Sakyamuni, 'The Wise one of the Sakya clan'). Variously dated, e.g. 566-486 BCE or c. 448-368 BCE, Gotama attained enlightenment and became the founder of the Buddhist religion: 3.11.34, 3.11.36, 4.3.22.

Buddhist prayers: 1.7.5, 3.4.26, 4.3.3, 4.4.8.
Amidista, 1.5.37.
Anapanassati Sutta, 1.2.27.
Asvalayana Sutra, 3.1.15.
Bodhicaryavatara of Shantideva, 2.3.47.
Dhammapada, 4.3.18.
Lotus Sutra, 1.5.39.
Mahadeviyakka (c.1130-1180), 1.8.33.
Mahavagga, 4.3.17.
Sutta-Nipata, 5.1.2, 5.1.3.

Bukhari (810-870). Complier of the one of the main collections of *hadiths* or traditions about the Prophet Muhammad: 3.7.1.

Bunyan, John (1628-88). English Dissenting preacher and author of *Pilgrim's Progess*: 1.1.27, 3.11.62.

Burgess, Ruth. Contemporary British writer of prayers: 1.2.37, 3.11.64, 3.11.65.

Burns, Robert (1759-96). Scottish poet: 2.3.39.

Calkin, Ruth Harms. Contemporary British writer of prayers: 3.4.18, 3.7.20.

Camara, Dom Helda Twentieth century Archbishop in North East Brazil, who was a champion of the poor and of non-violent social change: 1.4.29, 3.8.9, 4.2.12.

Campbell, George. Contemporary writer: 2.2.19.

Canada. *The Book of Alternative Services of the Anglican Church of Canada*: 1.6.10, 3.6.30.

Carden, John. Contemporary clergyman of the Church of England and author and compiler of prayers: 4.2.11.

Carmichael, Amy (1868-1951). Twentieth century. Worked most of her life in South India as a medical missionary: 2.4.28.

Cassidy, Sheila. Contemporary. Medical doctor, who became famous when she was arrested and tortured in Chile for treating a 'revolutionary'. Author of several devotional books: 3.9.8.

Caswall, E. (1814-78). Translator of Catholic hymns from Latin and other languages: 1.3.49.

Catherine of Genoa, St (1447-1510). Daughter of a Genoese aristocrat. After she and her husband underwent a religious conversion, she devoted herself to nursing destitute sick people: 3.7.39.

Catherine of Siena, St (c. 1347-1380). At the age of twelve she vowed her virginity to Christ and claimed to be in direct communication with Him. As an adult, she gathered disciples. Her best-known work is *The Dialogue* - a prolonged and often quite intimate conversation between God and herself: 1.9.26, 3.8.2.

Celtic prayers: 1.8.7, 2.2.6, 2.2.27, 2.2.31, 2.3.3, 2.3.4, 2.3.11, 2.3.25, 2.3.26, 2.3.35, 3.2.6, 3.7.24, 3.8.23, 3.11.60, 3.11.61, 5.1.8, 5.1.9, 5.2.20, 5.3.3, 5.4.14.

Chalice prayer: 1.9.19.

Chappell, Marjorie. Contemporary writer of prayers: 3.7.14.

Chinese prayers: 2.5.9, 4.5.7.

Chinmoy, Sri Kumar Ghose (1916-2007). Born in India, he entered an ashram at the age of 12. In 1964 he went to the USA and has taught meditation at the United Nations and in centres around the world. He has organised 'Peace Runs' and 'Peace Concerts' in many places: 3.6.18, 3.9.13, 4.4.9, 4.4.10.

Chuang-tsu, (also **Chuang chou**) c. 370-286 BCE). With Lao-tzu, one of the founders of Taoism: 1.8.8, 3.3.6.

Chun-Ming Kao. Twentieth-century Chinese Christian who was imprisoned by the Communists. He wrote about his experiences: 3.7.27.

Church of England
Alternative Service Book, 3.1.17, 3.4.29, 3.4.37.
Book of Common Prayer (1662), 1.7.9, 2.4.6.
Book of Common Prayer (1928), 2.4.7, 3.6.31, 3.6.32.
Common Worship, 3.4.27, 3.4.28.
Diocese of Bath and Wells Blessing Service for a Second Marriage, 3.4.13, 3.5.1.

Clark, Jason. Writer of Gaian or Earth prayers: 5.3.1, 5.3.2.

Cleeve, R. E. Contemporary writer of prayers: 1.1.39.

Coleridge, Mary (1861-1907). Novelist and poet. Descendant of Samuel Taylor Coleridge: 3.11.63.

Columba, St (c. 521-597). Christian abbot and missionary who established a community at Iona: 2.3.2.

Coolidge, Susan (Sarah Chauncy Woolsey) (1835-1905). Grew up in Cleveland, Ohio. Author of 'Katy' books for girls: 2.2.29.

Confucius (551-479 BCE). Latin for K'ung Fu-tzu. Chinese philosopher and moralist. After his death, his disciples complied a volume of his teachings, called the *Analects*: 3.11.49. See also I Ching.

Congregation of Abraxas. A Unitarian Universalist Order: 2.2.22, 2.4.10.

Cowper, William (1731-1800). English poet and hymn writer and opponent of slavery and British colonialism: 1.1.23.

Cox, Lilian. Contemporary writer of prayers: 2.5.15.

Cragg, Kenneth (1913-). Anglican Bishop and scholar on Islam: 1.7.26, 4.3.23.

Cranmer, Thomas (1489-1556) Archbishop of Canterbury under Henry VIII and Edward VI. Author of the 1548 and 1552 Prayer Books. He was martyred under Queen Mary: 3.6.21, 3.11.32. See also Church of England, *Book of Common Prayer*.

Cromwell, Oliver (1599-1658). Led the Puritan army against King Charles I. Became Lord Protector in 1653: 4.3.30.

Cummings, e. e. Twentieth-century American poet: 5.4.12.

Das, Surya (1950-). American Dzogchen Lama: 1.9.20.

Davies, A. Powell (1902-1957). Writer of prayers: 1.1.15.

Dawson, Brenda (d.1986). A primary school headmistress, who wrote some poems while a patient at St Christopher's Hospice: 3.7.2, 3.7.3, 3.7.4.

De Foucauld, Charles Eugene (1858-1916). Wealthy aristocrat and cavalry officer, who on recovering his faith eventually became a hermit, living among Muslims in the Sahara. He was assassinated in 1916. His simple way of life inspired the Little Brothers and Little Sisters: 1.9.9.

Devanesen, Chandran. Twentieth-century Indian Christian educationalist: 1.4.16, 1.7.31, 3.7.19.

Dimma. Seventh-century Irish monk: 3.8.31.

Dnyanadev (fl. 1290). Hindu poet and saint: 1.2.23.

Donne, John (1571/2-1631). Metaphysical poet. Ordained later in life and became dean of St Paul's in 1621: 1.7.20.

Dorsey, Thomas A. (1899-1993). He was born in Atlanta, Georgia in 1899. He started his music career in a small jazz band in Chicago but later went on to dedicate his life entirely to writing gospel songs. 1.8.13.

Dostoevsky, Fyodor (1821-81). Russian novelist: 5.2 9.

Dowling, Basil. Twentieth-century New Zealand writer: 1.7.23.

Drake, Sir Francis (1540-1596). Best known seaman of the Elizabethan age: 1.9.16, 2.3.45. 2.3.51.

Druid Song of Amergin: 5.3.9.

Dyck, Sally. Contemporary writer of prayers: 3.1.1.

Eckhart, Meister (1260-1327). Mystic: 1.1.30.

Egyptian Book of the Dead (c 3500 BCE): 1.4.26.

Egyptian (Ancient) prayer: 1.5.26 (Christian), 3.11.28, 3.11.48 (Egyptian religion).

Eknath (or Eknatha) (c. 1535-99). Born in Maharashtra. Hindu saint and Marathi poet, who also restored and edited the famous commentary *Jnaanesveri*: 1.8.25.

Ellerton, J. (1826-1893). Prolific hymn writer. Helped to prepare the 1889 edition of *Hymns Ancient and Modern*: 2.4.21.

Emerson, Ralph Waldo (1803-82). Lecturer, poet, essayist and teacher of New England Transcendentalism: 2.2.3.

Ephrem, St, the Syrian (c. 306-373). Devoted most of his life to biblical exegesis. Author of some hymns: 1.9.14, 3.9.3.

Epicurus, (341-270 BCE). Greek philosopher who taught the ethics of simple pleasures: 3.11.76.

Eskimo prayer: 3.1.10.

Esrefoglu (d. 1469). Muslim (Turkish) mystic: 1.3.30.

Essene Gospel of Peace: 5.2.3.

Ethiopian Jewish Prayer: 1.3.10.

Euripides (c. 480-406 BCE). Classical Greek dramatist: 1.4.19.

Farr, E. M. Contemporary writer of prayers: 3.8.25.

Felton, Tammy. Contemporary writer of prayers: 2.5.5.

Fénelon, François (1651-1715). Archbishop of Cambrai from 1695, whose letters of spiritual counsel have been much valued: 3.7. 26.

Fox, George (1642-91). He taught that truth is to be found in the inner voice of God speaking to the soul. He founded the Society of Friends: 4.1.18, 4.2.18, 4.3.34.

Francis of Assisi, St (1181-1226). He abandoned a knightly career for a life of poverty and care of the sick. Founded the Franciscans: 1.3.52, 3.9.18.

Frank, Anne (1929-1945). Born in Germany, she grew up in Holland where, with her family, she went into hiding from the Nazis, although eventually they were discovered. She died in a concentration camp. After her death her Diary became world famous: 4.3.15.

Frankl, Viktor E. Twentieth-century psychiatrist and concentration camp survivor: 1.3.44.

Freylinghausen, Johann (1670-1739). Hymn writer of the German Pietist movement: 2.4.13.

Frost, Brian. Contemporary writer of prayers: 1.8.48, 3.7.30, 4.2.21.

Furlong, Monica (1930-). Writer, especially on religious subjects: 4.2.5.

Gabriel, Charles H. Contemporary writer of prayers: 3.9.2.

Gandhi, Mohandas Karamchand, known as Mahatma ('Great Soul') (1869-1948). A Hindu spiritual teacher and practical leader of India in the struggle for independence. Wrote on a wide range of topics: 1.1.1, 4.1.3.

Gardner, Geoffrey. Contemporary hymn writer: 4.4.32.

George, Rosa. Contemporary writer of prayers: 3.2.13.

Ghosananda, Samdech Preah Maha (1929-2007). Contemporary Cambodian Buddhist leader: 4.3.11.

Gibran, Kahlil. Twentieth-century Lebanese spiritual writer, best known for The Prophet: 3.2.12, 3.4.4., 3.11.30.

Gilbert, Ellen Francis. Writer of prayers: 5.4.16.

Gingersoll, Robert. Contemporary writer: 4.1.8.

Girl Guide grace: 2.3.16.

Gladwin, Eric. Contemporary English poet and universalist: 1.1.6, 3.2.18, 3.5.6, 3.6.26, 3.6.36, 4.1.13, 4.1.14, 4.1.16, 5.4.9.

Gnanadason, Aruna. Contemporary writer of prayers: 4.5.3.

Gobind Singh, Guru (1666-1708). Tenth Sikh Guru and founder of the Khalsa: 4.1.22, 5.2.8.

Gordon, Charles (1833-1885). British general and Governor of Sudan. He was killed in the siege of Khartoum: 1.9.25.

Goure, Jim (d.1987). Writer of prayers and founder of United Research Inc, Black Mountain, NC 28711, USA: 1.7.4.

Green, Julian: 1.2.26.

Grellet, Stephen Contemporary writer: 4.3.8.

Gurney, Dorothy Frances (1858-1932). Granddaughter of Bishop Blomfield of London. Poet and hymn-writer: 3.4.32.

Hall, Joseph (1574-1656). Bishop of Exeter: 1.2.14.

Harcourt, Giles. Contemporary English clergyman and author and editor of prayers: 1.5.30, 1.7.27, 3.5.3, 3.6.9, 3.7.16, 3.7.17, 3.7.18.

Hasidism. Revivalist Jewish movement founded in Poland in the eighteenthth century by Ba'al Shem Tov (1698-1760) (see above), in reaction to Rabbinical Judaism. It taught that purity of the heart is more pleasing to God than learning: 1.1.12, 1.3.19. See also Nachman of Bratzlav and Levi Yitzchak.

Haskins, Minnie Louise (1875-1957). Poet: 2.5.1.

Hatch, Edwin (1835-89). Ecclesiastical historian at Oxford and writer of some hymns: 1.9.30.

Havergal, Frances Ridley (1836-1870). A woman of great saintliness who wrote a number of hymns: 1.9.27.

Hawaii prayer; 2.3.46, 3.4.19.

Hays, Edward. Contemporary Catholic priest who for many years was the director of a contemplative centre. Author of many books of prayers: 1.2.38, 1.8.42, 2.5.13, 3.1.7, 3.4.21, 3.4.22, 3.10.6, 3.11.26.

Hazrat Inayat Khan (1882-1927). Founder of the International Sufi movement: 1.7.17, 2.3.15.

Herbert, George (1593-1633). Courtier who became a model country parish priest. Poet and hymn writer: 1.5.28, 2.3.27, 3.6.16.

Herbert, C. Contemporary writer of prayers: 3.3.2.

Hick, John Harwood (1922-). Writer on philosophical theology. 4.1.26.

Hildegard of Bingen (1098-1179). Born into a noble family, she became a nun and eventually abbess of Rupersberg, near Bingen, on the Rhine. Her most famous work, *Scivias*, is a series of visions: 1.4.13, 5.4.6.

Hindu Scriptures: 3.11.42, 3.11.50, 3.11.83, 4.1.23, 4.3.31.
  Artharva Veda, 1.4.25, 3.4.34, 3.4.35, 3.11.75, 5.2.23, 5.3.12.
  Bhagavad Gita, 1.4.2, 1.5.54, 1.7.21, 3.8.5, 3.11.72.
  Blessing, 2.3.14.
  Brihad-Aranyaka Upanishad, 1.8.24.
  Hindu story, 3.11.42.
  Isha Upanishad, 1.3.18.
  Rig Veda, 1.4.11, 1.4.20, 1.5.5 (Gayatri Mantra), 2.4.24, 3.11.74, 4.1.5, 4.2.16, 5.4.7, 5.4.11, 5.4.13.
  Taittirya Aranyaka, 5.2.4.
  Tantric text, 1.3.15.
  Yajurveda, 4.2.9, 4.4.11.

Ho Chi Minh (1890-1969). Prisoner under the Communists in China: 3.8.8.

Hobin, Helen. (1993-) Prayer written when she was aged eight: 1.6.9.

Hollings, Michael (1921-). Catholic priest in London, who combined political and social awareness with traditional Catholic spirituality: 4.5.6.

Holtby, Winifred. Novelist: 3.6.5.

Hooper, Catherine Contemporary writer of prayers: 1.5.32.

Hopkins, Gerald Manley (1844-1889). Roman Catholic poet: 2.5.6, 3.11.29, 5.3.4.

Huddleston, Trevor (1913-). Anglican monk and archbishop who resisted South Africa's apartheid regime: 4.4.5.

Hugo, Victor (1802-1885). Poet, dramatist and leading French romantic: 3.4.8.

Hus, Jan (or John Huss) (1373-1415). Exponent of Wycliff's teaching, he was burnt at the stake for heresy: 1.9.4.

Hutchinson, Sir Robert (1871-1960). President of the Royal College of Physicians: 3.7.39.

I Ching (or Yi Ching). One of three pre-Confucian Chinese spiritual classics: 1.4.10.

Ibn Said (980-1037). Muslim philosopher. His works were translated in the West under the name of Avicenna: 1.5.25.

Ibn Hazm (994-1064). Spanish Muslim philosopher and poet: 1.5.27.

Iqbal, Sir Muhammad (1876-1938). Indian Muslim poet and philosopher, who sought to refashion Muslim thought in the light of Sufism and Western philosophy, especially of Bergson: 4.3.28.

Ingersoll, Robert: 4.1.8.

Irish blessing: 2.3.4.

Jagerstatter, Franz (d.1943). An Austrian farmer who was conscripted into Hitler's army, but was beheaded because he refused to take the military oath of obedience: 3.8.15.

Jain prayers: 3.9.24, 4.4.22, 5.2.22

Jal-al-Din Rumi. See Rumi.

Jami, Malwana Nur al-Din Abd al-Rahman (1414-92). Persian Sufi poet, known as the 'seal of the poets': 1.7.19, 3.7.19.

Janki, Dadi. Contemporary Administrative Head of the Brahma Kumaris World Spiritual University: 1.5.51, 3.2.21.

Japanese prayers: 1.1.21, 1.5.18, 2.2.16, 2.2.26, 2.5.8, 2.5.10, 2.5.12, 2.5.17, 2.5.18, 3.11.37, 4.4.12.

Jerome, St (c. 342-420). Scholar who translated most of the Bible into Latin (the *Vulgate*): 1.5.17.

Jesus Christ (born before 4 BCE and died about 30 CE). Jewish teacher and miracle-worker who was crucified by the Roman authorities. His immediate disciples believed that he was raised from the dead and they worshipped him as Lord. Christians believe him to be the incarnate Son of God: 1.1.22, 1.1.34, 3.8.18, 3.11.14, 3.11.16, 3.11.19, 4.3.24.

Jewish prayers: 1.1.35, 1.3.19, 1.5.20, 2.1.8, 2.3.30, 2.4.8, 2.4.9, 3.4.31, 3.11.68, 3.11.78, 3.11.79, 4.1.4, 4.3.32, 4.3.37, 4.4.24, 4.5.4, 5.2.16. See also *Hasidism*.

Johansen Berg, John. Contemporary British writer and compiler of prayers: 1.8.15, 4.3.37.

John Lame Deer. Sioux Indian: 2.3.32.

John Paul II (1920-2005). Born in Poland became Pope in 1978: 3.8.3.

Johnson, Samuel, Dr (1709-1784). Man of letters, literary critic, poet and lexicographer: 2.2.17.

Johnson, Joan. Contemporary writer of prayers: 2.2.13.

Judah Halevi (c 1075-1141). Jewish philosopher and poet, who spent much of his life travelling around the Jewish communities of Spain: 1.3.26, 1.3.27.

Julian of Norwich (c. 1342-1413). English anchoress and mystic. In May 1373, while she was suffering from a severe heart attack, she had a series of fifteen visions relating to the Passion of Christ, followed the next day by a final vision. She recorded these in the shorter text of her *Showings*: 1.3.13, 1.3.21, 1.5.43, 3.6.7.

Kabir (d. 1518). Poet of personal devotion to God. The differences between Hinduism and Islam were irrelevant to him: 1.3.42, 1.3.43, 1.5.34, 1.5.35, 3.11.23, 3.11.24, 4.1.20, 4.1.21.

Kagawa, Toyohiko (1888-1960). Japanese Christian evangelist and social worker. He was imprisoned in 1940 for his pacifism. He has been called one of the three greatest Christians of the twentieth century. Known for his novel, *Before the Dawn*: 2.3.10.

Keats, John (1795-1821). English poet: 5.4.2.

Keay, Kathy. Twentieth-century writer and compiler of prayers: 1.9.12, 2.3.44. 3.7.13.

Keller, Helen. She became blind and deaf in infancy and never experienced the reality of human speech: 1.2.12.

Kendall, Joan. Contemporary writer of prayers. 3.2.10.

Khwaja Moin-ud-din Chisthi (born c. 1137). Sufi saint and poet with a deep love for the poor. His tomb at Ajmer in Rajasthan attracts many Muslim pilgrims: 1.8.16.

Kierkegaard, Sören (1813-5). Influential Danish religious thinker, who emphasised the need for personal decision and commitment: 1.1.25, 1.7.24

Kingsley, Charles (1819-75). Social reformer and novelist: 3.3.4.

Krishnamurti, Jiddu (1895-1986). Indian religious figure, who stressed that truth can only be attained by complete self-awareness and self-knowledge. Krishnamurti Foundations exist in many parts of the world: 5.4.10.

Lalla. Fourteenth-century, Kashmiri woman mystic: 1.1.13.

Langland, William (c. 1330-c.1386). An unbeneficed clerk in minor orders who knew his Bible well. His *Vision of Piers Plowman* is a searching Christian narrative: 1.1.26.

Lao Tsu (b. 604 BCE?). Chinese sage reputed to have founded Taoism and to have written the *Tao Te Ching*, which expresses the essential teachings of Taoism (see below): 1.2.18, 1.3.7, 1.9.23, 3.10.7, 4.4.3.

Latin American prayer: 2.3.34.

Law, William (1686-1781). English Christian devotional writer. His most famous work, published in 1728, was *A Serious Call to a Devout and Holy Life*. He was a Nonjuror: 1.4.14.

Lawrence, David Herbert (1885-1930). English novelist: 3.11.4, 5.1.7.

Lawrence, Brother (1611-1691). After serving in the army for eighteen years, he entered the Carmelite monastery in Paris, where as a lay brother he was the community's cook, until blindness forced him to retire. After his death, letters and notes found in his cell were published in a book known as *The Practice of the Presence of God*: 3.6.15.

Leney, Norah. Her daughter, Susan, was at St Christopher's Hospice for nearly two years. After Susan's death, Norah's poems of mourning and reconciliation were published with the title *In a Lifetime* in 1975: 3.11.5.

Lesser, Fr Roger. Contemporary Catholic priest in India, who has written and translated many prayers: 1.1.40, 1.5.50, 1.5.51, 2.1.10, 3.6.28, 3.9.23, 3.10.12, 4.2.20, 4.3.16.

Levasseur, Conrad. Contemporary writer of prayers: 1.1.14.

Levi Yitzchak of Berditchev (1740-1809). A Hasidic (Jewish) spiritual leader: 1.3.25.

Lewin, Ann. Contemporary writer of prayers: 1.1.3.

Lincoln, Abraham (1809-1865). Sixteenth President of the United States of America, who maintained the Union during the Civil War: 1.9.6.

Livingstone, David (1813-73). Explorer and missionary to Africa: 2.3.13.

Longchenpa Rabjampa. Fourteenth-century Tibetan Nyingma Master: 3.7.10, 3.11.6.

Longfellow, Henry (1807-1882). American Unitarian poet: 2.5.3

Loyola, St. Ignatius (c. 1495-1556). Founder of the Society of Jesus (Jesuits) and author of *Spiritual Exercises*: 1.9.1.

Luke, St. First-century CE Evangelist: 1.1.34, 3.11.14, 3.11.19, 3.11.16.

Lutheran Manual of Prayer: 3.10.8.

Macdonald, George (1824-1905). Trained for the ministry but was dismissed for heresy. Best known for his stories and novels: 1.2.30, 3.7.15.

Magee, John Gillespie Jr. Canadian pilot killed in the Second World War: 3.6.20.

Maimonides, Moses (Rambam) (1135-1204). Jewish philosopher, doctor and codifier of Jewish legal teaching: 1.7.15, 3.7.38.

Malling Abbey. Christian convent in Kent, England: 1.2.29.

Manichaeism. A dualist and gnostic religion founded in the third-century CE in Iran by Mani: 1.8.40.

Manikka Vasahar (8th or 9th century). Tamil poet and holy man: 5.2.15, 5.2.22.

Manwaring, Randle. Contemporary writer of prayers: 3.7.21.

Maori chant.: 2.3.12.

Marcus Aurelius (121-180 CE). Roman Emperor, famous for *The Meditations* on Stoic philosophy: 1.2.15, 3.2.7.

Marks, Leo. Contemporary writer: 3.11.21.

Masahisa Goi. Author of the World Peace Prayer: 4.4.4.

Masefield, John (1878-1967). English poet: 2.5.16.

Matheson, George (1842-1906). Scottish hymn writer: 1.5.15, 4.1.30.

Matthew of Rievaulx. Mediaeval English monk: 3.4.5.

Matthews, Emily. Writer of prayers: 1.5.7.

Maule, Graham: Contemporary hymn writer 3.7.28.

Maurice, Frederick Denison (1805-72). Anglican theologian, who helped to form the Christian Socialists: 3.3.7.

McLaughlan, K. Contemporary writer and member of the Iona Community: 3.2.5.

McIlhagga, Kate (1938-). United Reformed Minister and member of the Iona Community: 1.2.35.

Mechtild of Magdeburg (1207-1294). Beguine nun and German mystic who lived a hermit-like existence, writing down her visions: 1.2.33, 1.3.24, 1.3.50, 1.5.40, 1.5.42, 4.3.9.

Meera Bai (Mirabai) (15th or 16th century). Rajasthani princess who was a Hindu devotee and poet: 1.5.38, 1.5.41, 1.8.37.

Melanchthon, Philip (1497-1560). One of Luther's first supporters: 3.8.24.

Mennonites. Followers of Menno Simons (1496-1561), who preached 'believers' baptism' and non-violence: 3.10.15.

Messengers of Unity: 4.2.2.

Milum, Lynne. Contemporary writer of prayers: 3.7.7. 4.2.1.

Monberg, Ulla. Contemporary English Christian writer: 2.1.4.

Montgomery, John (1771-1854). Free Churchman, journalist and hymn writer: 1.1.38.

More, Sir Thomas. Lord Chancellor of England. He opposed Henry VIII's Reformation and was executed by the king: 2.3.24, 3.9.11.

Morley, Janet. Contemporary English Christian writer: 1.3.39, 2.3.38.

Muhammad, ibn 'Abd Allah (570-632). The Prophet of Islam to whom the Qur'an was revealed: 1.5.8, 1.8.9, 1.8.30, 1.9.3, 1.9.17.

Muslim prayers: 1.1.9, 1.1.10, 1.1.11, 1.2.8, 1.2.10, 1.3.3, 1.3.4, 1.3.5, 1.3.6, 1.4.7, 1.5.3, 1.5.4, 1.5.27, 1.7.3, 1.8.3, 1.8.4, 1.8.28, 2.1.2, 2.3.6, 2.3.7, 2.3.36, 2.3.37, 2.4.14, 2.4.15, 2.4.16, 3.2.1, 3.2.2, 3.4.1, 3.4.3, 3.6.1, 3.7.1, 3.11.1, 3.11.43, 3.11.77, 4.1.2, 4.3.35, 5.2.7.

Nachman of Bratzlav (1772-1811). Hasidic rabbi and ascetic, who is known for his stories and parables: 4.5.5.

Nanak, Guru (1469-1539). First Sikh Guru and founder of Sikhism, who wrote numerous hymns in praise of God: 1.4.4, 1.4.6, 1.7.30, 3.6.10.

Native (North) American prayers: 1.4.31, 1.7.16.
Cheyene, 1.5.19.
Chinook psalter, 3.6.8, 5.2.19.
Iroquois prayer, 5.3.9
Lakota prayer, 1.4.30.
Navajo Blessing, 5.4.17.
Objibway, 1.5.33 (Art Solomon), 4.2.15.
Pawnee prayer, 5.3.11.
Tecumseh, Chief, 3.11.52.
Sealth, Chief, 5.3.10.
Sioux, 1.5.23, 2.3.32, 5.2.14.
Tewa People, 2.2.23.
Ute People, 5.3.7.
Zuni, 1.1.19, 5.3.6.
See also Black Elk.

Nestorian Church. It holds that there were two separate persons in the incarnate Christ. It derives from the teaching of Nestorius (d. c. 451), who was Patriarch of Constantinople from 428: 2.2.25.

New Guinea prayer: 1.8.34.

New Hebridean prayer: 1.8.23.

Newman, John Henry (1801-90). Leader of the Oxford Movement in the Church of England, Newman eventually converted to the Roman Catholic Church. He was made a Cardinal in 1879. Writer of poetry as well as of theology and history: 3.9.21.

Nezahualcoyotl (1402 -72). King of Texcoco, which is now part of Mexico: 3.11.38.

Nightingale, Florence (1820-1910). In 1854 she was appointed head of nursing in the Crimea, during the war there. Founder of trained nursing as a profession: 1.9.13.

Nouwen, Henri (1932-) Priest, peace campaigner and author: 4.4.19.

Ochs, Phil. Contemporary writer: 3.8.7.

Okri, Ben. Contemporary writer: 4.2.10.

Olufosoye, Timothy. Twentieth-century Archbishop of Nigeria: 2.3.5.

Oodgeroo of the Noonuccall (1920-1993). Well-known Australian poet, Kath Walker, who reverted to her tribal name in protest against the bicentennial celebrations of 1988. Author of several books of poetry: 3.7.36.

Orthodox Christian prayer: 2.4.18, 3.4.27, 3.11.45, 4.4.27, 5.1.5.

Ovid (43 BCE-17 CE). Influential Latin poet: 1.1.17, 1.9.11. 3.4.6.

Paterson, Evangeline. Contemporary writer: 3.2.4.

Paul, St (died c. 65CE). Born at Tarsus, brought up as a Pharisee and became a follower of Jesus after a vision. Apostle to the Gentiles and author of several letters, which form part of the New Testament: 1.9.5, 3.11.15, 3.11.55.

Pax Christi. Christian Peace Movement: 3.8.10, 4.4.17.

Pearse, Padraic. (1879-1916). Irish poet and playwright, who was executed for his leading role in the Easter Rising: 3.11.35.

Péguy, Charles (1873-1914). Christian spiritual writer and social reformer: 2.4.23.

Penn, William (1644-1718). English Quaker who founded Pennsylvania: 4.3.29.

Sharafuddin Maneri (1290-1381). Born near Patna in India, he is considered to be one of Bihar's most respected Sufis and was known as 'Teacher of the World'. His love of God was matched by service of others: 1.8.22.

Shepperson, Janet. Contemporary writer and member of the Corrymeela Community in Northern Ireland: 1.2.36.

Sheridan, Sybil. Progressive rabbi and author: 3.1.9.

Shikibu, Lady Izumi (c. 970-1030). Japanese writer: 3.11.37.

Shinto prayers: 1.5.16, 1.7.29, 4.1.12, 5.2.25, 5.2.26.

Shri Shivabalayogi Maharaj. Hindu teacher: 1.2.5.

Shrigley, G. A. Cleveland. Unitarian Universalist: 4.2.19.

Siha (c. 500-400 BCE). One of the Therigata nuns, who were female disciples of the Buddha, who encouraged them to use local dialects for their poems and prayers: 3.7.37.

Sikh scriptures (*Adi Granth*): 3.2.11, 3.4.33, 3.11.51, 3.11.53, 3.11.73, 4.1.19, 4.1.22, 4.4.25.
Japji, a hymn by Guru Nanak that is recited each morning by devout Sikhs, 1.4.6.
Mul Mantra, from Punjabi, meaning the concentrated and essential teaching of Sikhism. One of the first compositions of Guru Nanak. It is placed at the head of the Guru Granth Sahib, 1.4.4.
See also Guru Nanak, Guru Arjan, Guru Amar Das and Guru Gobind Singh.

Silvermarie, Sue. Contemporary American poet who has worked with Alzheimer patients: 3.7.6, 3.7.7.

Sivananda, Swami (1887-1963). Founder of the Divine Life Society and Mission. Teaches an Advaitin form of Hatha yoga: 1.8.32.

Smith, Steve. Contemporary writer: 3.7.31.

Solzhenitsyn, Alexander. Author, best known for *The Gulag Archipelago*: 1.5.11.

Starck, Johann (1680-1756). A leading member of the German Pietist movement: 3.1.14.

Stephen, St (died c. 35CE). First Christian martyr: 3.11.20.

Stevenson, Robert Louis (1850-94). Scottish travel writer and novelist: 2.4.12, 3.9.20.

Storey, Violet Alleyn. American writer: 3.2.26.

Sulpicius (c.363-420). Early Christian ascetic and graceful author, who wrote a life of St Martin: 2.2.9.

Suso, Henry (c. 1295-1366). Joined the Dominicans at 13. He endured years of depression when prayer seemed meaningless, but then had an intense mystical experience. His spiritual autobiography records his dialogue with God in times of both joy and sadness: 5.2.21.

Swann, Donald. Twentieth-century musician and Christian song and hymn writer: 4.1.15.

Symeon the New Theologian (949-1022). Byzantine mystic and spiritual writer. He was a formative influence on Hesychasm, the tradition of contemplative prayer especially associated with Mount Athos. He stressed 'felt devotion': 1.3.34.

Syrian Orthodox (Christian) prayer: 1.3.41, 2.2.20.

Tachibana-no-Sanki. A Shinto theologian during the Tokugawa Regime (1600-1868): 1.5.18.

Tagore, Rabindranath (1861-1941). The most widely read modern Indian poet, best known for *Gitanjali*. He founded what is now the University of Santiniketan: 1.1.4, 1.1.5, 1.1.31, 1.1.32, 2.1.6, 2.2.32, 2.4.5, 2.4.22, 3.1.16, 3.8.11, 3.8.16, 3.8.17, 3.10.3, 3.11.25, 4.2.14, 4.3.19, 5.2.10.

Tait, Campbell (1811-82). Archbishop of Canterbury: 3.2.24.

Tahiti hymn: 1.4.23.

Tao Te Ching. 'The Book of the Way and Its Power', (traditionally dated to the sixth century BCE, but may be a little later) attributed to Lao-tsu, is the foundation text of Taoism: 1.2.28, 1.4.9, 5.4.9.
See also Lao-tsu, 1.2.18, 1.3.7, 1.9.23, 3.10.7, 4.4.3.
and Chuang-tsu, 1.8.8, 3.3.6.

Tate, Nahum (1652-1715). With Nicholas Brady, he produced a 'New Version' of the Psalms in metrical verse: 1.3.51.

Taylor, Hudson (1832-1905). Pioneer missionary to China, who founded the China Inland Mission in 1865: 3.2.15.

Teilhard de Chardin (1881-1955). French Jesuit palaeontologist and theologian, best known for *The Phenomenon of Man* and *Le Milieu Divin*: 3.10.11.

Temple, William (1881-1944). Archbishop of Canterbury: 1.8.39.

Tennyson, Alfred Lord (1809-92). English Poet Laureate: 1.1.2, 2.5.2.

Teresa of Avila (1515-1582). An unruly child, she joined a Carmelite monastery, but after years of difficulty, at the age of forty she had some ecstatic experiences, which she interpreted as a spiritual marriage to Christ. She combined tireless administrative activities with an intense spiritual life, which is reflected in her *Book of God's Mercies*. With St John of the Cross, she founded a new order of Carmelities: 1.2.13, 1.2.20, 1.9.22, 2.3.48, 3.6.25, 3.7.33, 3.7.35.

Teresa, Mother (1910- 1997). After growing up in Albania, she went to India to teach in a convent school. After twenty years of this, she started working with the sick and dying in the slums of Calcutta and founded the Missionaries of Charity to carry on similar work across the world: 1.2.25, 3.8.6, 4.3.21, 4.3.38.

Thérèse of Lisieux (1873-1897). A Carmelite sister who described her interior spiritual life in her autobiography, *Story of a Soul*: 1.5.47.

Thich Nhat Hahn (1926-). Vietnamese Buddhist who now lives in France. A poet, Zen master and peace-worker: 2.2.4, 4.4.30.

Thomas a Kempis (c. 1380-1471). Born near Cologne, he entered the house of the Canons Regular near Zwolle. Spiritual writer and probably the author of *Imitation of Christ*: 1.4.29, 3.3.10.

Thomas, M. A. Twentieth-century Indian Christian theologian, who was a staff member of the World Council of Churches: 3.9.14.

Thurman, H (d. 1981), Poet, mystic, philosopher and theologian, who founded the Church for the Fellowship of All Peoples in San Francisco, which was the first interacial and interdenominational church in the USA: 3.9.16.

Tibetan Buddhist prayers: 1.7.5, 1.7.12, 3.7.10, 3.7.11, 3.11.6, 3.11.7, 4.3.2.

Tilak, Narayan Vaman (1862-1919). Indian Christian poet and holy man: 1.8.29.

Tiruvallur (c. 5th century CE). Tamil poet and author of *Tirukkural* or *Kural*: 5.1.1.

Todd, James M. Twentieth-century English writer and publisher: 3.3.12.

Traherne, Thomas (1637-74). Of poor parents, he was educated at Oxford and, soon after the Restoration, he was ordained as a clergyman of the Church of England, and joined a spiritual group. His poems show an intense love of nature and a mystical awareness: 2.2.1.

Tressler, Penny. Contemporary writer: 2.5.4.

Trine, Ralph Waldo (1866-1958). Metaphysician: 4.1.1.

Tukaram (c. 1607-1649). Hindu poet, who after an unhappy second marriage, turned to religion. He rejected all caste barriers and practised the presence of God in every detail of life: 1.5.48, 1.7.11, 1.7.13.

Tulsidas (1532-1623). Hindu poet and devotee of Rama. He retold the *Ramayana* in Hindi: 4.3.26 .

Turner, J. Stanleigh. Soldier: 2.3.22.

Tutu, Desmond Mpilo (1931-). Archbishop of Cape Town (1986-96), outspoken opponent of apartheid and author: 4.3.33.

Underhill, Evelyn (1875-1941). Scholarly student of the mystics, best known for her book *Mysticism* (1911): 1.7.6.

Unitarian Universalist prayers: 3.5.3, 4.2.23, 3.5.6, 5.2.24.

Uruguayan survivor: 1.8.26.

Urantia Book. Teaches that all people are one family, children of One God: 4.2.13.

Vanier, Jean. Founder of the L'Arche Community: 1.1.18.

Vardit Fertouk. As a child, wrote a prayer for peace: 4.4.5.

Vaughan, Henry (1622-1695). Christian poet: 1.3.14.

Vaughan, Charles (1816-1897). Anglican dean and author of many prayers: 4.4.14.

Vethathiri, Maharishi. Twentieth-century Kundalini Yoga Master: 4.2.3.

Virgil (70-19 BCE). Latin poet: 1.1.16.

Walker, Kit. See Oodgeroo of the Noonuccall.

Walsh, Ken. Contemporary English author of a collection of prayers called *Sometimes I Weep*: 1.5.10, 3.6.2, 3.6.3, 3.9.6, 3.10.2, 3.11.10.

Waring, Anna Laetitia (1823-1910). Born in Glamorgan and brought up as a Quaker, she converted to Anglicanism and became a well-known hymn writer. She also worked for the Prisoners' Aid Society: 1.8.44.

Watt, Jean M. Contemporary writer: 1.2.34.

Watts, Isaac (1674-1748). Famous hymn writer, who transformed psalmody into hymn singing: 3.11.33.

Wax, Lee. A Reform rabbi, she was ordained in 1994: 3.2.19, 3.2.20.

Wesley, John (1703-91). Founder of Methodism who is famous for his sermons and many letters: 1.9.7, 1.9.28.

West, Morris (1916-1999). Born in Melbourne, well known for his novels: 3.6.4.

White Eagle. Native American spirit who speaks through the mediumship of Grace Cooke. Members of the White Eagle Lodge follow a three-fold path of teaching, healing and communion: 1.5.52, 3.11.80.

White, Ro Eldin. Contemporary writer: 3.4.11. 3.4.12.

Whiting, William (1825-78). Master of Winchester Choristers' School. The only hymn he wrote he was the one for sailors 'Eternal Father, strong to save': 3.6.33

Whitman, Walter (1819-92). American journalist, essayist and poet: 2.3.9.

Whittier, John Greenleaf (1807-92). American Quaker poet. The hymn 'Dear Lord and Father of Mankind' is part of one of his poems: 1.2.32.

Widdup, R. RAF Chaplain: 2.3.20.

Wiggett, Harry Alfred. Twentieth-century South African priest: 2.5.11.

Wilkie, Ellen. Contemporary writer: 2.4.19, 3.4.19.

Williams, Harry (1919-2000). Dean of Trinity College, Cambridge, who became a monk, known especially for his sermons: 1.1.37.

Willis, Love Maria (1824-1908). American Unitarian hymn writer, mainly remembered for 'Father, hear the prayer we offer': 1.9.31.

Wilson, Lois. Twentieth-century Canadian church leader who was active in the ecumenical movement: 1.5.36.

Wilson, Steuart Hymn writer: 3.4.36.

Wint, Miriam Therese. Contemporary writer: 1.5.31.

Wittgenstein, Ludwig (1889-1951). Twentieth-century philosopher: 1.3.44.

Wordsworth, William (1770-1850). English Romantic poet: 2.4.4, 3.1.8, 5.2.5.

Wright, Alexandra. Liberal rabbi and writer: 3.4.2.

Xavier, St Francis (1506-52). Catholic missionary to India and Japan: 1.3.48.

Yakamochi. Japanese spiritual writer: 2.4.2.

Yeats, William Butler (1865-1939). Irish poet and dramatist: 3.2.9.

Yeger, Sheila: 5.1.10.

Yogananda, Paramahamsa (1893-1952). Founder of the (Hindu) Self-Realization Fellowship. He went to lecture in the USA in 1920 and stayed there, founding a Yoga Institute in Los Angeles. He travelled widely. He advocated Kriya-yoga - yoga based on practical efforts: 1.2.7, 1.3.22, 1.5.9, 1.6.4, 1.9.8, 2.5.19, 3.8.4, 3.9.4, 3.11.9, 4.1.9, 4.1.10, 4.1.11, 4.2.4, 4.3.4, 5.4.4, 5.4.5.

Zoroaster (Zarathustra). Variously dated. Zoroastrians date him to about 6000 BCE. Western scholars used to date him to the 6th century BCE, but others now date him about 1200 BCE. Believed he had seen God, the Wise Lord, *Ahura Mazda*, in a vision. God was opposed by the destructive power *Angra Mainyu*. Zoroaster called on people to serve the Wise Lord: 4.1.29.

Zoroastrian prayers: 1.4.21, 1.4.27, 1.7.14, 1.8.27, 2.3.40, 3.4.15, 3.9.25, 4.1.24, 4.3.1, 4.4.23.